The Indian Boundary
in the Southern Colonies, 1763-1775

The Indian Boundary

in the Southern Colonies, 1763-1775

by Louis De Vorsey, Jr.

THE UNIVERSITY OF NORTH CAROLINA PRESS • CHAPEL HILL

To Rosalyn, Megan, and Kirsteen

Acknowledgments

I wish to acknowledge the guidance and assistance received from Professor W. R. Mead of the Department of Geography, University College, London, in the preparation of my doctoral dissertation which served as the basis for this book. Without his patience and encouragement, I doubt that either would have seen completion. My thanks go also to Professor H. C. Darby, Chairman of that hospitable department, and a constant inspiration to anyone who would aspire to a serious study of historical geography.

Thanks also to the dedicated archivists and staffs at the British Public Record Office, British Museum, Institute for Historical Research, Royal Geographical Society, and other British institutions, who made my research such a pleasurable adventure. No less helpful were their counterparts in the United States, who, for the sake of brevity, are thanked via this general statement.

Further, I would thank my colleagues, Professor J. D. Eyre and Mr. D. R. Currey, who, with my sister, Miss Cora De Vorsey, lent invaluable aid in critical readings of the draft manuscript. Finally, thanks to my wife, Rosalyn, who was an indispensable assistant through all phases of my work.

Contents

Acknowledgments   vii

    I. *Introduction*   3

   II. *Competitors for the Land*   7

  III. *The Concept of a Boundary Line*   27

  IV. *The Virginia–Cherokee Boundary*   48

   V. *The North Carolina–Cherokee Boundary*   93

  VI. *The South Carolina–Cherokee Boundary*   112

 VII. *The Georgia–Indian Boundary Lines*   136

VIII. *The East Florida–Creek Boundary Line*   181

  IX. *The West Florida–Indian Boundary Line*   204

   X. *The Boundary on an "Accurate*
       General Map"   228

Bibliography   235

Index   261

List of Maps

Figure

1. *Tracing from John Stuart's Map of the Southern Indian District, 1764*   15

2. *Population distribution and growth in the Southeast*   24

3. *Tracing from Board of Trade map illustrating a preliminary proposal for an Indian boundary line*   33

4. *Contemporary map showing Proclamation Line of 1763*   37

5. *Tracing from Board of Trade map illustrating the Southern Indian Boundary Line in 1768*   63

6. *Tracing from John Stuart's map of the Lochaber and Hard Labour lines*   69

7. *Reference map showing Hard Labour and Lochaber lines*   70

8. *Tracing from map used by the governor of Virginia to illustrate the state of his colony's westernmost settlements in 1768*   72

9. *Tracing from John Donelson's map of 1771*   80

10. *The Virginia-Cherokee section of the Southern Indian Boundary Line*   82

11. *Reference map showing North and South Carolina Indian boundary lines*   96

12. *The North Carolina-Cherokee section of the Southern Indian Boundary Line*   103

13. *Tracing from a map of 1770 showing the demarcated portion of the North Carolina-Cherokee boundary*   104

14. *Map and profile of Mount Tryon, Polk County, North Carolina*   106

15. *The South Carolina-Cherokee section of the Southern Indian Boundary Line*   114

16. *The South Carolina-Cherokee boundary on the present-day and the contemporary map*   131

17. *Georgia-Creek boundary lines shown by Yonge
    and De Brahm*   142

18. *Georgia parishes, 1763*   147

19. *The Georgia-Creek section of the Southern
    Indian Boundary Line, 1768*   154

20. *Tracing from the original map of the Georgia-Creek
    boundary of 1768*   158

21. *The Georgia section of the Southern Indian
    Boundary Line, 1773*   164

22. *Tracing of the original map showing the northern
    portion of the Georgia "New Purchase" of 1773*   176

23. *Tracing of the original map showing the southern portion
    of the Georgia "New Purchase" of 1773*   177

24. *Contemporary map showing the colonies of East and
    West Florida*   183

25. *The East Florida-Creek section of the
    Southern Indian Boundary Line*   185

26. *Map showing the area to the west of the 1768
    boundary line which East Florida was
    trying to gain from the Creeks*   196

27. *The West Florida section of the Southern
    Indian Boundary Line*   211

28. *The Southern Indian Boundary Line as depicted
    on the Stuart-Purcell map of 1775*   231

29. *The Southern Indian Boundary Line*   232

*The endpaper: A Map of the Indian Nations in the Southern Depart-
ment, 1766 (by permission of the William L. Clements Library, Ann
Arbor, Michigan)*

*The Indian Boundary
in the Southern Colonies, 1763-1775*

I · *Introduction*

The subject of this book is a boundary line. Like many boundaries it was intended to separate people. The people in this case were the Indians and pioneers of the Southeast during the period immediately preceding the American Revolution. What follows is an account of the evolution of the Southern Indian Boundary Line, as this important boundary was called by those actively participating in its formation. A period of twelve years, from the Peace of Paris in 1763 until the political break between the seaboard colonies of America and the British Crown in 1775, saw the Southern Indian Boundary Line emerge on the map of the New World from the Ohio River south to the Florida peninsula and west to the Mississippi River.

While it might be said that this boundary was first conceived simply as an expedient, economic device to aid in maintaining peace with the Indians, it evolved into a geographic and conceptual force along the frontier zone of the Southeast. As such, the Southern Indian Boundary Line became the line along which two distinctive cultures were confronting each other in a contest for the southern quarter of North America. It was the principal point of focus for Anglo-Indian relations throughout the pre-revolutionary period in the Southeast. In many respects it closely reflected the true state of the forces which were operative in the frontier zone during this critical period.

Although a factor of great moment to the Indians, pioneer settlers, British administrators, and military leaders during the period of its conception and evolution, the Southern Indian Boundary Line has received only scant attention from historians of the present century and has escaped almost entirely the attention of the growing school of American historical geographers. Only one scholarly paper, published over sixty years ago, and two unpublished master's theses have been found which deal in detail with the

Southern Indian Boundary Line.[1] In no case had the author drawn upon the great fund of documentary and cartographic evidence available in British archives to illustrate the evolution and location of this important feature of pre-revolutionary frontier geography. Other authors who have included discussions or mentions of the Southern Indian Boundary Line in more general works have similarly omitted most of this evidence.

John C. Parish, however, is a notable exception to this criticism. He gathered a large amount of unpublished material pertaining to the boundary line in British archives while on leave from his teaching duties in the United States. In his posthumously published essay, "John Stuart and the Cartography of the Indian Boundary Line," Parish drew attention to this material, especially the cartographic, and concluded that those contemporaneous maps of it which are still extant left "no part of the Southern Indian Boundary Line which cannot be clearly located."[2] It must be stated, however, that the maps to which he referred were far from accurate in detail and can be translated to the map and landscape of the present day only with great difficulty.

This task of translation formed a large part of the labor which resulted in this book. The transfer of data from eighteenth-century maps to those of the present day can be thought to be simple and uncomplicated only by one who has never attempted it. Such a task was fundamental to this attempt to place the Southern Indian Boundary Line in its proper place on today's map. The maps that illustrate the stages in the evolution of the boundary in the chapters which follow are composites and frequently retain original spellings; they are derived from the analysis of many contemporaneous sources such as manuscript and printed maps, surveyors sketches, treaty articles, and descriptions.

Another invaluable and unique source of information concerning the boundary line was the many journals which recorded accurately and often almost verbatim the congresses held between

1. Max Farrand, "The Indian Boundary Line," *The American Historical Review,* X (July, 1905), 782-91. Lawrence G. Derthick, "The Indian Boundary Line In the Southern District of British North America, 1763-1779" (Master's thesis, University of Tennessee, 1930), and Cecil A. Duke, "The Indian Boundary Line South of the Ohio, 1763 to 1802" (Master's thesis, Vanderbilt University, 1930).

2. John C. Parish, *The Persistence of the Westward Movement and Other Essays* (Berkeley and Los Angeles, 1943), p. 145. One should except also John Richard Alden, who used an impressive body of British material in transcript form in preparing his excellent study, *John Stuart and the Southern Colonial Frontier* (Ann Arbor, Mich., 1944).

the colonies and southeastern Indian tribes to discuss and negotiate land and boundary problems. The statements and addresses made by Indian leaders were recorded with reasonable fidelity. The journals therefore are quoted frequently in the pages which follow to give the Indian a "voice" in the narrative. His very existence depended upon these negotiations concerning his most precious and sacred possession—the land. There can be little doubt that the tribal leaders understood the significance of the Southern Indian Boundary Line as well as the conditions which made it a necessity.

The British colonies occupying the mainland of eastern North America were loosely organized into two districts for the purpose of dealing with the Indian tribes during the mid-eighteenth century. These were the Northern and Southern Indian districts, each under the administration of a designated Superintendent for [of] Indian Affairs. The Ohio River was the line of division between the two districts, although there was some overlapping of interest, especially in the Illinois country. While the Southern Indian Boundary Line evolved within the Southern Indian District, its evolution was at times influenced by events occurring in the Northern Indian District. The most notable example of such influence was, of course, the Indian uprising led by Pontiac in the months following the Peace of Paris.

Geographically, the establishment of a surveyed and demarcated Indian boundary line in the Southern Indian District presented problems of immense proportions. The district spanned more than thirteen degrees of latitude and about fifteen degrees of longitude. Ten states including Georgia, the largest east of the Mississippi, have been created in its huge area.[3] Here Indians and white pioneers came into competitive contact along a zone which included the almost flat tidal marshes of the Gulf and Atlantic coasts, the rolling hills of the Piedmont, the steep slopes, precipices, and defiles of the southern Appalachian Mountains, the rugged but fertile vales of the Appalachian Valley, the rugged Cumberland Front and Plateau and which terminated on the banks of the Kentucky River as it flowed through the lush Lexington Plain and outer Blue Grass region to the Ohio River. By any standards, contemporary or present day, the distances covered and obstacles encountered in the surveying and demarcation of the

3. The states are Kentucky, West Virginia, Virginia, Tennessee, North Carolina, South Carolina, Georgia, Florida, Alabama, and Mississippi. Portions of Louisiana and Maryland were also included.

Southern Indian Boundary Line were enormous and presented challenges of gargantuan proportions to those individuals, white, red, and black, who accomplished the tasks.

Surveying parties were often engaged in their labor of blazing and marking the trees along the boundary through the trans-frontier wilderness for periods ranging from several weeks to five months. The work was arduous and the danger from wild beasts and hostile human beings considerable. Delays in communicating from the frontier to the populous tidewater region could extend to several days or even weeks and the voyage from the colonies to England and return might involve several months. This time lag in communications placed a premium on local initiative and lent to those individuals located in or near the frontier a great opportunity to shape the course of empire to meet local requirements and conditions. The important role of individuals in the evolution of political boundaries is clearly demonstrated in the case of the Southern Indian Boundary Line.

The problems of vast distances and agonizingly slow communications coupled with a tradition of intercolonial rivalry had a strong bearing on the evolution of the Southern Indian Boundary Line in still another way. Courses of action were pursued in the frontier wilderness by agents of the frequently competing colonies which bore little if any semblance to programs issued from the Crown in London. In many respects, therefore, the Southern Indian Boundary Line evolved as a set of colonial links only loosely welded into a chain by the British central authority. Herein lay perhaps its greatest weakness.

II · Competitors for the Land

The middle decades of the eighteenth century saw the empires of Britain, France, and Spain joined in a contest for the control of eastern North America. It was a contest that had wide ramifications. Not the least important of these was the growing awareness of the Indians of their strategic position in the struggle for their homeland. The Iroquois Federation of the north realized early the value of this strategic position and was often able to play the British against the French to the advantage of the federation. This early exercise of political manipulation seemed to assist in an equally early development of a high degree of political sophistication and organization among these northern tribes.

The southern tribes, too, had ample opportunity to play one European power against the other during the seventeenth and early eighteenth centuries. In this art they lagged but a short distance behind their northern neighbors.

The momentous Albany Convention of 1754 provided a forum where Indian attitudes and opinions could be heard by the most influential British colonial leaders of the day. During the formal orations that formed an important part of the convention, a Mohawk Indian spokesman gave words to one of the chief causes of Indian concern and anxiety. He candidly observed that: "The governor of Virginia and the governor of Canada are both quarreling about lands which belong to us, and such a quarrel as this may end in our destruction. They fight who shall have the land."[1]

1. Colonial Office Records, America and West Indies (original correspondence etc.), Vol. 6, p. 183, British Public Record Office, London.
The bulk of the original source materials used in the preparation of this book are found in the British Public Record Office. Of particular interest and value were three classes of records: America and West Indies (C.O. 5), Colonies General (C.O. 323), and Maps and Plans (C.O. 700). America and West Indies (C.O. 5) includes such materials as the original correspondence and entry books of the Board of Trade and the secretary of state. Acts, sessional papers, and miscellanae

This sentiment was to be repeated in a variety of situations by most major tribal leaders in the Southeast during the following decades. Increasing Indian concern over their tribal hunting grounds was to emerge as one of the two or three most important themes running through Anglo-Indian relations during the later eighteenth century.

In a clear recognition of the significance of the Indian fears regarding the unregulated expansion of white settlements onto their hunting grounds, the governors assembled at Albany recommended "that the bounds of those colonies which extend to the south sea be contracted and limited by the Alleghenny or Apelachian Mountains." However, no such action was taken by the British government at this early date.

Before proceeding further, it is advisable to consider in some detail the manner in which the Indians were distributed over the Southeast in the mid-eighteenth century.

THE SOUTHERN INDIANS IN MID-CENTURY

Most of the coastal plain and piedmont Indian tribes had ceased to be barriers to white settlement by the middle decades of the eighteenth century. Many had expired in epidemics or wars, others had retreated into the interior, or still others like the Pam-

---

are arranged under the following subdivisions: Carolina (Propriety); North Carolina; South Carolina; Connecticut; East Florida; West Florida; Georgia; Maryland; Massachusetts; New England; New Hampshire; New Jersey; New York; Pennsylvania; Rhode Island; Vermont; Virginia; Proprieties. In all, 1,450 volumes and bundles dating from *ca.* 1606 to 1807 are included in this artificial class of documents. For brevity, footnote citations to these materials will appear in a form giving the class (C.O. 5) followed by a volume number (C.O. 5-6) and page reference (C.O. 5-6, p. 183).

The class of papers known as Colonies General, Original Correspondence (C.O. 323), is made up of documents which usually concern more than one colony or no colony in particular. The earlier part of C.O. 323 includes the valuable series of Board of Trade papers called Plantations General. Colonies General, Original Correspondence (C.O. 323) includes 1,868 volumes dated from 1689 to 1943.

Of singular interest and value in the preparation of this book were the maps of early America found in the Public Record Office. These were acquired from a variety of sources, the most important being the Colonial Office Records. In all, there were about 1,600 maps catalogued under the classification Maps and Plans (C.O. 700). During the course of the author's research in the Public Record Office the map collection was being re-indexed and a new system of map referencing was being introduced. Such designations as M.R. and M.P.G. for maps in the Public Record Office result from this new system and may be unfamiliar to readers who have not worked in the Public Record Office in recent years or are familiar only with references in the old system.

unkys in Virginia had become "so far civilized as to wear the European dress and in part follow the customs of the common planters."[2]

The tribes which retained a distinctive identity and represented an important factor to be reckoned with along the advancing frontier south of the Ohio River during the second half of the eighteenth century were described in some detail by Edmund Atkin. Atkin served as the first Superintendent for Indian Affairs in the Southern District of America. In 1755 he prepared a report which John Richard Alden described as containing "shrewd analyses of French and British Indian policies" in the Southeast.[3] Among other things Atkin drew attention to the numbers of fighting men in each tribe as well as the strategic nature of tribal locations in the Southeast. He listed the tribes as follows:

The Cherokees—
    Commonly distinguished by the names Upper,
    Lower and Middle above three thousand men   3,000
The Catawbas—
    but little more than three hundred perhaps
    twenty   320
The Chicasaws—
    not more than four hundred and eighty in all
    places, to wit
        In the nation   350
        At their camp on the borders of the Upper
        Creek Nation   80
        Upper Savano River   50   480
The Creeks—
    Lower Nation, living apart, and by some called
    Coweta's about twelve hundred men   1,200
    Upper Nation distinguished by the name of
    Tallapoosies Abecas and Alibamas (as by an
    acco. taken in [Nov.] 1749)   1,180
    Savanoes, from the north, incorporated among
    those three tribes   185   2,665
Of the Alibamas—
    four little towns having 155 men, next and very
    near the French Fort, are entirely in the French

2. C.O. 5-1330, p. 272.
3. *John Stuart,* p. 69.

interest, as well as probably the Savanoes, but
are all obliged to observe the same terms with
us, as the rest of the Nations   155

                                           Total   6,365

The Chactaws . . . lost to us at present   3,600[4]

Atkin included several valuable observations on the strategic
importance of the locations of the various tribes in his report. Only
the one describing the Cherokee tribal area will be mentioned here.

This is a most important country by its nature and situation, lying in
a very extraordinary and remarkable manner among the mountains in
the midst of the heads of several large rivers, that have communication
with different and remote parts on all sides; to wit, the Savane [Savan-
nah] and other rivers, that flow eastward into the Atlantic Ocean; the
Chatahuchee and Flint Rivers, that uniting near Apalatchee flow southward into the Gulph of Mexico; and the branches of the Hogohege or
great Cherokee River [Tennessee], that flows westward into the Mississippi and is joined by the Ohio River that hath its source northerly
so far as Lake Erie, and the country of the Sennekas, to which there
is a straiter and more direct passage from the Cherokee Towns,
by very short and easy transitions from one stream to another of the
numerous branches of the Ohio nearest to the back of Virginia, Maryland, and Pennsylvania. The high ridge of mountains which runs behind them N.E. and S.W., continues on the back of No. Carolina a
due westerly course from the Cherokees parallel with the Hogohege
[Tennessee] River; there being no mountains whatever to the southward of the Lower Cherokee Towns near the latitude 34, as is represented in almost all maps. From the lower to the upper Towns, the
passage through the mountains is so narrow that two horses can scarce
go abreast. So that the Cherokee country is the best formed by nature
for dominion of the Inland Indian nations on this side of the Mississippi
and the Lakes.[5]

It can be seen from this extract that Atkin appreciated the
potential strengths of the southern Indians. A sense of their own
strength did not escape the Indians as they were courted first by
one great power and then the other. Thomas Pownall, colonial
governor and geographer, in 1755 called the Indians "the most

4. Wilbur R. Jacobs (ed.), *Indians of the Southern Colonial Frontier: The
Edmund Atkin Report and Plan of 1755* (Columbia, S.C., 1954), pp. 42-43. The
general locations of the tribes can be observed on the map of 1764 which is included as Fig. 1. Atkin is not cited in John R. Swanton's comprehensive *The
Indians of the Southeastern United States* (Washington, D.C., 1946).
5. Jacobs, *Indians of the Southern Colonial Frontier*, p. 48.

dangerous enemies in such a wilderness where . . . [they] are masters and possessed of every hold and pass."[6] This same expert saw the English colonies of America "in not only a weak defenceless state, but exposed to, and almost at the mercy of a very powerful enemy." To build any fortification network short of one approximating "another Chinese wall," Pownall pointed out, was folly of the most disastrous sort. Rather than building garrisons and fortifications to safeguard the settlements, he advised leaving "the Indians in full and free possession of their dwelling houses and hunting grounds, which the English have in the most solemn manner confirmed to them by treaty."[7]

Accurately assessing the advantage which Britain's superior industrial and maritime base afforded her in the competition for North America, Pownall continued:

As the being supplied with European goods is to the Indians the first essential interest of their politicks: Is the sole and actual object of their alliance with us, and the only real and permanent motive of their attachment to us; and according to the custom of these people all public transactions are executed by exchange of presents, all public friendship preserved and animated by public hospitality and liberality. The first and fundamental object of the English measures should be to provide for these in a regular and sufficient manner, the being able to do this is our peculiar advantage and superiority over the French. . . .[8]

Alden summarized the significance of Britain's economic superiority in the struggle by stating, "The French might have gained the alliance of all the Indians between the Gulf of St. Lawrence and the Gulf of Mexico, had it not been for the fact that the English were consistently able to furnish the Indian with better trade goods at cheaper prices."[9] In the following chapters the validity of these observations is often emphasized. Matters of trade and land were almost always closely linked in the negotiations between the colonists and Indians of North America. By the mid-eighteenth century it was increasingly apparent that the Indians of eastern America were on the horns of a dilemma. On the one

6. C. O. 5-18, p. 309. For a discussion of Pownall's ability as a geographer see his *A Topographical Description of the Dominions of the United States of America* . . . , ed. Lois Mulkearn (Pittsburgh, Pa. 1949).

7. C.O. 5-18, p. 313.

8. *Ibid.,* pp. 313-14. For an excellent review of the significance of Indian gifts, see Wilbur R. Jacobs, *Diplomacy and Indian Gifts: Anglo French Rivalry Along the Ohio and Northwest Frontiers, 1748-1763* (Stanford, 1950).

9. Alden, *John Stuart,* p. 4.

hand, they required numerous articles of European manufacture such as firearms and woolen cloth which could only be obtained from their white neighbors who were, on the other hand, their competitors in a growing struggle for the possession of the continent. John Stuart, who succeeded Atkin as Indian superintendent in 1762, mentioned the Indian's dependence on European goods in his unpublished report of 1764, where he observed:

The original great tie between the Indians and Europeans was mutual conveniency. This alone could at first have induced the Indians to receive white people differing so much from themselves into their country. . . . A modern Indian cannot subsist without Europeans; and would handle a flint ax or any other rude utensil used by his ancestors very awkwardly; so what was only conveniency at first is now become necessity and the original tie strengthened.[10]

The trader who supplied these necessities to the Indian in return for his pelts and hides was but the vanguard of the encroaching army of European planters and husbandmen who followed and threatened the extinction of the Indian and his way of life. How to enjoy the utensils and luxuries of European workshops and yet retain his vast living space of virgin field and forest for his own use became the great problem of the Indian of the southern interior during the second half of the eighteenth century.

In due course the dilemma facing the Indian was, in a modified form, to perplex the British leaders and policy-makers who were charged with shaping the course of the British Empire. Simply stated, the problem facing the Crown was to foster and encourage the growth and prosperity of the American colonies of the seaboard and yet to prevent a disastrous conflict from arising as the expanding colonies encroached upon the land claimed by the Indian tribes. Such a conflict would have led to an enormously expensive military effort unacceptable to an economy-minded government in the postwar period of the 1760's.

Before investigating the programs which were proposed to establish a modus vivendi between the Anglo-American and Indian subjects in the southern district of George III's newly secured empire, it is necessary to review briefly the numbers, location, and character of the Indians living there at the time of the Peace of Paris when the control of eastern America passed to Great Britain.

Although there are a number of sources which help to provide

10. C. O. 323-17, p. 512.

a generalized picture of the location of the Indians in the Southeast during the eighteenth century, much work that would fill in the details remains undone. For example, the construction of a series of maps to show the location and numbers of the southeastern Indians at selected points in time would be most revealing, especially if juxtaposed with those showing the white population distribution pattern (included here as Fig. 2). In the absence of such a set of maps, many of the materials published by the Bureau of American Ethnology are a source which, although diffuse, are extremely valuable as a background for the study in hand.[11]

John Stuart, the superintendant for Indian affairs in the southern department for fifteen years following his acceptance of the post in 1763, was probably the best-informed expert on Indian affairs in the Southeast during this period. He was also a cartographer of some note and had a keen sense of the importance of maps in the administration of his important office.[12] One of his first maps, showing the vast area of his department, was prepared to accompany and illustrate his valuable "Report on the Indians of the Southern Department" and was forwarded to the Board of Trade on March 9, 1764.[13] A tracing from this important map is included here as Figure 1.

11. Of particular interest are: James Mooney, *Myths of the Cherokee* ("Nineteenth Annual Report of the Bureau of American Ethnology," Pt. I [Washington, D.C., 1900]. Mooney includes two maps, "The Cherokee Country" and "The Cherokee and their Neighbors . . . ," which are valuable.

Charles C. Royce, *Indian Land Cessions In the United States* "Eighteenth Annual Report of the Bureau of American Ethnology" [Washington, D.C., 1899]). The introduction to this annual report by Cyrus Thomas is seriously in error in the section devoted to the colonial period and should not be relied upon.

John R. Swanton, *Indian Tribes of the Lower Mississippi Valley and Adjacent Coast of the Gulf of Mexico* (Bureau of American Ethnology, Bulletin 43 [Washington, D.C., 1911]); *Early History of the Creek Indians and their Neighbors* (Bureau of American Ethnology, Bulletin 73 [Washington, D.C., 1922]); *The Indians of the Southeastern United States* (Bureau of American Ethnology, Bulletin 137 [Washington, D.C., 1946]); *The Indian Tribes of North America* (Bureau of American Ethnology, Bulletin 145 [Washington, D.C., 1952]).

Swanton has provided reprints of a number of early maps which accompany certain of the bulletins and enhance the value of these materials greatly. Plate 7, with bulletin 73, is titled "Part of the Purcell Map compiled not later than 1770 in the interest of British Indian Trade by John Stuart, H.M. Sup't of Indian Affairs original in the Edward E. Ayer Collection, Newberry Library, Chicago, Ill." This map is incorrectly identified and dated by Swanton, as explained in the concluding chapter of this study.

12. Parish, "John Stuart and the Cartography of the Indian Boundary Line," in *The Persistence of the Westward Movement and Other Essays*, pp. 131-46.

13. The map has become separated from the report, which is filed as C. O. 323-17 in the Public Record Office, London. The map is located in the British

In Stuart's words, this map showed "the territory claimed by each [tribe], and their Boundaries with the respective Provinces according to their Pretension."[14] He went on to point out the map's limitations by stating: "I do not offer this to your Lordships as an accurate map of the Provinces and Sea Coast, nor it is from actual surveys, but it will convey a juster idea of the Indian Countries, and their situations than any I have as yet seen. I have made it out from my own observation and such intelligence as I have been able to procure and could depend on. . . ."[15]

This map, probably drawn by Stuart, does in fact represent "a juster idea of the Indian Countries" and shows better than any other source this writer has encountered the extent of the lands claimed by the tribes of the Southeast in 1763. It is, therefore, an indispensable guide in any attempt to form an impression of the pattern which the Indians formed over the landscape of the Southeast in the period between the Peace of Paris in 1763 and the American Revolution in 1775. Its distorted lineaments, which tend to exaggerate the strength of the tribes and extent of tribal lands, are indicative of Stuart's attitude toward the Indians at the time that the British assumed control of the region from the French and Spanish. There was no attempt to underestimate or play down the Indian strength; on the contrary, the map emphasized the Indian power and position at that date. It was, by the Superintendent's admission, a subjective depiction but nonetheless meaningful and revealing. It will serve well as a guide in helping the present-day reader to see the problem as the contemporaries living with it visualized it on the eve of the period which witnessed the evolution of the Southern Indian Boundary Line.

It is not enough, however, that we see the pattern of distribution formed by the southeastern Indians; it is now necessary to investigate its component features by taking a closer view of the Southern Indian tribes which formed it.

Museum where it is filed as Additional MSS. 14,036, f. 8. It was not until 1961 in the course of research for this study that these two valuable sources were identified as forming Stuart's complete report. They should be brought together in a published form.

14. C. O. 323-17, p. 463.

15. *Ibid.* William P. Cumming, *The Southeast In Early Maps* (Chapel Hill, N.C., 1962), p. 234, states that, "DeBrahm may be the author of this [Indian District 1764] and the Indian Nations 1766 map." Stuart's remarks quoted above would suggest that the 1764 map was his own work. It would appear probable that he was capable of producing it, so there seems little reason to deny him the authorship of this valuable cartographic source.

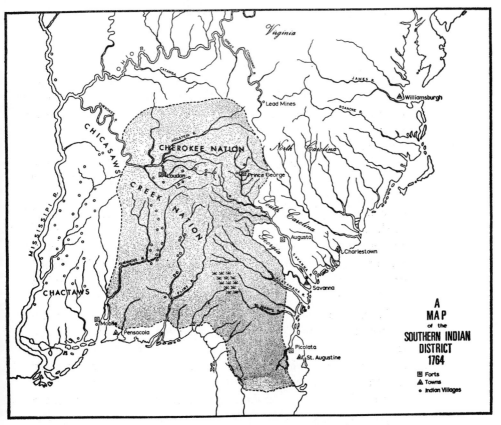

Fig. 1.   Tracing from John Stuart's map of the Southern Indian District, 1764. (From British Museum, Additional MSS. 14,036, fol. d.)

During the mid-eighteenth century the Indians of the Southeast were more numerous than those found living to the north of the Ohio, and on the whole they were less warlike than the Iroquois. Their settlements were more compact, and they possessed rudimentary systems of government which were developing at an increasingly rapid rate in response to growing contacts with their white neighbors. The governor of South Carolina in 1758 suggested that the Indians "be considered as so many nations whose friendship it deeply imports to the Crown of Great Britain to preserve." He went on to ask rhetorically, "and may not the same means which prove so beneficial in Europe be adopted with great prospect of success in America?"[16] Although the governor was exaggerating the Indian's state of political maturity by comparing their tribes to European nation states, he was voicing the opinion of many administrators who were encouraging the Indians to act in concert and to curb the individual Indian's behavior in accordance with agreements made between the white colonies and Indian tribes. Rather than clearly defined "nations" as colonial administrators were wont to call them, the major tribes of the Southeast were loose federations of villages which were often linked in geographic groupings called "divisions." The Cherokee, for example, were often divided into the "Overhills," "Valley," "Middle," and "Lower," with each of the four divisions composed of a number of villages or, as they were often called, "Towns." Each village usually had one leader, frequently chosen for his prowess in battle or on the hunt, or sometimes in recognition of wisdom and experience or family ties. Although the title "king" or "emperor" was frequently applied to outstanding tribal leaders by Europeans, there were in reality no such dignitaries among the Indians. The tribal official most like a king was probably the elected chief of the Catawba. This tribe was very much under the influence of South Carolina and the governor of that colony closely supervised the elections. By the middle of the eighteenth century the Catawbas were greatly reduced in strength and were easily controlled by South Carolina. The internal political life of the larger tribes such as the Creeks and Cherokees was very complex, with individuals, factions, and tribal divisions often in conflict.[17] These tribal schisms are difficult to analyze in detail here, but the Anglo-Americans soon learned to take advantage of them by

16. C. O. 5-376, p. 47. Fred Gearing suggested that duress caused by South Carolina's dealing with individual Cherokee villages as one whole political unit, wherein the constituent units were mutually accountable for one and another, helped in moving the Cherokee toward statehood; see Gearing, "The Rise of The Cherokee State as an Instance In a Class: 'The Mesopotamian' Career To Statehood," in William N. Fenton and John Gulick (eds.), *Symposium on Cherokee and Iroquois Culture* (Bureau of American Ethnology, Bulletin 180 [Washington, D.C., 1961]), pp. 127-34.

17. Although Atkin may have been exaggerating slightly, his comments on this point are of interest: "The upper and lower Cherokees differ from each other, as much almost as two different nations. The upper (among whom the Emperor resides) being much more warlike, better governed, better affected to us, and as sober and well behaved as the others are debauched and insolent. . . . They seldom take part even in each others wars; which is also the case with the upper and lower Creeks. . . . The middle Cherokees are much more like the upper than the lower." Quoted by Jacobs, *Indians of the Southern Colonial Frontier*, p. 49.

supporting friendly and amenable Indians against their tribal rivals to gain influence for the furtherance of their own schemes.

Discussing the Indian way of life, William Bartram, the eighteenth-century explorer and naturalist, provided an informative, contemporary description of the typical Indian village of the Southeast. He wrote from first-hand knowledge when he stated:

> An Indian town is generally so situated, as to be convenient for procuring game, secure from sudden invasion, a large district of excellent arable land adjoining, or in its vicinity, if possible on an isthmus betwixt two waters, or where the doubling of a river forms a peninsula; such a situation generally comprises a sufficient body of excellent land for planting corn, potatoes, beans, squash, pumpkins, citruls, melons etc. and is taken in with small expense and trouble of fencing, to secure their crops from the invasion of predatory animals.[18]

The Indian male disdained agricultural pursuits in his public utterances and credited only warfare and hunting as fit undertakings for a man. The evidence indicates, however, that all of the southern Indians engaged in agriculture; the women, children, and older men did most but by no means all of the work entailed. The agricultural methods were crude but the land was productive, harvests plentiful, and yields were adequate in most years.[19]

The Indian dependence on agriculture was recognized by the Anglo-Americans, who made the Indian "plantations" and storehouses military objectives whenever they fought with the tribes. Stuart indicated the importance of agriculture among the tribes of his district in his valuable unpublished report on the Indians by stating: "At the proper season the inhabitants of the town join, in cultivating and planting the lands belonging to it; from which

18. Francis Harper (ed.), *The Travels of William Bartram, Naturalist's Edition* (New Haven, Conn., 1958), p. 325.

19. De Brahm's account of the Cherokee country in 1756 gives a hint of the temptation which the almost virgin Indian lands represented to far-seeing colonials at that period. He observed: "Their [Cherokee's] vallies are of the richest soil, equal to manure itself, impossible in appearance ever to wear out; the putrified matter from the mountains are in rainy seasons washed down into the vallies, and leave the mountains bear of good soil, the land in the vallies by this means (besides being well watered with rivulets) is become a real matrice to receive from phlogiston the impregnation of niter, so that there is present a perpetual renewal of what encourages vegetation. Should this country once come into the hands of the Europeans they may with propriety call it the American Canaan. . . . This country seems longing for the hands [of] industry to receive its hidden treasures, which nature has been collecting and toiling since the beginning ready to deliver them up. . . ." Quoted by Samuel C. Williams, *Early Travels in the Tennessee Country, 1540-1800* (Johnson City, Tenn., 1928), p. 193.

labor none but the sick and disabled are exempt. All manner of distinction is upon this occasion laid aside. After which every family depends upon the produce of the land alloted it."[20]

Bartram's commentaries on the Cherokee towns, which he visited, abound with colorful descriptions of the agricultural landscape; this one describes the area near the present Franklin, North Carolina:

After riding about four miles, mostly through fields and plantations, the soil incredibly fertile, arrived at the town of Echoe, consisting of many good houses, well inhabited; I passed through and continued three miles farther to Nucasse, and three miles more brought me to Whatoga; riding through this large town, the road carried me winding about through their little plantations of corn, beans, etc. up to the council house, which was a very large dome or rotunda, situated on the top of an ancient artificial mount and here the road terminated; all before me and on every side appeared little plantations of young corn, beans etc. divided from each other by narrow strips or borders of grass, which marked the bounds of each one's property, their habitation standing in the midst.[21]

Bernard Romans went so far as to state that, "The Chactaws may more properly be called a nation of farmers than any savages I have met with."[22]

Agriculture was clearly vital to the Indians' way of life in the Southeast, but their attitudes toward the land were those of a people with a hunting and gathering economy. In his report Stuart emphasized the importance of this attitude in dealing with the Indians. He stated: "The whole business of an Indian life is war and hunting. As hunters they require a much greater extent of territory in proportion to their numbers, than nations that subsist by agriculture: which makes them extremely tenacious of their lands and jealous of encroachments.[23]

Just as the loosely organized system of tribal government was often bewildering to Europeans, so was the Indian attitude toward land ownership. Stuart explained this communalistic tenure system as follows:

20. C. O. 323-17, pp. 490-91.
21. Harper, *Bartram's Travels*, p. 221.
22. Bernard Romans, *A Concise Natural History of East and West Florida* (facsimile reproduction of the 1775 edition, Gainesville, Fla., 1962), p. 71. Frequent references to cattle, swine, and fowl indicate that the Indian appetite for flesh was often satisfied without resorting to the noble pursuit of the hunt.
23. C. O. 323-17, p. 489.

Each individual has a right to, and looks upon himself as proprietor of all the lands claimed by the whole nation. This will account for the umbrage taken by Indians at purchases made and titles obtained by private persons and even by provinces: since no Indian whatsoever, let his influence or power in his own country be ever so great, can give away any more than his own right in any piece of land; which in the Cherokee Nation would be no more than as one is to 13,500. . . .[24]

The necessity of obtaining the agreement of large numbers of tribesmen to land cessions was to complicate and add greatly to the expense of the many Indian "congresses" held by the Superintendent in his effort to establish the Southern Indian Boundary Line.

Stuart's report and the numerous Indian treaties, which played such a central role in the evolution of the Southern Indian Boundary Line, make it clear that the tribes listed by Atkin in his report of 1755 were those which controlled the interior of the continent south of the Ohio and east of the Mississippi during the second half of the eighteenth century. Before proceeding to a discussion of the British realization and appreciation of their control, which formed the background of the boundary negotiations to be considered in the following chapters, it is necessary briefly to consider these tribes in terms of their numbers and location during the period 1763-1775.

The Cherokee.—In 1764 Stuart estimated that the Cherokee villages could muster a total of 2,750 fighting men. Using a factor of one fighting man for approximately five Indians, this would place the Cherokee total at 13,750 which is close to the 13,500 mentioned by Stuart.[25] The Cherokee occupied about forty towns which were commonly divided into four groups or divisions known as: (1) the Lower Towns, located in the Keowee and Tugaloo river valleys; (2) the Middle Towns, located on the upper reaches of the Little Tennessee River; (3) the Valley Towns, located to the north of the Hiwassee River; and (4) the overhill Towns, located on the lower reaches of the Little Tennessee. Contemporary sources frequently combined the Valley Towns with the Overhill.

The strategic importance of the Cherokee location, astride the Appalachian Mountains in the heart of the present states of Tennessee, North and South Carolina, and Georgia, was emphasized

24. *Ibid.*, p. 490.
25. *Ibid.*, p. 465. Although estimates vary widely, this total seems reasonable and is usually accepted.

by both Atkin and Stuart. The Cherokee were influenced and affected by the neighboring colonies of Virginia, North and South Carolina, and Georgia during the period covered by this study. In turn, the affairs of these colonies were profoundly influenced by their potent Cherokee neighbors, who were in a position to deny access to vast areas of but little used and loosely held hunting grounds.

Considered more civilized than the other southern tribes, the Cherokee were proud of a racial and cultural unity and of being "one people." There is, however, frequent evidence to indicate that unity of purpose and action was more of a myth than fact and that schisms between the tribal divisions were frequent. A system of seniority seems to have extended a slightly greater authority to the chiefs of the Overhill town of Chote, who were often referred to as "Emperor"; but, as noted above, these dignitaries possessed but little coercive power.

The Catawba.—The Catawba had been reduced to a small group able to muster only about sixty fighting men in 1764. By the best estimates their total number was between 300 and 350 during the pre-revolutionary decade. They were granted a reservation of land on the Catawba River between North and South Carolina in 1763 and were very much under the protection and control of the latter colony. Effectively by-passed and surrounded by the advancing tide of white settlement, the Catawbas represented no barrier to westward expansion during the period which saw the evolution of the Southern Indian Boundary Line.

The Creeks.—The Creeks or "Muscokee" (Muskogee) formed a loose confederacy of people who populated an extensive area of the Southeast. The variety of racial elements involved and the wide dispersal of their settlements made the Creeks even less unified than the Cherokee. In his report of 1764, Stuart identified forty-one Creek towns capable of mustering about 3,600 warriors as forming the "nation." The two largest divisions of the tribe were: (1) the Upper Creeks, inhabiting towns in the valleys of the Coosa and Oakfuskie rivers and (2) the Lower Creeks, inhabiting towns in the valleys of the Chattahoochee and Flint rivers. A third division of the tribe was evolving during the later years of the period and came to be identified by the name Seminole during the 1770's. The Seminoles were an offshoot of the Lower Creek division, who were moving into the area of the modern state of Florida. During the twelve-year period of this study the Creek strength was roughly divided between the Upper and Lower Creeks on a two-thirds, one-third basis, with the Upper division mustering about 2,000 warriors. The total population of the confederacy probably reached 17,000 or 18,000, if all associated groups are included.

Romans left no doubt as to the polyglot nature of the Creek tribe when he wrote:

A mixture of the remains of the Cawittas, Talepoosas, Coosas, Apalachias, Conshacs or Coosades, Oakmulgis, Oconis, Okchoys, Alibamons, Natchez, Weetumkus, Pakanas, Taensas, Chacsihoomas, Abekas and some other tribes whose names I do not recollect . . . call themselves Muscokees and are at present known to us by the general name of Creeks, and divided into upper and lower Creeks; also those they call allies and are a colony from the others living far south in East Florida.[26]

The Upper and Lower divisions acknowledged each other as brethren and frequently, but by no means always, pursued the same policies. The Seminoles to the south were rapidly moving toward a complete separation. It is suggested that the word "Seminole" was used by the Creeks to indicate their fellows who had broken from the tribe and failed to obey its councils.[27]

It can be seen in Figure 1 that the Creeks were located in the "deep" South and were principally engaged in contacts with the colonies of Georgia, East Florida, and West Florida during the period of this study.

26. Romans, *Natural History of Florida*, p. 90.
27. Romans' spelling of some of these tribal names may be unfamiliar to the reader of today. The following list places the more widely known names alongside of Romans.' The page numbers refer to the place in Swanton's *The Indians of the Southeastern United States* where each tribe is discussed:

Cawittas	Coweta (p. 126)
Talepoosas	Tallapoosa Yuchi (p. 214)
Coosas	Coosa (p. 124)
Apalachias	Apalachee (p. 89)
Conshacs or Coosades	Cusabo (p. 128)
Oakmulgis	Akmulgee (p. 168)
Oconis	Oconee (p. 165)
Okchoys	Okchai (p. 166)
Alibamons	Alabama (p. 86)
Natchez	Natchez (p. 158)
Weetumkus	Wiwohka (p. 207)
Pakanas	Pakana (p. 170)
Taensas	Taensa (p. 188)
Chacsihoomas	Chakchiuma (p. 105)
Abekas	Abihka (p. 81)

The Choctaws.—The most numerous of all the southern tribes were the Choctaw; they were more dependent upon agriculture and consequently had less extensive hunting grounds under their control. Estimates vary widely, but it is probable that the Choctaw were capable of mustering about 5,000 fighting men from their numerous towns located along the upper reaches of the Pearl and Pascagoula rivers. Stuart mentioned that he gained a portion of his knowledge of this tribe, which had long been under a strong French influence, from two members of the tribe while they attended the Indian Congress at Augusta in 1763.

The Choctaw seem to have possessed even less cohesiveness in their internal organization than the Creeks. The French identified an eastern and western division, but during the British period of control in the far Southeast, three divisions were usually recognized. These were: (1) the Upper Choctaw Towns, located on the branches of the Upper Pearl River and composing about one-half of the total strength of the tribe; (2) the Lower Choctaw Towns, located along the branches of Tombigbee River to the east with about one-quarter of the tribe's number; (3) the Six Towns located along the branches of the upper Pascagoula River accounted for a final one-quarter of the tribe's total strength.

Contacts with the Choctaw regarding land matters were chiefly the concern of West Florida.

The Chickasaws.—Stuart, like most British observers, was full of admiration for the "brave little nation of Chickasaws," which had earned its high regard among the English by strongly resisting the French. The tribe had been reduced by a long period of warfare with the French and Choctaw as well as other Indian enemies. Stuart credited the main group, located about forty miles to the north of the Choctaw, with about 450 gun men. He also mentioned the two emigrant groups which had settled on the Savannah River and among the Creeks earlier. These, he noted, were looked down upon as traitors by the members of the main group, which still inhabited the ancestral homeland near the upper Tombigbee River.

The Chickasaw, probably as a consequence of their small number and exposed position, had a high degree of unity. They were far removed from areas being actively settled by Europeans during the pre-revolutionary period and were usually more concerned in trade than land and boundary matters with the white men.

Mention must be made of the so-called Small Tribes or Nations which were found along the eastern bank of the lower Mississippi River. Stuart listed these as the: "Beluxis, Humas, Attucapas, Bayuglas, Tunicas, Peluchas, Osugulas and Querphas."[28] Of these the Querphas were noted as being the most numerous with five villages. The Osugulas were credited with three and the Tunicas with two villages.

This, very briefly sketched, was the pattern formed by the approximately 60,000 Indians who claimed almost all of the southeastern quarter of the continental empire which the British had won from the French and Spanish.

THE ADVANCE OF WHITE SETTLEMENT

It was into this "Indian Country," of vast extent and sparse population, that white settlers from the British colonies advanced with renewed vigor as the French and Spanish relinquished their claims during the second half of the eighteenth century. This advance quickly produced an uneasiness among the Indians of the region, who saw in it a serious threat to their way of life. That the advance of white settlement was a very real phenomenon can be seen by a comparison of the four population maps of Figure 2. The increase in numbers and extension of white population toward the interior is striking, to say the least. To the Indians of the Southeast it may well have seemed like a white tide threatening to sweep them away before it.

The reasons for this increase and migration of European and African Americans have been discussed at great length elsewhere and will be briefly summarized here. The great growth in numbers indicated by the maps of Figure 2 was the result of both natural increase and immigration. The significance of immigration is

28. C.O. 323-17, p. 488. Stuart's spelling of some of these tribal names may be unfamiliar to the reader of today. The following list places the more widely known names alongside of Stuart's. The page numbers refer to the place in Swanton's *The Indians of the Southeastern United States*, where each tribe is discussed:

Beluxis	Biloxi (p. 97)
Humas	Houma (p. 139)
Attucapas	Atakapa (p. 93)
Bayuglas	Bayogoula (p. 95)
Tunicas	Tunica (p. 197)
Peluchas	Opelousa (p. 168)
Osugulas	Pascagoula (p. 170)
Querphas	Quapaw (p. 176)

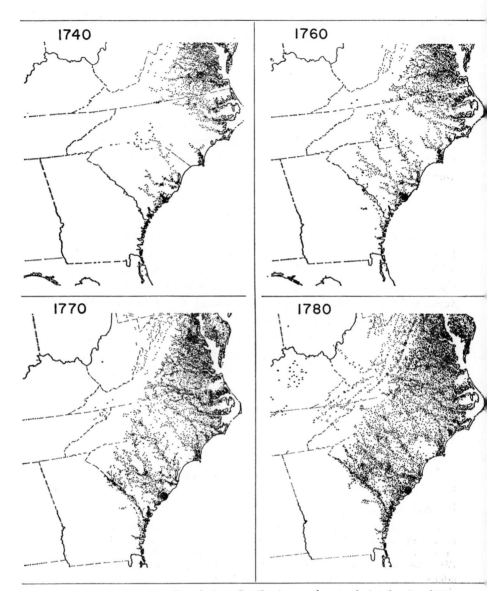

Fig. 2. Population distribution and growth in the Southeast. 1 dot = 200 colonists. (From Friis, *A Series of Population Maps,* used with the permission of the American Geographical Society.)

emphasized when it is realized that no less than one-third of the seaboard colonists were foreign born in 1760.[29]

By present-day standards the population density of even the most populous colonies was not high. There were, however, strong forces generated from within these colonies which drove many individuals to leave the security of the tidewater for the piedmont and successively the piedmont for the mountains and valleys beyond. The most important factors which have been advanced to explain this westward migration are soil exhaustion and decreased crop yields, rising land values in more densely settled eastern areas and older communities, abundant cheap land of good to high quality in the West, speculative land ventures in the West, internecine conflicts of the tidewater and piedmont settlements, generous land laws of colonial governments wishing to populate exposed frontiers, the granting of bounty lands for military and other service, restrictive land systems and tenure in older, settled areas, attractive reports and propaganda concerning the West, and the inability of dissenting individuals and groups to adapt to the often rigid pattern of society in the East.[30] The Indians were but little concerned with the causes of this advance toward their hunting grounds and sacred tribal lands. The advance was the important thing; it was real and accelerating and they knew it threatened to inundate and destroy them and their way of life. British administrators also recognized the westward tide of the seaboard colonists which was approaching flood stage in the wake of British victories over the French in the interior.[31]

Lewis Evans, the eighteenth-century geographer, described the pattern formed by the growing British settlements at the outbreak of the French and Indian War (1754-1763):

The settlements made by the English are bounded on one side by the ocean, and on the other by no certain line or distance; for in some places they are not above 30 or 40 miles from the heads of the tide and in others 150 or 200. . . . The scattered settlements thence to

29. Curtis P. Nettels, *The Roots of American Civilization: A History of American-Colonial Life* (New York, 1938), p. 383. For a graphic demonstration of population growth during the colonial period see the cartogram presented by Ralph H. Brown, *Historical Geography of the United States* (New York, 1948), p. 50.

30. Herman R. Friis, *A Series of Population Maps of the Colonies and the United States, 1625-1790* (American Geographical Society, Mimeographed Publication No. 3 [New York, 1940]), p. 12.

31. See the extract from the Board of Trade Report on the Peace of Paris, 1763, quoted below on p. 30.

Ohio along Yoghiogani and Monaungahela are lately broke up by the incroachments of the French in that quarter. Those on Green Briar and its branches, and downward to the fork, and thence southward by Stahlmakers, at the head fork of the Holston River, to the line dividing Virginia and Carolina, complete the line, and yet remain undisturbed. This may be supposed to include our remotest settlements; but for many miles in breadth they are very widely scattered; not so much for want of people to improve and plant, but schemes in almost every colony to prevent them.[32]

Devastated and abandoned during the war, most of these transmontane settlements were soon reoccupied with the re-establishment of British control over the area. The period from the cessation of the French and Indian War to the American Revolution was one of persistent expansion in the Southeast, especially into the valleys of the area which was to become the states of West Virginia, Kentucky, and Tennessee. A less well-chronicled but perhaps equally significant movement was that taking place as pioneers moved southward to occupy the youthful colony of Georgia and the newly created colonies of East and West Florida.

Inevitably these movements of pioneer settlers toward the interior and southern coasts led to the invasion of lands claimed and defended by the Indians who hunted and lived on them. The problem of how to guide the growth and increased prosperity of her seaboard colonies and still avoid an open conflict with the Indians was to form a major preoccupation for the British during the period between 1763 and 1775. The policy chosen to solve this problem involved the establishment of a boundary line which would clearly separate the lands reserved for the use of the Indians from those available for occupation and exploitation by peoples of European origin and their African slaves. It is to the concept of such a boundary line that attention must now be turned.

32. Lewis Evans, *Geographical, Historical, Political, Philosophical and Mechanical Essays* . . . (Philadelphia, 1755), p. 2. Evans was discussing the settlements along the Youghiogheny and Monongahela rivers in Pennsylvania and those on the Greenbrier and Holston behind the colony of Virginia.

III · *The Concept of a Boundary Line*

The French and Indian War made the British increasingly aware of the strength of the tribes located in the American wilderness. This awareness began to crystalize in the shape of policies which would, it was argued, win the allegiance of the Indians to the British cause and obviate an enormously costly military operation which might otherwise be required to reduce them. Both the French and Spanish were waging an effective propaganda campaign to convince the Indians that the English wished nothing less than their total extermination to allow the pre-emption of the whole continent east of the Mississippi by the land-hungry colonists of the seaboard. As Pownall had pointed out in 1755, the English exhibited "an insatiable thirst after landed possessions." This he saw as "the sole ground of the loss and alienation of the Indians from the English interest and this is the ground the French work upon."[1]

Following the fall of Fort Duquesne in 1760, the governor of Virginia was ordered to refrain from making land grants of any kind on the upper Ohio and its tributaries. In imposing this prohibition on the westward growth of the colony, the Board of Trade acted in the belief that Indian claims to the areas concerned had to be dealt with effectively before orderly and secure settlement along the frontier could result.[2] Although the precise nature and extent of the Indian claims were not uniformly understood, the very fact that there were such claims greatly influenced policies being formulated by British ministers. As early as January, 1763, the Secretary of State for the Southern Department, Lord Egremont, observed:

1. "Memorial Stating the Nature of the Service in North America 1755—and Proposing A general Plan of Operation founded thereon" by T. Pownall in C. O. 5-18, p. 303.

2. A more complete and documented discussion of this point will be found in the next chapter.

His Mty [has] it much at heart to conciliate the affection of the Indian nations, by every act of strict justice, and by affording them his royal protection from any encroachment on the lands they have reserved to themselves, for their hunting grounds, & for their own support & habitation; and I may inform you that a plan, for this desirable end, is actually under consideration.[3]

Egremont presented a paper titled "Hints relative to the Division and Government of the conquered and newly acquired Countries in America" to the Board of Trade on May 5, 1763.[4] It has been suggested that "Hints" was written by Henry Ellis, governor of Georgia and knowledgeable Indian expert. He expressed a view popular with George III's chief advisors when he wrote:

It might also be necessary to fix upon some line for a western boundary to our ancient provinces beyond which our people should not at present be permitted to settle hence as their numbers increased they would emigrate to Nova Scotia or to the provinces on the southern frontier where they would be useful to their mother country instead of planting themselves in the heart of America out of the reach of governments and where from the great difficulty of procuring European commodities they would be compelled to commence manufactures to the infinite prejudice of Britain.[5]

The mercantilist attitude toward the American colonies was clearly phrased in "Hints," as was the concept of a boundary to restrain their westward growth. The thought of interior colonies removed from easy access by sea was an anathema to many English merchants and policy-makers of the mid-eighteenth century. A generation earlier the author of an anonymous tract entitled "Some Considerations relating to the present Condition of the Plantations; With Proposals for a Better Regulation of Them" had detected a predilection among the "Americans" which was equally anathematic. Writing in about 1730 the author of "Some Considerations" observed, "the people born there [America] are too apt to inbibe notions of independency of their mother Kingdom."[6] It was

3. Quoted from C. O. 5-214 by Alden, *John Stuart,* p. 244.
4. C. O. 323-16, p. 189 ff.
5. *Ibid.,* p. 194. Verner W. Crane, "Hints Relative to the Division and Government of the Conquered and Newly Acquired Countries In America," *The Mississippi Valley Historical Review,* VIII (March, 1922), 367-73. Crane states that "the Hints" may fairly be regarded as the key document in the series which culminated, more or less fortuitously in the proclamation of October 7, 1763.
6. C. O. 5-5, p. 313.

generally understood that such "notions of independency" often arose in those areas farthest removed from the harbors and navigable streams of the seaboard.

John Cartwright, writing about the American colonies in 1775, observed that: "Nations are most free and happy when their extremities are near enough to the vital seat of government to feel its pervading principle in its full warmth and activity, and by the spring of their own re-action to pour into the heart again full-flowing tides of health, life and vigour."[7]

The suggested boundary line would, it was felt, serve to forestall any serious ruptures with the mother kingdom which might be precipitated by the growth of interior populations entirely removed from maritime commerce. Ellis, the governor of Georgia, was aware of the part such a boundary could play in diverting the growing population of the middle colonies to his own sparsely populated frontier colony as well as to the soon-to-be-organized Floridas farther south.

Clearly, the idea of a continuous boundary line to separate the British American colonies of the Atlantic seaboard from the powerful Indian tribes of the interior appealed to a numerous and important segment of those in a position to shape the future course of empire in the New World. In addition, the fur trade interests were still strong and could be expected to support a policy which would, in effect, create a gigantic Indian reserve wherein the hirsute harvests of the forests could not be diminished by the encroaching planter's clearing ax and plow.

A TENTATIVE BOUNDARY PROPOSED

On the same day that he presented the "Hints" to the Board of Trade, the secretary of state officially informed its members of the happy conclusion of the peace negotiations with France and Spain. He then requested that the board prepare a general report relative to the newly ceded territory which had been added to the empire. In his request to the board, Egremont observed that it might be found necessary to erect forts in the Indian country to guarantee their pacification. On this topic he continued by observing:

. . . yet His Majesty's justice and moderation inclines him to adopt the more eligible method of conciliating the minds of the Indians by the

7. Harold M. Baer, "An Early Plan for the Development of the West," *The American Historical Review*, XXX (April, 1925), 541.

mildness of his government by protecting their persons and property and securing to them all the possessions, rights and privileges they have hitherto enjoyed and are entitled to, most cautiously guarding against any invasion or occupation of their hunting lands, the possession of which is to be acquired by fair purchase only and it has been thought so highly expedient to give them the earliest most convincing proofs of His Majestys gracious and friendly intentions on this head that I have already received and transmitted the Kings commands to this purpose to the governors of Virginia, the two Carolinas and Georgia, and to the Agent for Indian Affairs.[8]

Early in the following month the Board of Trade issued its lengthy report on the Peace of 1763 with recommendations for the organization of the newly won territories in North America. In outlining the advantages which had accrued to the Crown of Great Britain by the terms of the peace treaty, the board mentioned first the important northern fisheries and then observed that, "another obvious advantage of the cession will be the supplying of all the Indian Tribes upon the continent of North America with European commodities immediately through the hands of English traders."[9] Following this observation the report noted that, "another advantage . . . is the secure settling of the whole coast of North America . . . from the mouth of the Mississippi to the boundaries of the Hudsons Bay settlements . . . by the industry of emigrants from Europe or from the overflowing of your Majestys ancient colonies."[10] In an illuminating elaboration of this statement the report continued:

Nothing is more certain than that many of Your Majesty's ancient colonies appeared to be overstocked with inhabitants, occasioned partly from an extremely increasing population in some of those colonies whose boundaries had become too narrow for their numbers, but chiefly by the monopoly of lands in the hands of land jobbers from the

8. C. O. 323-15, p. 101. The communication to the southern governors and Indian superintendent took the form of a circular letter dated March 16, 1763 (C. O. 323-15, p. 104) in which it was stressed that the winning of the Indian's confidence was imperative. The southern Indians were to be met in a general congress as soon as possible. The new political situation would be explained to them in as delicate a manner as possible in order to counter the French and Spanish propagandist's efforts. This congress was held at Augusta in November, 1763, and marked the beginning of a long series of negotiations that led to the delineation of the Southern Indian Boundary Line. For a published version of this letter, see William L. Saunders (ed.), *The Colonial Records of North Carolina* (Raleigh, 1886-1890), VI, 974.

9. C. O. 5-65, p. 63.

10. *Ibid.*, p. 64.

extravagant and injudicious grants made by some of Your Majesty's governors, whereby a great many of Your Majesty's subjects were either forced into manufactures, being excluded from planting by the high price of land (a situation which they otherwise would have preferred) or forced to emigrate to the other side of the mountains, where they were exposed to the irruptions of the Indians as well as the hostilities of the French contrived to excite at first, by the Indians in their alliance, and at last by regular troops in Nova Scotia, and a dread of the like calamities on the side of Georgia from the Indians and Spaniards, have hitherto prevented the salutory progress of these new settlements, and the happy consequences which otherwise might have been expected from them.[11]

Completing their review of the advantages which had accrued as a result of the peace treaty, the Lords of Trade urged the speedy establishment of civil governments in the newly ceded territories. In the more remote areas such as the Indian hunting grounds, "where no perpetual residence or planting" was intended, a free trade regulated by "such military force . . . judged necessary as well for the protection of trade and the good of your majesty's Sovereignty and the general defence of North America" was to be established.[12] This Indian reserve, "where no settlement by planting is intended immediately at least to be attempted," was to be an answer to the Indian apprehensions regarding their lands. It would be theirs alone and free of "any particular form of civil government." The pressure for increased economy in the administration of the postwar empire was to minimize the number of military posts maintained in the Indian country at a later date.[13]

Rather than outline any program for the regulation of trade in the Indian reserve, the board chose to wait until reports from the military commander and superintendents for Indian affairs could be obtained and studied. They did not, however, hesitate in recommending to the king that his "several governors of [his] ancient colonies" be ordered to cease making any "new grants of land beyond certain fixed limits to be laid down in the instructions for that purpose."[14] To illustrate the limits of this enormous Indian reserve as well as the bounds of Florida and Canada, the Board of

11. *Ibid.,* pp. 64-65.
12. *Ibid.,* p. 67A.
13. The impracticability of any attempt to pacify the Indians by fortifying interior positions was stressed by Thomas Pownall in 1755. See pp. 10 and 11 above for Pownall's statements.
14. C. O. 5-65, p. 67.

Trade included a map with its report.[15] This map appears to be
the first attempt at plotting the Indian boundary line, which was
becoming a central feature in the developing British imperial policy
for North America.

Figure 3 is based on a tracing made from the original map,
which has been separated from the Board of Trade report. The
original is a large engraved map showing most of the North American continent as it was known to the cartographers of the mid-
eighteenth century. The tracing can only hint at some of its more
obvious errors and distortions, such as the fragmented Florida
peninsula. The eastern portion of the map is colored and contains
several lengthy extracts from the peace treaty. The suggested
Indian boundary line is shown by a red line. The boundary for
the southern district begins at the confluence of the Gt. Conaway
[Kanawha] River with the Ohio and follows the Kanawha River
south to the Virginia-North Carolina boundary line.[16] From the
headwaters of this river, which is clearly shown as being west of
the mountains, the line cuts overland across North and South
Carolina to the upper Flint River. The Flint River was also to
divide Florida into an eastern and western division. The northern
boundary of West Florida to the Mississippi completed the bounds
of the Indian reserve, which the Board of Trade proposed to
establish early in 1763.

Admitting to a profound ignorance of the geography of southern
North America, "particularly of that part which lies between the
great mountains and the Mississippi, of which there are not extant
any charts or accounts on which we can depend," the Board of
Trade had given form to a boundary line, which, if adopted, would
exclude the land-hungry American colonists from almost all of the
transmontane country between the Ohio River and the thirty-
first parallel.

15. "An Accurate Map of North America Describing and Distinguishing the
British, Spanish and French Dominions. . . . According to the Definitive Treaty
Concluded at Paris 10 February 1763 etc.," Eman Bowen, Geogr. to His Majesty
and John Gibson engraver, M.R. 26, P.R.O.

16. Although the eighteenth-century maps and documents describing this area of
the present-day states of West Virginia and Virginia frequently use the names
"Kanawha" (or its variants) and "New" indiscriminately, modern usage is
somewhat more precise. The Kanawha or Great Kanawha River is the name
applied to the stream formed by the junction of the New and Gauley rivers in
Fayette County, West Virginia. It flows for about 97 miles in a northwesterly
direction to the Ohio River. The New River is formed by the junction of the
North and South forks in Ashe County, North Carolina. It flows generally northward for about 255 miles to join the Gauley and form the Kanawha.

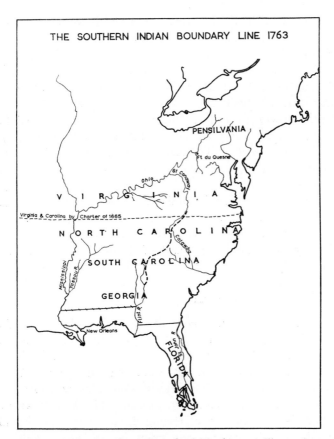

Fig. 3. Tracing from Board of Trade map illustrating a preliminary proposal for an Indian boundary line. (P.R.O., M.R. 26.)

The secretary of state informed the Board of Trade in July that the king had approved the plan for the creation of the three new governments of Canada and East and West Florida as illustrated on their map. He observed, however, that the large Indian reserve might become a source of trouble if left outside of any civil authority. It was feared that the area would become a refuge for criminals and possibly tempt other powers to lay claim to the area "as derelict lands."[17] To avoid these evils Egremont requested the board to consider extending the limits of Canada to embrace the Great Lakes to the Mississippi and "also that all lands

17. C. O. 5-65, p. 18.

whatsoever ceded by the late treaty, and which are not already included within the limits of His Majesty's ancient colonies or intended to form the governments of East and West Florida, . . . be assigned to the government of Canada, unless your Lordships should suggest any other distribution which might answer the purpose more effectually."[18]

On the general plan of an Indian reserve to be protected from encroachment by Europeans, the king indicated his entire approval.[19] The Board of Trade, however, advised against the inclusion of the Indian reserve in the bounds of an extended Canada or any other province and urged that the interior "be reserved, for the present for the use of the Indians."[20] Thus during the summer months of 1763 the British government seemed close to adopting a program which would result in the creation of an Indian boundary line approximating the Board of Trade's tentative boundary shown on Figure 3.

A BOUNDARY PROCLAIMED

An Indian uprising under the inspired leadership of Chief Pontiac had broken out in May of 1763 and the full impact of the loss of most of the interior military garrisons had probably been appreciated in London by the late summer of that year.[21] Without mentioning the Indian rising directly, Lord Halifax wrote to the Board of Trade on September 19 to state: "His Majesty approves your Lordships proposition of issuing immediately a proclamation to prohibit for the present, any grant for settlement within the bounds of the countries intended to be reserved for the use of the Indians. . . ."[22]

In outlining the purposes of the proclamation, the new secretary of state made it clear that it would be an omnibus document to declare the provisions for bounty lands to the reduced veterans who had served against the king's enemies in North America and to: (a) set the limits of the new colonies of Canada and the two Floridas, (b) establish these colonies, (c) prohibit private pur-

18. *Ibid.*
19. *Ibid.*, p. 19.
20. C. O. 323-16, p. 329.
21. Howard H. Peckham, *Pontiac and the Indian Uprising* (Princeton, N.J., 1947), is an excellent study of this important episode. Fred J. Hinkhouse, *The Preliminaries of the American Revolution As Seen in the English Press 1763-1775* (New York, 1926), p. 37.
22. C. O. 323-16, p. 329.

chases of land from the Indians, (d) establish a free Indian trade under a system of licensing, and (e) empower the king's military officers and Indian agents to seize criminals and fugitives in the Indian reserve. On October 4 a draft of the requested proclamation was forwarded and on October 7, 1763, the document was promulgated.[23]

The Proclamation of 1763 was undoubtedly one of the most important instruments of British policy concerning North America during the eighteenth century. As indicated above, a wide range of topics were included in this omnibus instrument, which is still the subject of debate among historians interested in the critical decade which saw the growth of colonial opposition to the Crown. In this study only those elements of the proclamation which seem most directly relevant to the evolution of the Southern Indian Boundary Line will be investigated.

Included in the prolix wording of the proclamation were the following phrases relating to "a western boundary . . . beyond which our people should not at present be permitted to settle":

. . . that the several nations or tribes of Indians with whom we are connected, and who live under our protection, should not be molested or disturbed in the possession of such parts of our dominions and territories as, not having been ceded to, or purchased by us, are reserved to them, or any of them, as their hunting grounds.

The governors of the newly proclaimed colonies of Quebec, East Florida, and West Florida were enjoined not to grant any land beyond the "bounds of their respective governments, as described in their commissions." Since the bounds of the older colonies were not so neatly fixed and in some cases extended to the great south sea (as the Pacific Ocean was known), the problem of delineating a western boundary for them was more difficult. Rather than describing the boundary line which the Board of Trade had suggested in its report of June, the proclamation included the following prohibition to the governors of the elder colonies:

That no governor or commander-in-chief in any of our other colonies or plantations in America, do presume for the present, and until our further pleasure be known, to grant warrants of survey, or pass patents

23. The proclamation was published in full with a map in the October, 1763, issue of *The Gentleman's Magazine* (London). It can also be found in Charles J. Kappler, *Indian Affairs—Laws and Treaties* (Washington, 1903-1929), IV, 1172, or Merrill Jensen (ed.), *American Colonial Documents to 1776,* Vol. IX of *English Historical Documents* (London, 1955), pp. 640-43.

for any lands beyond the heads or sources of any of the rivers which fall into the Atlantic Ocean from the west and northwest; or upon any lands whatever, which not having been ceded to, or purchased by us . . . are reserved to the said Indians, or any of them.

Thus with a few strokes of the pen the watershed of the Appalachian Mountain system was to mark temporarily the westernmost limit of the colonies.

It was further stipulated that individuals could not make any purchases of land or establish settlements in the Indian country. Land was to be purchased from the Indians only in the name of the Crown, "at some public meeting or assembly of the said Indians, to be held for that purpose by the governor or commander-in-chief of our colonies respectively within which they shall lie."

In the case of settlements already located in the Indian reserve the proclamation was brutally explicit. It stated:

And we do further strictly enjoin and require all persons whatever, who have either wilfully or inadvertently seated themselves upon any lands within the countries above described, or upon any other lands, which not having been ceded to, or purchased by us, are still reserved to the said Indians as aforesaid, forthwith to remove themselves from such settlements.

The only area where permanent settlement had already crossed the watershed of the Southeast was along the Virginia frontier. The effect of the proclamation on the settlers there is discussed in the chapter devoted to the evolution of the Indian boundary line in that colony.

No official map was prepared to accompany the proclamation of 1763 but one was drawn for the October issue of *The Gentleman's Magazine,* which published the full text of the document. This map is included as Figure 4. It is clear from a comparison of Figures 3 and 4 that the Board of Trade had abandoned the boundary proposal which had been included in their report of June 8. It would seem probable that the knowledge of the long-feared Indian uprising which had broken out under Pontiac's leadership caused the board to seize the expedient of an easily described watershed boundary. Also it can be seen that the "Lands Reserved for the Indians" extended ever farther to the east than had the earlier proposal. The New River valley, which was settled by Virginians, was the most notable of the areas surrendered to the Indians by the terms of the proclamation. On the map show-

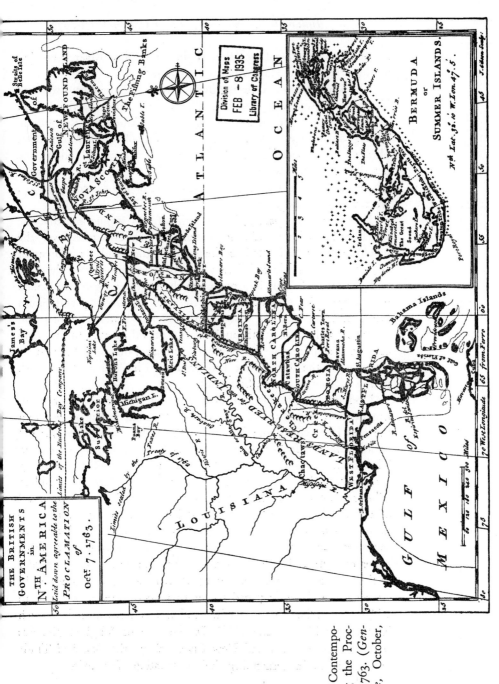

Fig. 4. Contemporary map showing the Proclamation Line of 1763. (*Gentleman's Magazine*, October, 1763.)

ing the Proclamation Line (Fig. 4) the name New River is applied to the whole New-Kanawha river system.[24]

The Proclamation Line is often shown in elementary texts and historical atlases as representing the western limits of the British colonies during the period preceding the American Revolution. This is an incorrect assumption which overlooks a very important phrase in the proclamation. This is the phrase which follows the description of the watershed line and reads: "or upon any lands whatever, which not having been ceded to, or purchased by us . . . are reserved to the said Indians."

It is to be emphasized, in the light of this stipulation, that the Proclamation of 1763 did not extend British dominion over the whole of the area located to the east of "the heads or sources of any of the rivers which fall into the Atlantic Ocean from the west and northwest." This is a point which has often been overlooked in non-specialist presentations. Vast areas in Georgia and South Carolina located to the east of the watershed were claimed and retained by the Indians throughout the period of 1763 to 1775 and only in Virginia was the Southern Indian Boundary Line to be extended to the west of the Proclamation Line during the British period of control in the Southeast.

Undoubtedly, Pontiac's Indian uprising lent an added note of urgency to the drafting of the proclamation but it can be seen that the area reserved for the Indians south of the Ohio River was not greatly changed from that suggested by the Board of Trade earlier. The Proclamation Line was, to a large extent but not entirely, the product of expediency; it was meant to reassure those Indian tribes not yet allied with Pontiac. Nor was the order for the removal of settlers already established on land claimed by the Indians entirely new or without precedent. It was noted in the *Records of the Moravians,* on August 6, 1763, that: "In the Charleston newspaper of June 25th there is a most favorable declaration in behalf of the Indians, dated December 19, 1761, in which all governors in America are earnestly urged to see that no one settles on land to which the Indians have a claim, and if any have settled on such land they will be removed."[25] In the case of Virginia pioneers settled in the Holston and New River valleys, the Board of Trade was consistent in demanding their evacuation after 1760.

24. See note on p. 32, above.
25. Adelaide L. Fries (ed.), *Records of the Moravians in North Carolina, 1752-1775,* I (Raleigh, N.C., 1925), 274.

There seems little doubt, however, that the Proclamation Line was a temporary stopgap measure rather than a viable boundary meant to separate permanently George III's red and white subjects in the New World. Washington was probably correct in his evaluation when he wrote:

I can never look upon that proclamation in any other light (but this I say between ourselves) than as a temporary expedient to quiet the minds of the Indians . . . any person, therefore, who neglects the present opportunity of hunting out good lands, and in some measure marking and distinguishing them for his own, (in order to keep others from settling them), will never regain it.[26]

Hinsdale showed that Franklin also concluded that the proclamation was entirely the product of the need to pacify the Indians at a critical time. The same authority stressed the effect of the procla-X mation and the British land policy which followed it by pointing to the Declaration of Independence, which charged that the king had: "endeavored to prevent the population of these states; for that purpose obstructing the laws for the naturalization of foreigners; refusing to pass others to encourage migrations hither, and raising the conditions of new appropriations of lands."[27]

In view of the energetic manner in which the king's civil servants pursued the quest for extended boundary lines and land cessions from the Indians in the twelve-year period preceding the Declaration of Independence, this indictment seems exaggerated. Abbott stated that the Proclamation Line was generally regarded as the temporary measure it was. She pointed out that, "direct colonial opposition did not come until 1768 when the line was scheduled to become a permanent policy."[28]

It is significant to note that the Indians too were aware of the direction in which the British Crown was moving during the summer of 1763. The officer in charge at Augusta, Georgia, received a "talk" from the headmen of the Lower Creeks which was dated September 16, 1763. In this talk the Indians stated:

It seems you keep your talk very private, but there is nothing to be hid from we red people: there was a red man from the Tuckabatchies

26. Worthington Chauncey Ford, *The Writings of George Washington*, II (New York, 1889), 220.

27. B. A. Hinsdale, "The Western Land Policy of The British Government From 1763 to 1775," *Ohio Archeological and Historical Publications*, I (Dec., 1887), 207-29.

28. Phyllis Ruth Abbott, "The Development and Operation of an American Land System to 1800," (Ph.D. dissertation, University of Wisconsin, 1959), p. 48.

went down with the white people, and when he got to Augusta, the white people desired him to go back immediately, and he came away according to their desire; as he returned back he overtook a gang of pack-horses, and kept company with them to the Oakmuljees, and a white man told him several things, but whether it be true or not we cannot tell, this man that brings us this news, is an old man, and would not tell lies; we have heard, that the governor of Charles-Town intends to buy our lands from us, as far as Ogeechie, and as high up as Broad River; and the governor of Savannah intends to buy from us, as far as the fork of Alatamaha; and the governor of North-Carolina intends to buy as far as the Okonies.[29]

Clearly, talk of land purchase and cession was very widespread in the southern frontier even before the proclamation was promulgated. It is not surprising that the topic of a boundary line to separate the Indian hunting grounds from the areas open to white settlement was introduced early into the deliberations of the Southern Indian Congress held between the governors of Virginia, North Carolina, South Carolina, and Georgia and members of the Chickasaw, Choctaw, Cherokee, Creek, and Catawba tribes at Augusta, Georgia, on November 5, 1763.[30] The fourth article of the "Treaty For the Preservation and Continuance of a Firm and Perfect Peace and Friendship . . . ," signed at this congress, delineated the first section of the Southern Indian Boundary Line.[31] It will be shown that the Southern Indian Boundary Line and not the ephemeral Proclamation Line separated the British colonies from the Indian tribes of the Southeast on the eve of the American Revolution.

THE BOUNDARY IN THE PLAN OF 1764

As indicated above, the Board of Trade had admitted in early 1763 that more information was necessary before a definitive program for the administration of the Indian reserve could be proposed. They mentioned the military commander and the superintendents for Indian affairs as particular experts who had been requested to make reports on the general topic of Indian affairs.[32]

29. *Journal of the Congress of the Four Southern Governors, and the Superintendent of That District, with the Five Nations of Indians, at Augusta, 1763* (Charles-Town, 1764), p. 12.

30. *Ibid.*, p. 38.

31. This section of the boundary was to divide Georgia from the Creeks and is discussed in detail in the chapter dealing with that colony.

32. C. O. 5-65, p. 67.

The reports received from these experts contributed materially to the substance of the "Plan for the Future Management of Indian Affairs," which was produced by the Board of Trade in 1764.[33] Several of the forty-three articles of the Plan of 1764, as it is commonly designated, established rather strict controls for the Indian trade. These provisions were strongly opposed by the Indian traders and other commercial interests. Included in the proposed regulations was a tax to be placed on the fur trade to help support the administration of the scheme. Such a tax would have required parliamentary approval before the Plan of 1764 could become law and operative. The Stamp Act disturbances which flared during the period coupled with vigorous opposition from the traders made the necessary parliamentary consideration inexpedient and the Plan of 1764 never became law.

The failure to obtain parliamentary approval for the Plan of 1764 seemed to have little effect on the execution of its provisions regarding land and boundary matters in the Southeast. John Stuart, stated in 1768, that "The Plan for the future management of Indian Affairs formed by the Right Honble. Board of Trade . . . has constantly been the light by which I have steered my course in conducting the affairs of the department. . . ."[34]

Articles 41, 42, and 43 of the Plan of 1764 had a direct bearing on land and boundary matters and served as "the light" by which Stuart steered his course through the numerous Indian congresses he organized and conducted in the Southeast from 1763 to 1768. Article 41 stated:

That no private person, society, corporation or colony be capable of acquiring any property in lands belonging to the Indians whether by purchase of or grant or conveyance from the said Indians excepting only when the lands lie within the limits of any colony, the soil for which has been vested in proprietors or corporations by grants from the Crown. . . .

Article 42 provided:

That proper measures be taken with the consent . . . of the Indians to ascertain and define the precise and exact boundary and limits of the lands which it may be proper to reserve to them and where no settlement whatever shall be allowed.

33. *Ibid.*, p. 131.
34. C. O. 5-69, p. 214.

Article 43 stated:

That no purchase of lands belonging to the Indians whether in the name and for the use of the Crown, or in the name and for the use of Proprietors of Colonies be made but at some general meeting, at which the principal Chiefs of each Tribe claiming a property in such lands are present and all tracts so purchased shall be regularly surveyed by a sworn surveyor, in the presence and with the assistance of a person deputed by the Indians to attend each survey; and the said surveyors shall make an accurate map of such tract describing the limits, which map shall be entered upon record with the deed of conveyance from the Indians.[35]

These provisions from the Plan of 1764 and not the loosely worded proclamation of 1763 served as guidelines to the evolution of the Southern Indian Boundary Line.

The following chapters will undertake a more detailed study of that evolution. The study will concentrate on the British colonies directly concerned in the play of forces that led to the establishment of a continuous boundary line, in large measure surveyed and demarcated, through the frontier of the Southeast from the Ohio River on the north, to the Florida peninsula on the south and the Mississippi River on the west.

As Reynolds pointed out, "every frontier is actually two: the frontier of those who were advancing and the frontier of those who are being advanced upon."[36] The frontier of the American Southeast in the latter eighteenth century was also an ambivalent frontier, with the Indian in retreat before the inexorable advance of European culture. In the pages which follow an attempt has been made to present the Southern Indian Boundary Line from both the Indian and European point of view in order to avoid the pitfall of presenting the concept of a uniparous evolution. De Voto warned historians of the danger of neglecting the Indian in frontier studies when he wrote:

A dismaying amount of our history has been written without regard to the Indians, and of what has been written with regard to them much treats their diverse and always changing societies as uniform and static. Indian history, has, as it were, fallen between two specialities. Anthropologists have preferred archeological and ethnological in-

35. C. O. 5-65, p. 131.
36. Robert L. Reynolds, "The Mediterranean Frontiers, 1000-1400," Walker D. Wyman and Clifton B. Kroeber (eds.), *The Frontier In Perspective* (Madison, Wis., 1957), p. 23.

quiries to historical ones; in most of their treatises "the period of white contact" is likely to be the one most perfunctorily explored. Moreover, in such historical inquiries as they make, they tend to overvalue Indian traditions, which are among the least trustworthy of human records. Historians are wary because the records are scanty, very often unreliable, and sometimes nonexistent, and the axiom that without documents there can be no history yields but reluctantly to the other axiom that when documents are lacking history must find other instruments to use. But also, I believe, there is some inherent tendency to write American history as if it were a function of white culture only.[37]

THE INDIAN CONCEPT OF A BOUNDARY

The lack of a written Indian language during the eighteenth century precluded their leaving a heritable source of documentary residue to provide the grist most common to the historian's mill. Belts of beadwork wampum were often used to transmit important messages and hieroglyphics were sometimes used to record important events, but these remains are fragmentary and often impossible to interpret accurately. In this study, treaty articles and speeches delivered by Indian leaders at the many Indian congresses held in the Southeast have been employed to gain an insight into Indian attitudes and motives regarding their land. Writing of these Indian treaties, Van Doren observed that "for both matter and manner [they] are after two hundred years the most original and engaging documents of their century in America."[38] In addition to the treaties and recorded speeches made by Indians at the congresses, there are messages commonly referred to as "talks" which the Indians sent to colonial officials. These were usually transcribed in written form by Indian traders, military officers, interpreters, or other literate, English-speaking individuals who were in close contact with the Indians. The Colonial and Dominions Offices Records now housed in the British Public Record Office, London, contain a great volume of this material, which has been investigated for the preparation of this study. Insofar as has been possible an effort has been made to understand the life, the societies, the cultures, the thinking and the feeling of the Indians, as urged by De Voto.

This effort is as important to the geographer attempting to

37. Bernard A. De Voto, *The Course of Empire* (Boston, 1952), p. xv.
38. Julian P. Boyd, *Indian Treaties Printed by Benjamin Franklin, 1732-1762* (Philadelphia, 1938), p. viii.

recreate an element of the political geography of the frontier of two centuries ago as De Voto argues it to be for the historian. Kirk, a geographer, pointed out, "it is clear that they [historical geographers] must recreate not only Phenomenal Environments as they were or are but also the Behavioral Environments of the Communities whose spatial actions they are trying to interpret."[39] That the materials and techniques essential to an accurate recreation of the behavioral environment are those more often associated with the historian than the geographer in no way detracts from the validity and usefulness of these materials in providing the solutions to geographic problems of the past. As Kirk further observed, a great number of geographic problems resolve into a study of decision-taking situations.[40] The congresses held between the Indian tribes and colonies of the American Southeast during the period 1763-1775 represented "locational" decision-making situations of the first rank since they affected that element which Spykman identified as making the state different from all other social structures—territory.[41] Spykman also observed that, "survival for such a unit [state] means preserving political independence and retaining control over a specific territory whose limits are defined by an imaginary line called a boundary."[42] Although the Indian tribes represented political states in only their most rudimentary forms, the Indians evinced a passionate desire to retain their territorial bases which they identified as vital to their continued existence as a people. Stuart observed in 1765 that: "The fixing and ascertaining a distinct Boundary between the Indians and all the Provinces is essential to the tranquility of this district; it is a point which greatly concerns them, and to which they are extremely attentive."[43]

The terms "boundary" and "frontier" remain sources of controversy among many geographers but most authorities agree with Boggs, who wrote, "the term 'boundary' denotes a line such as may be defined from point to point in a treaty, arbittal award, or boundary commission report."[44] Such lines are often demarcated

39. William Kirk, "Problems of Geography," *Geography,* XLVIII (Nov., 1963), 368.

40. *Ibid.,* p. 370.

41. Nicholas John Spykman, "Frontiers, Security, and International Organization," *The Geographical Review,* XXXII (July, 1942), 437.

42. *Ibid.*

43. C. O. 5-66, p. 367.

44. S. Whittemore Boggs, *International Boundaries—A Study of Boundary Functions and Problems* (New York, 1940), p. 22. For the purpose of this study

on the earth's surface by a system of recognizable markers or depicted on maps of the areas concerned. Clearly the Indian exhibited a high degree of environmental appreciation and understanding, which allowed him to identify and comprehend a designated river or line of blazed trees as marking the outermost limit of his tribe's domain. Such demarcated boundaries were easily conceived of as being "like a stone wall or a tree which you are not to climb over" by the southern Indians.[45]

The extent to which these aboriginal Americans were able to form a concept of boundary lines delineated in prolix treaty articles and drawn on manuscript maps was an important element in the evolution of the Southern Indian Boundary Line. There seems to have been little attention paid to the "map sense" of the American Indians of the eighteenth century by either ethnologists or geographers of the present day. Indeed, at first glance the Indians would seem almost without a need for nor an understanding of such sophisticated social encumbrances as political boundaries and maps to depict them. As Mooney pointed out in his discussion of the Cherokee, "there were no fixed boundaries and on every side the Cherokee frontiers were contested by rival claimants."[46]

During the second half of the eighteenth century, however, the southern Indians were becoming increasingly aware of boundaries which were accepted as separating their hunting grounds from one tribe and another as well as from the white colonies. Frequent references to boundaries such as the Tombigbee River separating the Choctaw and Creek tribes occur in the literature illustrating the evolution of the Southern Indian Boundary Line. As an ancillary to his primary task of establishing the Southern Indian Boundary Line to separate tribal lands from the colonies of his district, the southern superintendent for Indian affairs was frequently engaged in efforts designed to regularize and delineate intertribal boundaries as well.

Concerning the Indian's cartographic capabilities, it would seem that his close contact with the natural environment and his peripatetic way of life had equipped him with an innate ability to

---

the term "frontier" will be understood to indicate a zone in which the phenomena associated with the growth or contraction of an ecumene are present and noticeable. See Ladis K. D. Kristof, "The Nature of Frontiers and Boundaries," *Annals of the Association of American Geographers,* IL (Sept., 1959), 269-82, for a full discussion of these terms.

45. C. O. 5-73, p. 273.
46. Mooney, *Myths of the Cherokee,* p. 14.

depict his landscape in a manner which often amazed European contemporaries. Governor Glen of South Carolina, commenting on the cartographic skill of the Cherokee, observed: "I have not rested satisfied with a verbal description of the country from the Indians but have often made them trace the rivers on the floor with chalk, and also on paper, and it is surprising how near they approach to our best maps."[47] Stuart, too, reported having the Choctaw delegates to the Indian congress held at Augusta in 1763 assist him in locating and naming the villages of their tribe on a map. Writing about the Indians west of the Mississippi River, a French authority observed:

Although the Indians have no more knowledge of geography than of the other sciences, they make delineations upon skins, as correctly as can be, of the countries with which they are acquainted. Nothing is wanting but the degrees of latitude and longitude. They mark the northern direction to the polar star, and conformably to that mark out the windings and turnings of the rivers, the lakes, marshes, mountains, woods, prairies and paths. They compute distances by day's or half day's journey.[48]

Thomas Pownall commented on the "map sense" of the eastern Indians in his widely circulated *Topographical Description,* in which he stated:

Indeed all the Indians have this Knowledge to a very great Degree of practical Purpose. They are very attentive to the Positions of the Sun and Stars, and on the Lakes can steer their Course by them. The different Aspects which the Hills exhibit on the North Side, from that which the South has impressed on their Eyes, suggest, habitually, at the Moment, in every Spot, an almost intuitive Knowledge of the Quarters of the Heavens which we, mechanically, mark by the Compass. This, at the first Blush, may appear incredible to some; but it may be explained even to the most incredulous. Can any, the most inattentive Observer, be at a Loss to pronounce, in a Moment, which is the North or South Side of any Building in the Country. The same Difference between the South or North Aspect of a Mountain or a Hill, or even a Tree, is equally striking to the Attention of an Indian; and is much more strongly marked by that Accuracy with which he views these Objects; he sees it instantly, and has, from Habit, this

47. William L. McDowell (ed.), *Documents Relating to Indian Affairs, May 21, 1750–August 7, 1754* (Columbia, S.C., 1958), p. 536.

48. Jean Baptiste Trudeau, "Remarks on the Manners of the Indians Living High Up the River Missouri," trans. Samuel L. Mitchell, *The Medical Repository,* VI second hexade (1809), p. 56.

Impression continually on his Mind's Eye, and will mark his Courses as he runs, more readily than most Travellers who steer by the Compass. The Ranges of the Mountains, the Courses of the Rivers, the Bearings of the Peaks, the Knobs and Gaps in the Mountains, are all Land Marks, and picture the face of the Country on his Mind. The Habit of travelling mark to him the Distances, and he will express accurately from these distinct Impressions, by drawing on the Sand a Map which would shame many a Thing called a Survey. When I have been among them at Albany, and enquiring of them about the Country, I have sat and seen them draw such.[49]

Both De Brahm and Bartram included references to the Indians "natural knowledge in Geometry" in contemporary accounts of the Southern Indian Boundary Line in East Florida and Georgia.[50]

Although it was seldom credited on the maps drawn to illustrate the various boundary surveys undertaken with the co-operation of the southern tribes, it is probable that much of the supplementary detail included in them came from information provided by the Indian members of the surveying parties.[51] It would further seem probable that these same Indians, upon returning to the tribal council fires after the completion of these surveys, were quite capable of communicating the locations and significance of the new boundaries they had helped demarcate. In conclusion, it would seem that the rank and file of the southern Indian population probably enjoyed as clear an understanding of the location and significance of the Southern Indian Boundary Line as did their white opposite numbers in the southern colonies concerned.

The following chapters will investigate the evolution of the Southern Indian Boundary Line between the colonies of Virginia, North Carolina, South Carolina, Georgia, East Florida, and West Florida and their neighboring Indian tribes.

49. Pownall, *A Topographical Description* p. 126.
50. Harper, *Bartram's Travels*, p. 27. British Museum, King's MSS, 210, fol. 66.
51. Bartram provided an interesting account of a boundary survey in Georgia where an Indian took over the lead of the surveying party after a dispute concerning a faulty compass. Harper, *Bartram's Travels*, p. 26.

IV · The Virginia-Cherokee Boundary

PRELIMINARIES TO THE VIRGINIA-CHEROKEE BOUNDARY

The first public discussion dealing with a Virginia-Cherokee boundary line took place at the general Indian congress held at the Augusta, Georgia, frontier post on the upper Savannah River in November, 1763. Significantly, the Cherokee spokesman, Chief Attakullakulla, introduced the subject in his address to the assembled southern governors. He stated that, "the lands towards Virginia must not be settled nearer the Cherokees than the southward of New River; hunting is their trade, and they have no other way of getting a living."[1] The Cherokee were clearly claiming that their hunting grounds extended to the area lying between the Holston and New River systems in what are today the westernmost counties of Virginia. This claim, although lacking precision in the *Journal* of the congress, was more clearly expressed by the superintendent for Indian affairs in his report and map of 1764. He described the Cherokee hunting grounds as extending "to Holstein's [*sic*] River and to its most northern source, one of its principal branches takes rise in Augusta County in Virginia the others in the mountains that run behind North Carolina which gives them an extent this way of 220 miles."[2]

The map (Fig. 1) which accompanied and illustrated his report of 1764 leaves little doubt that the superintendent was recognizing the claim voiced by the Cherokee at Augusta a few months before.[3]

In his reply delivered to the Indians at Augusta the superintendent quickly reached the heart of the land problem and stated:

1. *Journal of the Congress* . . . , p. 31. It should be understood that although certain areas, such as the lower Holston valley, were later determined to fall under the jurisdiction of North Carolina, they were at this time considered to be in Virginia's sphere of influence.

2. C. O. 323-17, p. 459.

3. This valuable map was separated from the report and is now found in British Museum, Additional MSS, 14,036, fol. d.

You have complained of settlements being made on the part of Virginia to the westward of New River, and desire no further settlements may be made there. In order to comply strictly with the great king's instructions, copies of which you have among you, and that we may in no shape deceive you, we will explain the state of those settlements.

By a former governor, and above twenty [years] since, a large grant of lands in that part of the country was made to one Col. Patten, who under that grant sold out parcels of the land to people who settled there: in these settlements you have acquiesced without complaint to this time, as they are at a great distance from your country. Another large grant was also made by the great king just before the breaking out of the war with the French; but those disturbances prevented any persons settling under that grant, and by the kings late instructions to the governor of Virginia no land can be granted even so far as the eastern banks of that river [the New River], so that you have nothing further to apprehend on that account.[4]

The main reasons for the Indian congress at Augusta were the conciliation and reassurance of the Indians to convince them of the magnanimous intentions of the English toward them and their lands. It would seem that the superintendent's statements accomplished these objectives adequately since the Cherokee "acknowledged of their own accord, that they had claimed more than were their hunting grounds, and what they now desired was, that they might not be molested in hunting as far as the spring head of the Holston River."[5]

Before tracing more precisely the evolution of the Virginia-Cherokee section of the Southern Indian Boundary Line, it is necessary to review the earlier contacts between the Cherokee and Virginia concerning land matters.

Until the middle years of the eighteenth century contacts between the Cherokee and Virginians were infrequent and usually confined to trade matters.[6] Joshua Fry reported in 1751 that "With the Cherokee Virginia never had any war, or league of peace; but a trade has been carried on with them for many years to the content and advantage of both sides; and they never set up any claim

4. *Journal of the Congress* . . . , p. 36. For a description of the grant to James Patton (Col. Patten) which Stuart mentioned see "List of Early Land Patents and Grants Petitioned For in Virginia up to 1769," *The Virginia Magazine of History and Biography*, V (1897), 173.

5. *Journal of the Congress* . . . , p. 37.

6. W. Neil Franklin, "Virginia and the Cherokee Indian Trade, 1673-1752," *East Tennessee Historical Society's Publications*, IV (1932), 3-21.

to lands in this colony."[7] Developing the theme of Virginia-Indian contacts more fully, Fry went on to summarize several of the early treaties which had been negotiated by the colony with its Indian neighbors. Significantly, the Cherokee were not directly concerned in any. Most of the treaties mentioned concerned the Iroquois Federation, which controlled the area of the upper Ohio Valley. Following his review of these treaties, which covered the period from 1684 to 1744, Fry mentioned the observations of several early explorers of the transmontane area behind Virginia. These explorers' reports plus his own considerable knowledge of the area led him to conclude, "that the country between our settlements and the Mississippi is uninhabited or at most has only some inconsiderable Indian villages."[8]

In explaining the absence of Indians in the vast area which later became the state of Kentucky, Fry stated "That there are no Indian Nations living in it, is owing to the strength and disposition of the Six Nations [Iroquois Federation], who at this time make incursions on the Catawbas living in North Carolina merely for the sake of killing them, traversing on foot for this purpose a country of the extent of eight or nine degrees of latitude."[9] Significantly, in 1734 a Cherokee request to be allowed to settle members of the tribe on a "branch of Roanoke River that from thence they may enjoy the conveniency of a free trade with this colony [Virginia]" was refused because "they [the Cherokee] might be disturbed by the Northern Indians who hunt yearly thereabouts."[10] The Iroquois control over the area behind Virginia was tacitly admitted by Cherokee and Virginian alike during the first half of the eighteenth century.

This condition did not remain static; Fry, who was writing at the mid-point of that century, drew attention to the changing bal-

7. "Report on the Back Settlements of Virginia," C. O. 5-1327, p. 171. For a published version of this report see Delf Norona (ed.), "Joshua Fry's Report on the Back Settlements of Virginia (May 8, 1751)," *The Virginia Magazine of History and Biography,* LVI (Jan., 1948), 22-41.

8. *Ibid.* Fry was very well acquainted with transmontane Virginia. He is probably best known for his contribution to the important map titled, "A Map of the Inhabited Part of Virginia. . . ." For a description of this map see William P. Cumming, *The Southeast In Early Maps* (Chapel Hill, N.C., 1962), plates 57 and 58 and pp. 219-20.

9. C. O. 5-1327, p. 169. J. R. Swanton observed in his *The Indians of the Southeastern United States,* p. 65: "It is not a little surprising to discover that the Lexington Plain, the 'blue grass country,' was not occupied for any considerable period by any body of Indians in the historical era."

10. C. O. 5-1429, p. 99.

ance of power in the interior. He quoted from a well-accepted authority of the day to explain this altering balance in the power structure of the Indian tribes when he wrote:

There are no Indians either within or near the bounds of Virginia, as far as I know, of any considerable force, but the Cherokee living back of North and South Carolina, and the Six Nations in the province of New York; and these but more especially the latter have much decreased since our [first] knowledge of them. Mr. Golden in his history of the Six Nations says that they are now not above a tenth of their number, they were when they first waged war with the French of Canada.[11]

The events which transpired during the quarter-century following Fry's observations made it clear that the Iroquois grip on the area south of the Ohio River was growing increasingly weak. This decline in Iroquois control was paralleled by an increased Cherokee interest in this area. The southern tribe was becoming aware of a growing competition for land to the south, east, and west of its core area. White colonists were threatening on the east as the frontiers of South Carolina and Georgia advanced and hostile Indian tribes were exerting pressure on the Cherokee's southern and western flanks. As the Cherokee attempted to exploit the hunting grounds previously controlled by the Iroquois, they increasingly came into contact with the frontiersmen leading the advance of Virginia settlements into the same areas.

Fry described the extent of those settlements at Mid-century as follows:

The Virginia settlements have been greatly extended within the last thirty years, for before that time there were few inhabitants above the falls of the rivers. At present the country is not only well peopled, but beyond it even to the Alegany Ridge, that is to the head springs of all our rivers which run into the Atlantick Ocean, the south head branches of Roanoke being excepted are but thinly settled.

Beyond the Alegany or Mississippi Ridge on the New River and its branches are seated about one hundred families, but the settlements that way with proper encouragement will in a short time greatly increase.[12]

The "Alegany or Mississippi Ridge" referred to here by Fry was what is today commonly known as the Blue Ridge. This

11. C. O. 5-1327, p. 171.
12. *Ibid.*, p. 170.

mountain range separates the New–Kanawha River system, which is a tributary of the westward flowing Ohio, from the easterly flowing streams of the piedmont in Virginia and North Carolina.[13]

These settlements along the upper reaches of the New and Holston rivers did receive "proper encouragement" from the government of Virginia and appeared to increase as Fry predicted they might.[14]

It is advisable at this point to consider some of the motives underlying the extension of Virginia population and settlements into the transmontane country drained by the Ohio River system. These motives were many and varied, extending across a wide spectrum from profiteering to imperial defense. Rather than undertake a lengthy examination of them, it will suffice to consider in review those motivating factors which seemed most significant to the contemporaries closest to the westward movement in Virginia. This movement was bringing European homesteaders into contact with the Indian hunters of the interior.

The series of population maps composing Figure 2 provide a graphic impression of the westward migration of Europeans into the ridge and valley province of Virginia during the mid and late eighteenth century but can do little to explain the reasons for this movement. There is, of course, no single reason which can explain this phenomenon of frontier advance. It might be said that there were almost as many reasons for the migration as there were individuals engaged in it. There are, however, two factors which emerge as fundamental in any attempt to understand the migra-

13. This is clearly shown on two maps associated with Fry, *supra*, note 8, and the map showing the Virginia-North Carolina Boundary of 1749, M.P.G. 361, P.R.O.

14. John Mitchell, the eighteenth-century geographer and author of what has often been termed the most important map in American history, commented on these transmontane settlements as follows: "And on the south side of the Ohio, we are not only well settled on Wood River [New River] . . . but likewise on Holston River that lies upwards of 150 miles to the westward of that place." Quoted from "Remarks on the Journal of Batts and Fallan in their Discovery of the Western Parts of Virginia in 1671," British Museum, Additional MSS, 4432.

On his better-known map Mitchell noted the following: " 'Holston River Settled' and 'Well Settled' in the area between the upper Holston and New Rivers."

A facsimile of this map, first printed in 1755, has been prepared by the U.S. Geological Survey as plate 5 in their Bulletin 817. Cumming, in his *Southeast In Early Maps*, presents a portion of the Mitchell map as plate 59. Hunter Miller presents an attractive colored facsimile of the 1775 edition of the Mitchell map at the end of Vol. III of his *Treaties and Other International Acts of the United States* (Washington, D.C., 1931).

tion in Virginia during the mid-eighteenth century. These were
(1) the passion for the acquisition of productive land, and (2)
the strategic requirements of an empire embarked on a struggle
for the control of eastern America.

In the words of an authority on the subject of westward expansion in eighteenth century America, "the prime determinative
principle of the progressive American civilization of the eighteenth
century was the passion for the acquisition of land."[15] This passion was expressed differently by differing individuals, some of
whom attempted to gain control over huge tracts for speculative
ventures on an enormous scale whereas others desired nothing more
than what was necessary to provide a livelihood for themselves and
their families.

Although frequently the subject of criticism, the speculative
schemes which proliferated in western Virginia made contributions that were important to the advance of the frontier of white
settlement in that area. The exploration of routes of access and the
production of maps to illuminate the area which had remained
terra incognita to the English through much of the first half of
the eighteenth century were examples of positive contributions performed by those, like the Ohio Company of Virginia, who were
interested in speculative schemes. Bailey saw this venture as "the
opening English wedge in the Ohio country."[16] Mulkearn echoed
this view and drew attention to the company's "surviving letters
and documents, its journals and maps [which] provided us with
innumerable details of our early frontier history."[17] Christopher
Gist, employed by the company to explore the Ohio Valley during
1750 and 1751, compiled an extremely valuable account of his observations. The editor of the published version of Gist's *Journals*
stated that "the explorations were the earliest made so far west,
for the single object of examining the country, as they are the first
also of which a regular journal was kept."[18] The Ohio Company
was only one of a number of speculative organizations which

15. Archibald Henderson, "The Creative Forces in Westward Expansion: Henderson and Boone," *American Historical Review*, XX (Oct., 1914), 88.

16. Kenneth P. Bailey, *The Ohio Company Papers, 1753-1817* (Ann Arbor,
Mich., 1947), p. 2.

17. Lois Mulkearn, ed., *George Mercer Papers Relating to the Ohio Company of
Virginia* (Pittsburgh, Pa., 1954), p. viii.

18. William M. Darlington, *Christopher Gist's Journals with Historical Geographical and Ethnological Notes and Biographies of His Contemporaries* (Pittsburgh, Pa., 1893), p. 29.

envisaged the occupation of the transmontane area as potentially profitable and worthy of promotion.[19]

An increased awareness of the French threat in the transmontane country was responsible for policies which were meant to counter French ambitions by increasing Virginia's strength in the area of the upper Ohio basin. A succinct statement of such a policy appeared in a Board of Trade report dated 1748. With reference to the Virginia frontier, the report stated:

That the settlements of the country lying to the westward . . . will be for His Majesty's interest and advantage . . . [His] subjects will be . . . enabled to cultivate a friendship and carry on a more extensive commerce with the Nations of Indians inhabiting those parts and such settlement may likewise be a proper step towards disappointing the views and checking the encroachments of the French by interrupting part of the communication from their lodgements upon the Great Lakes to the River Mississippi.[20]

While such an official attitude enabled influential speculators to obtain enormous land grants, it soon became apparent that this form of enfeoffment seldom led to the desired peopling and strengthening of the frontier. Increasingly critical comments were made in an effort to expose the evils of untramelled land acquisition by individuals and groups for speculative purposes. Typical of such criticism were the remarks found in a representation dated 1754. It stated: "That the granting or patenting vast tracts of land to private persons or companies without condition of speedy settlement has tended to prevent the strengthening of frontiers of the particular colony in which such tracts lye and been prejudicial to the rest."[21] It is not surprising that the anonymous author of this tract, along with many other people of position, was urging that a western limit be fixed for the seaboard colonies to halt such injudicious land-granting before chaos was created in the interior. This representation suggested that these limits should be established: "That the bounds of these colonies which extend to the South Seas [Pacific Ocean] be contracted and limited by the Aleghenny or Apalachian Mountains; and that measures be taken from settling, from time to time, colonies of His Majesties Protestant

19. The *doyen* of American frontier historians, Frederick J. Turner, mentioned several in his "Western State-Making in the Revolutionary Era," *The American Historical Review,* I (Oct., 1895), 70-87.

20. C. O. 5-1366, p. 411.

21. "Representation of the State of the Colonies in North America," British Museum, Additional MSS. 33,029, fol. 156.

Subjects westward of said mountains in convenient cantons to be assigned for that purpose."[22]

Population increase and soil exhaustion in the older settlements of the seaboard provided an increasing tide of families who, with their belongings and livestock, flowed into the transmontane country by several routes. Billington drew attention to the significance of decreasing land prices as the pioneers moved southwestward along the most important route—the "natural highway" of Virginia's Great Valley. Land prices decreased from over £15 per hundred acres on an average in Pennsylvania to the less than £5 which was being charged for the productive land of westernmost Virginia.[23] These low prices drew groups of settlers like a magnet to the areas drained by the New and Holston River systems.

The author of the valuable eighteenth-century work *American Husbandry* stated: "The want of fresh land in Virginia, for the tobacco planters to spread themselves over, occasioned many settlers to pass the Allegany [*sic*] Mountains, and fix themselves on the rivers that fall into the Ohio."[24] John Mitchell, too, emphasized the demands of the tobacco-raising industry, which he stated required a limitless supply of fresh land "fit to produce that exhausting weed." To furnish this supply of land for what he called "the only considerable branch of trade in all North America," Mitchell pointed prophetically to "those rich lands upon the Mississippi and Ohio."[25]

Even as the tide of settlers reached the headwaters of the Holston River, certain informed individuals were anticipating the movement into the rugged ridges, valleys, and plateau which lay beyond. Fry observed in his report of 1751 that:

The lands towards the heads of the rivers and a great way beyond our settlements are mountainous but there are fruitful vallies and much also of the high land is exceedingly rich.

Mr. Thomas Walker . . . went westward till he came into a flat country and could discover no more mountains that way; and the men who went with John Howard say that they saw on the Mississippi

22. *Ibid.*
23. Ray Allen Billington, *Westward Expansion: A History of the American Frontier* (New York, 1949), p. 90.
24. *American Husbandry* (London, 1775), I, 279.
25. John Mitchell, *The Present State of Great Britain and North America with Regard to Agriculture, Population, Trade and Manufacturers* (London, 1767), p. 145.

and its large branches more good land than they judged is in all the English Colonies as far as they are inhabited.[26]

Fry and others who were acquainted with the mountainous environment flanking the Cumberland Plateau to the west of Virginia's frontier saw the area not as a barrier to settlement but rather as an area where "fruitful vallies and exceedingly rich land" would serve as a prelude to the incalculably productive plateau and central lowlands beyond.

Other contemporaries were aware of serious problems inherent in the advance of white settlers into the transmontane interior. Thomas Pownall exhibited a keen understanding of the role the Indians would be likely to assume as the frontier advanced. In considering the immediate problem of the Anglo-French struggle for domination, he wrote the following in 1755:

The native inhabitants (the Indians) of this country are all hunters: all the laws of nations they know or acknowledge are the laws of sporting, and all the idea they have of landed possession, is that of a hunt. The French settlers of Canada universally commend hunters and so insinnuated themselves into a connection with these natives.

While the French kept themselves thus allied with the Indians as hunters and communicated with them in, and strictly maintained all the laws and rights of sporting the Indians did easily and readily admit them to a local landed possession: A grant which rightly acquired and applyed they are always ready to make as none of the rights or interests of their nation are hurt by it; but on the contrary they experience and receive great use, benefit and profit from the commerce that the Europeans therein establish with them: Whereas on the contrary the English with an insatiable thirst after landed possessions have got deeds, and other fraudulent pretenses grounded on the abuse of treaties, and by these deeds claim possession even to the exclusion of the Indians, not only from their hunting grounds (which with them is a right of great consequence) but even from their house and home, as by particular instances from one end of the continent to the other might be made to appear: upon these pretences they have drove the Indians off their lands: the Indians unable to bear it any longer told Sir William Johnson that they believed soon they should not be able to hunt a bear into a hole in a tree but some Englishman would claim a right to the property of it as being his tree: And whatever the great proprietors, Patentees and land jobbers may

26. C. O. 5-1327, p. 171. For a published source containing the "Journal of Dr. Thomas Walker," see J. S. Johnston, *First Explorations of Kentucky* (Louisville, Ky., 1898).

affirm or affect to prove or however angry they may be with those who declare this; this is the sole ground of the loss and alienation of the Indians from the English interest and this is the ground the French work upon.[27]

As the events which culminated in Pontiac's Rebellion of 1763 made clear, Pownall had indeed identified the Indian as a source of future problems of great magnitude for the advancing white pioneers.

The war with the French interrupted the advance of Virginians into the lands "on the waters of Mississippi" and attacks by these enemies with their Indian allies occasioned a large-scale retreat of the frontier residents. In Virginia the pioneers fell back to the safety of "stocade forts" erected along the Greenbrier River and other defensible locations. One of the westernmost settlements, that of Samuel Stalnaker on the upper Holston River, was shown on a map of *ca.* 1761 as "Sternacres Settlement Destroyed by the Shawanese Indians." Upstream from Stalnakers appeared the caption "Abandoned Plantations."[28]

Land speculators, too, were affected by the war since it made it impossible for them to comply with requirements for improvement and settlement which were necessary to validate the grants they held. Only that huge speculative grant held by James Patton, which was discussed at the Augusta congress in 1763, was recognized as being valid at that date.[29] Smaller grants of not more than 1,000 acres had been made to individuals as late as 1760. One of the last was that made to John Chiswell for "one thousand acres on both sides of New River."[30] Chiswell operated a lead mine on his property along the upper New River opposite to the mouth of a tributary called Cripple Creek. Chiswell's Mines became a landmark often referred to in Indian negotiations concerning the Virginia-Cherokee section of the Southern Indian Boundary Line.[31]

27. C. O. 5-18, pp. 302-3. Fry might have added that the Indians seldom objected to the traders and packhorsemen of his own nationality who resided in many of the larger Indian "towns." Presumably they were not viewed as competitors for the land as white planters and herdsmen were.

28. "A Map of the Cherokee Country," John Stuart fecit [*ca.* 1761], British Museum, Additional MSS. 14,036, fol. 5. See also Cumming, *The Southeast In Early Maps,* p. 231.

29. C. O. 5-1330, pp. 292-94.

30. C. O. 5-1348, p. 169.

31. Henry Howe stated in his *Historical Collections of Virginia* (Charleston, S.C., 1845), p. 515, that: "The lead mines of Wythe [county] are about 13 miles easterly from the Court House, on New River, opposite the mouth of Cripple

The fall of the stronghold, Fort Duquesne, at the site of the present-day city of Pittsburgh in 1760 extinguished the Gallic threat which had blocked the advancing Virginians during the French and Indian War. Unchallenged English control of the upper Ohio basin did not, however, signal a resumption of the old pattern of speculative land grants in the area. In 1760 the Board of Trade instructed the governor of Virginia to refrain from making further grants of any kind upon the Ohio or any of its tributaries.[32] The governor was successful only in obtaining permission to allow those displaced by the war to return to their homes already established in the area. In 1760 it was clear that the Virginia frontier was destined to be considered in a new light by George III's advisors.

When the governor sought permission to issue land grants to bona fide new settlers (as opposed to land speculators) who wanted to move into the transmontane frontier in 1761, the Board of Trade refused. This refusal was explained on the grounds that the Indian claim to the area had not been adequately extinguished and any such increase in Virginia's settlements might provoke them to war against the English. The Virginia governor appeared to have agreed with the Board of Trade's prohibition against grants to speculators but continued to maintain that bona fide settlers should be granted land in the New River basin where, he argued,

Creek. Formerly they were worked with great profit; but the discovery of lead in the far west has operated disadvantageously to the interest of the proprietors of these works, situated as they are, so far inland and away from easy means of transportation. These mines were discovered very early and were worked in the Revolution. The first proprietor was Col. Chiswell an English gentleman, who built a frame house—the first erected in this section of the country—which is now standing, in a delapidated condition near the mouth of Mill Creek. The Col. attempted unsuccessfully to extract silver from the ore. He killed a man in a quarrel and died in prison."

In his answers to a questionnaire relative to his colony's condition, Francis Fauquier, governor of Virginia, mentioned the lead mines on the New River in 1763. He stated that: "There have been mines both of copper and lead discovered but neither of them worked except one mine very rich in lead lying on a branch of New River in the road to the Upper Cherokee Nation, the proprietors of this are now beginning to work it, of which number I was one myself but quitted it on a doubt whether lead would bear the expence of so long a land carriage as is necessary to bring it to market. The mine is certainly rich in lead, and was thought to contain a considerable quantity of silver, but by the experiments yet made it does not contain a sufficient quantity to answer the expence of extracting it."

Thomas Jefferson also mentioned these lead mines in his *Notes On The State of Virginia* (New York, 1964), pp. 23-24.

32. C. O. 5-1367, pp. 204-6.

the Indians held no valid claim.[33] He specifically denied any Cherokee claim to the area.

When the Proclamation of 1763 made the Crown's recognition of the Indian claims to the whole of the interior west of the Blue Ridge watershed the basis for future land policy in America, the governor again argued Virginia's point of view. He pointed to the long tenure of many of the frontiersmen who had entered the transmontane country in response to official encouragements earlier and requested that these settlers along the New and Holston rivers be excluded from the order to quit which was embodied in the Proclamation. Alden summarized Governor Fauquier's arguments as follows:

Since Fauquier sympathized with the pioneers who had complied with Virginia law and since he lacked power even to prevent squatters from occupying the Kanawha [New River] region, he prudently let the matter drop. The pioneers remained, but at the same time declined to pay quitrents, because their titles were in serious doubt. Such was the status of the Kanawha Valley settlements until 1766 when John Stuart reopened the whole question.[34]

In a lengthy letter to the secretary of the Board of Trade, the

33. C. O. 5-1330, p. 24.

34. Alden, *John Stuart*, p. 267.

Before letting the matter drop Governor Fauquier wrote a letter which must have caused considerable consternation among the members of the Board of Trade. In this letter dated Feb. 13, 1764 (C. O. 5-1330, pp. 292-94), the governor drew attention to several problems which had been created by the Proclamation of October 7, 1763. These problems concerned the fate of Virginians who had been encouraged by three provincial acts to settle "on the waters of Mississippi" a decade before. After pointing out that the Cherokee had renounced any claim to the area in their statements made at the congress in Augusta, he concluded by observing: "Indeed it is believed that they never at any time had any right to lay claim to them [lands to the eastward of Holston River], and I do not know that any tribe of Indians whatever do lay claim to the land in question, as their hunting grounds; at least this I am sure of that no such claim has been made since I have had the honor to preside in this Colony."

Perhaps the most vexing problem of all was that created by the extremely complex geography of the Appalachian watershed which was the crux of the Proclamation of 1763 as it affected the land problem in Virginia. Governor Fauquier wrote: "It may be necessary to observe to your Lordships, that the head branches of the waters which empty themselves into the Atlantic Ocean on which by the Proclamation I am at liberty to grant patents for lands interlock with the head branches of the waters which are discharged by the Mississippi into the Gulf of Mexico on which I am restrained from granting patents."

Rather than attempt to provide answers to the governor's thorny questions, the Board of Trade drew up a set of additional instructions for the governors of Pennsylvania and Virginia which ordered that all settlers located west of the Proclamation Line be removed.

superintendent of Indian affairs included a detailed review of the state of Anglo-Cherokee relations to the summer of 1765.[35] Touching on the relationship existing between the tribe and the Colony of Virginia the superintendent observed:

The fixing and ascertaining a distinct boundary between the Indians and all the Provinces is essential to the tranquility of this district; it is a point which greatly concerns them, and to which they are extremely attentive.

The murder of their people by the back settlers of Virginia has not so bad an effect and the consequences are not so much to be apprehended as of encroachments on their lands. The Indians can comprehend that the wicked actions of a few individuals ought not to be considered as a proof of the intentions of the whole community, and will be well satisfied to have the perpetrators brought to justice; But grants of land claimed by them, they know to be the acts of whole Provinces which alarms them and they consider as incontestable proofs of our bad intentions and want of faith.

It is not the Cherokees alone who think themselves injured; the jealousy of all the nations is awakened and the bad impressions left on their minds by the French, confirmed by these encroachments.[36]

In conclusion, the superintendent indicated that it would probably be necessary to hold a congress with the Cherokee to settle these problems and to establish a peaceful relationship with them.

THE INITIATION OF NEGOTIATIONS FOR A VIRGINIA-CHEROKEE
BOUNDARY

During 1765 and 1766, negotiations between the Cherokee and the colonies of North and South Carolina concerning the fixing of a boundary between the Indians and those colonies were frequently punctuated by allusions to a continuation of this Carolina boundary to include Virginia. A letter reporting the successful demarcation of the South Carolina-Cherokee boundary included the following mention of a proposed Virginia line:

The Cherokee propose running the line from where it terminated a straight course, to Colonel Chiswell's Mines, which I believe will be north, as nigh as I could make it; They say, that it must be very evident, that as they have given all their claims of lands in Virginia, below Chiswell's Mines and in South Carolina, below Dewis's Corner, that a straight line, from Reedy River to the Mines, must consequently

35. C. O. 5-66, pp. 356-71.
36. *Ibid.*, p. 367.

cut off a great deal of their land in No. Carolina; that part of their hunting ground lies 40 miles eastward of where they now nominate their boundary; but that they do not love disputing with the White People concerning a trifle; therefore they made them a present of it.

It would be very necessary, that a surveyor should first sight the line, from Reedy River a north course, in order to know where it will terminate in Virginia, and whether or not, it will take away any of the settlements.[37]

This Cherokee proposal is shown on Figure 11 as the "second Cherokee Proposal."

This proposal for a boundary line, as well as others which originated with the Cherokee, invariably named Chiswell's mine as the termination "on the Virginia side."[38] It will be recalled that Chiswell's lead mines were located along the east bank of the New River or several miles to the northeast of the headwaters of the Holston River, where the Cherokee had terminated their claim in 1763. Alden saw in this shift from the Holston to the New River a repudiation of the "informal agreement made by Attakullakulla and Fauquier at the Congress of Augusta."[39] Significantly, this Cherokee extension of their claim to lands in the area behind Virginia passed without challenge.

During June, 1766, the Cherokee refused permission to allow an agent of Virginia to establish a public trading store at the Long Island of the Holston (at the site of the present-day city of Kingsport, Tennessee). In stating their reasons for this refusal, the Cherokee were reported to have claimed that the area near the Long Island was among their best hunting grounds, and that a trading store and settlement there would represent an irresistible temptation to younger Indians who might steal horses or kill cows and cause serious trouble. Although it was not clearly stated, the Cherokee seemed well aware of the strategic significance of the Long Island and the military threat which a stockaded Virginia post located there might pose for their towns located farther down the Great Valley. The Virginians were told that they might settle near Chiswell's lead mines and trade from there.[40]

It can be seen that the Cherokee were developing a policy which provided for a continuous boundary line to separate their hunting

37. *Ibid.*, pp. 398-99.
38. *Ibid.*, p. 417.
39. Alden, *John Stuart*, p. 267.
40. C. O. 5-66, p. 394.

grounds from the colonies of South and North Carolina and Virginia. While the details of the boundary line with Virginia were still the subject for discussion and negotiation, it was clear that the Cherokee had advanced their claim from the Holston River to the New River during the three years following the congress at Augusta.

On the other hand, Virginia was more oblique in its policies. In a lengthy general report on the state of Indian affairs in his district written in 1766, the superintendent of Indian affairs reported winning the co-operation of North Carolina in the continuing effort to extend the Cherokee boundary line to the north of its termination in South Carolina. He also stated that he had "not been favoured with any [reply] from Lieutenant Governor Fauquier" of Virginia to his correspondence on the matter of a boundary line behind that colony.[41] Alden pointed out that the superintendent had written to the Virginia executive on three separate occasions during 1766 but received no reply.[42] Fauquier and other Virginia leaders were not anxious to have a Cherokee boundary established which would limit that colony's access to the west. Although the governor did not honor the Indian superintendent with a statement of Virginia's policy on the matter, he was actively engaged in petitioning the authorities in London on behalf of the pioneers settled on the upper Holston and New Rivers. He expressed the Virginia opinion that these pioneer settlements "on the waters of Mississippi" should be allowed to remain and further requested that the whole of the area between North Carolina and Pennsylvania, as far west as the Ohio River, be thrown open to settlement by the Virginians. The leaders of Virginia continued to maintain, albeit in a dilatory manner, that no Indian tribes were resident in this area and that at most it was visited by Indian hunters only sporadically.

During the spring of 1768 the Board of Trade delivered "A Report to the Crown on the Management of Indian Affairs in America . . . ," in which the intention of the imperial government regarding Indian boundary lines was clearly stated. This report undertook "a consideration of . . . what system it may be now proper . . . to pursue with respect to that vast and extensive country in North America, which, on account of the Indian War raging within it was made by the Proclamation of the 7th of Octob. 1763,

41. C. O. 5-67, p. 46.
42. Alden, *John Stuart*, p. 267.

Fig. 5. Tracing from Board of Trade map illustrating the Southern Indian Boundary Line in 1768. (From P.R.O., M.P.G. 280.)

the object of mere provisional arrangement."[43] The Lords of Trade stated that the Indians of "that vast and extensive country" were still discontented because of the continued encroachment of their

43. C. O. 5-69, p. 60.

lands and abuses practiced by unscrupulous Indian traders. The crux of the proposed solution to the land problem was the Indian boundary line, which was to be speedily completed and ratified throughout the colonies. To provide the king with "a more perfect view" of the boundary lines the Board of Trade included a map with their report.[44] A tracing from this original map "in which we have endeavored to trace those lines out, with as much accuracy as the general Maps of America will admit," is included as Figure 5.

It can be seen on Figure 5 that the Virginia-Cherokee boundary was to run from where the North Carolina Indian line terminated at Chiswell's mines on the "Conhawa" (New-Kanawha) River due north to the mouth of that river where it met the Ohio. This boundary reflected a major change in the policy of the Board of Trade on this important issue since they had proposed in 1763 that the Kanawha River should be the western boundary of Virginia (see Fig. 3). This westward shift of the boundary indicated the Board of Trade's acknowledgement of the presence of Virginia settlements in the New River valley which would be allowed to remain undisturbed. The Kanawha-New River boundary also showed clearly that the board had decided to discount the Iroquois claim to the area south of the Ohio River in favor of the Cherokee, who lived near at hand and used the area for hunting.

In a letter addressed to both Indian superintendents, on April 15, 1768, the following instruction regarding the Indian boundary line was included: "That the line described in the Report of the Board of Trade shall be ratified and confirmed in every part and the colonies required to inact the most effectual laws for preventing all settlement beyond such line."[45]

The Indian superintendents had no power to see that laws preventing settlement beyond the boundary were passed. But they could and did begin to organize Indian congresses so that the boundary line could be completed to separate the Indian tribes and colonies throughout the length of the American frontier.

THE DELINEATION OF THE HARD LABOUR LINE

A Southern Indian District Congress was convened at Hard Labour in South Carolina during October, 1768. The boundaries already established behind South and North Carolina were ratified at this meeting. During the proceedings of the congress, the In-

44. M.P.G. 280, P.R.O.
45. C. O. 5-69, p. 120.

dian superintendent reviewed the location of the proposed boundary for Virginia. He stated that it was to run "from Chiswell's Mine on the Great Conhaway [New-Kanawha] to the confluence of said river with the Ohio in a straight line a north course." This was the boundary which the Board of Trade had specified in their report. In reply to the superintendent's address the ranking Cherokee chief, Oconostota, announced that the Indians had expected that the river itself would form a natural boundary between their tribal hunting grounds and Virginia. He continued: "[it] will be impracticable to mark the trees in the winter, the line runs due north, through a country full of mountains, which will soon be covered with snow and ice it is uninhabited and in winter will neither afford shelter for men, or food for horses; but early in the spring I promise my father [Superintendent Stuart] that I will go and finish the line myself."[46]

This boundary, which received the Cherokee's approval, did indeed run through an extremely rugged area which is now the western part of the state of West Virginia. Receiving ratification at Hard Labour on October 14, 1768, the boundary from Chiswell's Mines to the Ohio River became known as the Hard Labour Line.

Late in 1768 an event which took place hundreds of miles away in the Northern Indian District threw the whole problem of a Virginia-Cherokee boundary line once more into confusion. This was the Indian congress held by the superintendent of that district with the northern tribes at Fort Stanwix, New York. Sir William Johnson, the northern Indian superintendent, had been instructed to establish a boundary line between the Indian lands and colonies of his district in accordance with the Board of Trade's wishes on this subject. This northern boundary was to begin on the Ohio River opposite the mouth of the Kanawha River, where the Southern Indian Boundary Line was to terminate. Plainly, the Board of Trade had chosen to recognize the Cherokee claim to the area south of the Ohio River in preference to that of the Iroquois. As Alden stated:

It is clear that Shelburne and the Board of Trade intended that the Kanawha should serve as the line between Virginia and the Cherokees. It is equally certain that Shelburne's instructions favored the Cherokees as against Virginia because the Indians placed their pretensions before the home government through Stuart and because Virginia made no specific objection either to Stuart or to officials in London.[47]

46. C. O. 5-70, p. 77.
47. Alden, *John Stuart*, pp. 269-70.

It will be recalled that the Kanawha River had been an important element in the boundary line originally proposed by the Board of Trade during the early months of 1763. The Kanawha River line did not please the northern superintendent, who had originally suggested that the boundary with the tribes of his district be extended to the Tennessee River in recognition of the long-standing Iroquois claim to the area forming the present state of Kentucky.[48] This tenuous claim was based on past military victories over the southern tribes and, as indicated above, it was becoming clear that Iroquois strength was on the wane. Their ability to hold such a vast area so far distant from their tribal coreland was questionable and the ceding of it to the British king in return for expensive gifts was probably recognized as the most expedient course of action by the Indians. Such a cession would relieve the Iroquois of the dangerous necessity of having to defend their title against the stronger southern tribes should they challenge it, as well as insure them of a handsome compensation from the British who would have found refusal difficult.

Difficult or not, the Board of Trade had decided against acceptance of the Iroquois claim south of the Ohio River and had clearly indicated this decision to both Indian superintendents. For some reason Sir William Johnson, the northern superintendent, "allowed" the Iroquois to persuade him to include the country south of the Ohio River with the cession of land which they made to the king at Fort Stanwix in November, 1768. In the deed of cession, which was signed at the historic Fort Stanwix Indian Congress, the controversial country south of the Ohio was described in the following terms: "We have likewise continued it [the boundary] south to Cherokee [Tennessee] River because the same is and

48. In a letter to the Board of Trade dated Nov. 18, 1764, Sir William Johnson, the northern superintendent of Indian affairs, outlined the territory of the Iroquois Federation as follows: "In right of conquest they claim all the country (comprehending the Ohio) at the back of Virginia, thence to the Head of Kentucke River and down the same to the Ohio above the rifts, thence northerly to the south end of Lake Michigan. . . . However these more distant claims being possessed by many powerful nations, the inhabitants have long begun to render themselves independent by the assistance of the French and the great decrease of the Six Nations; but their claims to ye Ohio and thence to the Lakes is not in ye least disputed by the Shawanese, Delawares etc. who never transact any sales of land or other matters without their consent. . . ." C. O. 323-18, p. 99.
In a letter to Benjamin Franklin, George Croghan, the well-known Indian trader, reported in 1765 that the Indians "would most cheerfully" surrender that part of their land which lay on the Ohio River behind the colony of Virginia. He added that this area was now of no use to them as hunting grounds. C. O. 5-66, p. 84.

we do declare it to be our true bounds with the Southern Indians [Cherokee] and that we have an undoubted right to the country as far south as that river, which makes our cession to his majesty much more advantageous than that proposed."[49] The reason for Johnson's "absolute disregard" of his orders on this point would involve a lengthy discussion beyond the scope allowed in this study. It will suffice to state that the effect of his action threw the whole problem of a Virginia-Cherokee boundary once more open for further discussion and negotiation. The Virginians were at last spurred to exert themselves in attempting to obtain an extension of the already delineated Hard Labour Line.

The Virginians intended their petitions for an extension to the Hard Labour Line for both the southern superintendent and authorities in London. The aims of Virginia on the topic of an Indian boundary line were outlined in the instructions sent by the governor late in 1768 to the two commissioners appointed to act for the colony on the matter.[50] They were to inform the southern superintendent that the Hard Labour Line would be very injurious to the king's service and to those people who had been legally encouraged earlier to settle to the west of this boundary. The governor continued by stating that Virginia, had she been consulted, would have shown that the Cherokee had "no just title to the lands recently ceded at Fort Stanwix." In conclusion, the commissioners were instructed to obtain a further delay in the scheduled spring meeting with the Indians so that the whole matter could be presented to the king and his ministers "in order to get the boundary extended to the Cherokee [Tennessee] River."[51]

In pursuing their assignment the boundary commissioners for Virginia went to the length of persuading two important Cherokee chiefs to accompany them to Charleston for a meeting with the southern superintendent. In the presence of the superintendent the Indians indicated that they would agree to an alteration in the Hard Labour Line which would allow the settlements located on the upper Holston to be included in Virginia's bounds. The super-intendent refused to make any decision on the proposed alteration but promptly contacted his superiors in London for instructions.

Replying to the Virginia claim that the colony had not been

49. C. O. 5-1347, p. 41.
50. H. R. McIlwaine and John P. Kennedy (eds.), *Journals of the House of Burgesses of Virginia, 1619-1776* (13 vols.; Richmond, 1905-1915), *1766-1769*, p. xxxi.
51. *Ibid.*

given an opportunity to state its views on the Indian boundary, the superintendent tersely reminded the colony that he had frequently requested Governor Fauquier's co-operation in the matter, which had never been forthcoming.[52] The superintendent, however, did state that he would "with great cheerfulness resume a negotiation for a new line when H.M. shall please to signify his pleasure."[53]

The superintendent suggested to his superiors in London a new boundary which would include all of the Virginia settlements. This new boundary was to be negotiated at Virginia's expense and was described as follows: ". . . to begin at the point where the North Carolina line terminates and run thence a west course to Holstein's [Holston] River, where it is intersected by the line dividing the provinces of North Carolina and Virginia, and thence in a North East by North course to the confluence of the Kanhaway and Ohio Rivers."[54] This new boundary would begin at the point where the delineated North Carolina Indian boundary intersected the Virginia-North Carolina boundary rather than at Chiswell's Mines, some miles farther north. From this intersection it was to be surveyed due west until it reached the Holston River. From the Holston River the line would be surveyed to the mouth of the Kanawha River on the Ohio. Stuart illustrated his proposal clearly on a map which he forwarded to London in 1771.[55] Figure 6 is based on this original map and shows the proposed boundary, which was ratified in 1770 with the earlier Hard Labour Line of 1768. Figure 6 should be compared with Figure 7, which shows these two boundary lines plotted on a present-day map of the area. It can be seen that the superintendent depicted the North Carolina Indian boundary incorrectly on his map, which shows it as terminating on the west side of the New (Great Conhaway on 1771 map) River rather than at Chiswell's Mines along the east bank of that stream. This might have resulted from a reliance on the imperfect maps of the day or it may have been a deliberate attempt to minimize the apparent change in the line. In either case, the map made

52. *Ibid.*, p. xxxiii. Lawrence G. Derthick stated that "Until Fauquier's death in the spring of 1768, the affair continued to be a state of confusion for which the governor was directly to blame." Quoted from "The Indian Boundary Line In the Southern District of British North America, 1763-1779," (Master's thesis, University of Tennessee, 1930), p. 66.

53. McIlwaine and Kennedy, *Journals of the House of Burgesses, 1763-1769,* p. xxxiii.

54. C. O. 5-227, p. 45.

55. M.P.G. 348, P.R.O.

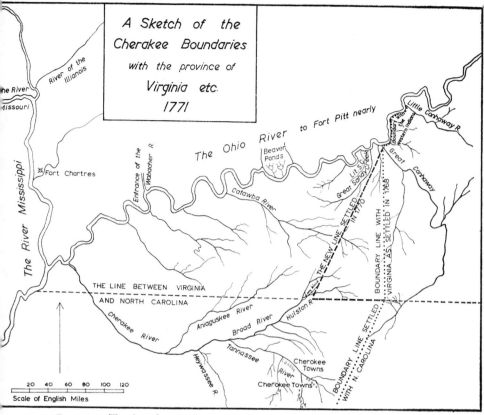

Fig. 6.   Tracing from John Stuart's map of the Lochaber and Hard Labour lines. (P.R.O., M.P.G., 348.)

plain the fact that Virginia's boundary had been shifted to the west to embrace a considerable gore of territory so that all of the legally established Virginia settlements would be included.

The Crown's acceptance of the superintendent's new boundary scheme is not surprising in the light of the representations which Virginia had made on the subject. The Virginians had understandably laid a great stress on the Fort Stanwix cession, which they saw as effectively extinguishing any Indian claims to the country south of the Ohio River. It will be recalled that they had consistently denied any Cherokee pretension to a claim in the area which later became Kentucky. To illustrate the Virginia contentions, Governor Botetourt forwarded an important manuscript map

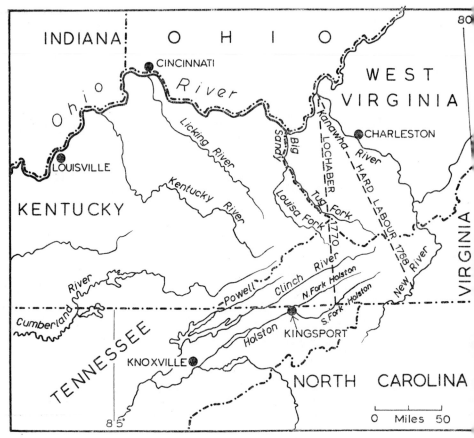

Fig. 7.   Reference map showing Hard Labour and Lochaber lines.

to London. He described this late in 1768 as a map "of the lands purchased at Fort Stanwix and those which remain to be purchased of the Cherokees in order to secure peace betwixt them and us in all eternity."[56]

A study of this revealing map, which has served as the source for Figure 8, shows that the area embracing the upper Holston River is captioned "the lands . . . to be purchased of the Cherokee."[57] The area to the east, embracing the basins of the New,

56. C. O. 5-1347, p. 30.

57. C. O. 700, Maps Virginia 18. See also the informative discussion of this map included in John C. Parish, "John Stuart and the Cartography of the Indian

Green Brier, and Kanawha rivers, however, is captioned "Those lands were granted and partly settled in consequence of a purchase made at Lancaster in the year 1744 and further confirmed at Loggstown in 1752." The area which was indicated as "granted and partly settled" was entirely within the new line that the Indian superintendent suggested. It is probable that the London-seated policy-makers sincerely felt that the boundary being suggested by the king's superintendent of Indian affairs embraced all of the area which the Virginians were claiming. It can be concluded that in December of 1768 all indications were that Virginia was in agreement with the boundary line that the superintendent had suggested.

While negotiations were being carried on for an orderly extension of Virginia's territory to the west of the New River basin a less orderly but, in the last analysis, more important change was taking place in the Virginia frontier. This change resulted from a less than orderly influx of new settlers into the area beyond the New River. The reason for this increase is perhaps to be found in the following extract from the *Virginia Gazette* of December 1, 1768: "The Six Nations and their tributaries have granted a vast extent of country to His Majesty, and settled an advantageous boundary line between their hunting grounds and this and other colonies to the southwards as far as the Cherokee River."[58] The personal account of James Smith is perhaps typical of the manner in which hundreds of frontiersmen were effected by this news of the Fort Stanwix Cession. He stated:

In the year 17[68] I heard that Sir William Johnson, the kings agent for settling affairs with the Indians, had purchased from them all the land west of the Appalachain Mountains, that lay between the Ohio and the Cherokee River; and as I knew by conversing with the Indians in their own tongue, that there was a large body of rich land there, I considered I would take a tour westward, and explore that country.[59]

Boundary Line," *The Persistence of the Westward Movement and Other Essays,* p. 136.

58. *Virginia Gazette,* Dec. 1, 1768, quoted in Samuel C. Williams, *Dawn of Tennessee Valley and Tennessee History* (Johnson City, Tenn., 1937), p. 134.

59. Quoted by Williams, *Early Travels in the Tennessee Country, 1540-1800,* p. 204. It is very likely that many discontented "Regulators" from North Carolina were making their way west at about this time also. An entry in the Fries, *Records of the Moravians in North Carolina,* I, 379 for Aug. 24, 1768, mentioned "A party of men from Orange Country passed through our village. They were going to Holston's River to look for land—though there may be another reason."

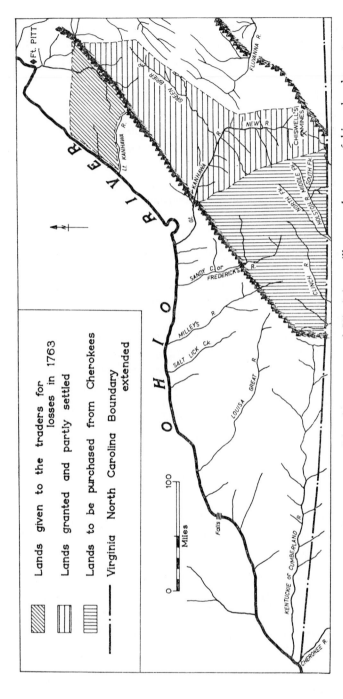

Fig. 8. Tracing from map used by the governor of Virginia to illustrate the state of his colony's western-most settlements in 1768. (P.R.O., C. O. 700, Maps, Virginia/18.)

Some indication of the rapidity with which the land along the upper Holston River was being occupied in this period is given in the account of a group of frontiersmen who traversed the area in 1769. Upon meeting a large party of Indians along the Holston they beat a hasty retreat to the more settled areas. The chronicler of early Tennessee, Ramsey stated:

They turned about and went back up the river ten or fifteen miles and concluded to return home. About twenty miles above the North Fork [of Holston], they found . . . a cabin on every spot where the range was good and where only six weeks before nothing was to be seen but a howling wilderness. When they passed by before, on their outward destination, they found no settlers on Holston, save three families on the head springs of that river.[60]

To the north of the Ohio in Pennsylvania, too, the tide of pioneers was flowing westward at an increasing rate during the months following the Fort Stanwix cession. George Croghan, one of the central figures in Pennsylvania's westward expansion, observed:

You will not be surprised when I assure you, that Mr. Penn has sold since the Congress [at Fort Stanwix], all the good land within his grant to the westward of the Allegany mountains. What number of families has settled since the congress, is to the westward of the high ridge, I cannot pretend to say positively, but last year [1769], I am sure, there were between four and five thousand, and all this spring and summer the roads have been lined with wagons moving to the Ohio.[61]

The southern superintendent stated during his discussions with Virginia relative to an alteration of the Hard Labour Line that . . . "all the settlements to the westward of Samuel Starnacres [Stalnakers on the upper Holston] have been made since Sir Willam Johnson's purchased at Fort Stanwix."[62]

The author of an anonymous contemporary work on the British colonies in North America referred to the influence of the Fort Stanwix Indian cession on the advancing Virginia frontier. He concluded:

This purchase was made not with a view to encourage any settlements beyond the mountains, but only to satisfy the Indians; the tenor of the Proclamation of 1763 was adhered to, and the governor of Virginia

60. J. G. M. Ramsey, *The Annals of Tennessee* (Charleston, S. C., 1853), p. 94.
61. Quoted in Clarence Walworth Alvord, *The Mississippi Valley in British Politics* (Cleveland, 1917), II, 113.
62. Quoted in Williams, *Dawn of Tennessee Valley*, p. 335.

ordered to admit of no colonization within the specified limits. But such orders could not be obeyed; for the country was found so fertile and pleasant, that fresh numbers every day thronged thither; and the expediency of establishing a government over them was found daily greater.[63]

It can be seen that even while an alteration of the Hard Labour Line was being discussed and decided upon the pioneers of Virginia were surging down the Holston Valley into areas well beyond the new limits under discussion. As the author of the paragraph above stated, "the expediency of establishing a government over them was found daily greater." It is probable that an awareness of this newly advanced frontier caused a reassessment of the boundary problem in Williamsburg during the winter months of 1769.

VIRGINIA PROPOSALS FOR A BOUNDARY

On December 13, 1769, the Virginia House of Burgesses issued a memorial which once again brought the topic of an Indian boundary line into doubt. Commenting on the boundary line proposed by the Indian superintendent, the Burgesses observed:

That the said line if extended from the intersection of Holston's River, the point which would terminate the line dividing this colony from North Carolina to the mouth of the Great Kanhaway [Kanawha], would be near two hundred miles in length, and must pass through a country abounding with high and rugged mountains, extremely difficult and dangerous of access, and intersected by many water courses; that the present posture of Indian affairs would make a strong guard of armed men necessary for the protection of those who might be commissioned to run such a line, as it must necessarily pass through a country uninhabited, and through which those Indians who seem at present most inclined to hostilities do frequently take their routes.[64]

Following this statement, which was reminiscent of the Cherokee description of the same area, the Burgesses proceeded to claim that this boundary would cut off legally established settlements. This claim was contradictory to the earlier Virginia claims which had been illustrated in the map forwarded to London earlier. The Burgesses would seem to have been attempting to include the new

63. *American Husbandry,* p. 281.
64. McIlwaine and Kennedy, *Journals of the House of Burgesses, 1766-1769,* p. 335.

settlements made along the Holston, Watauga, Nolachucky, and Powell rivers during late 1768 and 1769 under the aegis of the colony as "legally established settlements." They further seemed devoted to obstructing any proposal that would result in a restriction of Virginia's free access to western lands. In accordance with this intention, the Burgesses concluded their memorial by suggesting that Virginia's western limit be delineated by a continuation of her North Carolina boundary due west to the Ohio River.[65]

The southern Indian superintendent promptly corrected the Virginians by pointing out: "A continuation of the line dividing your colony and North Carolina from the point where it intersects Holston's River, in a due western course, can never touch the Ohio but will run within less than sixty miles of the Cherokee Towns and fall upon the Cherokee [Tennessee] River a little below Chuola or the Chickasaw landing."[66] The superintendent further pointed out that the boundary line between Virginia and North Carolina followed the parallel of 36°30' north latitude and that the Cherokee towns were reckoned to be located between 35° and 35°40' north latitude. A boundary such as that proposed by the Burgesses was untenable since, according to the superintendent, it would cut the Cherokees off from their hunting grounds and create a competitive condition between the Indians and whites which would be "an insurmountable obstacle." As a postscript the superintendent added ominously that the Indians were very apprehensive of encroachment and seemed ready once again to band together in a general resistance to the British.

The forceful arguments of the Indian superintendent were considered by a committee of the Burgesses which undertook a com-

65. The error of assuming that the Virginia-North Carolina boundary would, if extended due west, intersect the Ohio River would indicate that the Burgesses were employing a map similar to that which Botetourt had forwarded to London. The colonial boundary is shown on this map as striking the Ohio River near the mouth of its tributary the Cherokee [Tennessee] River. This error seems inexcusable since even Mitchell's map of 1755 showed the Virginia-North Carolina boundary correctly striking the Mississippi River well below the mouth of the Ohio.

66. McIlwaine and Kennedy, *Journals of the House of Burgesses, 1770-1772,* p. xi.

The Virginia boundary commissioners, Lewis and Walker, suggested this boundary to the southern Indian superintendent on Jan. 16, 1770. They stressed that the due west boundary would best serve the interests of the Crown and the inhabitants of the colony. In their conclusion they stated that "this boundary will give room to extend our settlements for ten or twelve years, will raise a considerable sum by the rights, much increase the quit rents and enable the inhabitants of Virginia to live without manufacturing such materials as they raise." *Ibid.,* p. xxxvii.

prehensive review of the boundary problem during the spring of 1770. On June 15 the committee offered a resolution which was adopted by the Burgesses. In brief, the resolution recognized the validity of the superintendent's arguments and signalled Virginia's abandonment of the proposed "due west" boundary. The Burgesses urged the executive to join in the speedy settlement of the superintendent's proposed line from the Holston to the mouth of the Kanawha River.[67]

Before considering the delineation of this boundary line, it should be mentioned parenthetically that the retreat from Virginia's traditional claim to the transmontane west was not without precedent. Indeed, there were many in Virginia who viewed unlimited western expansion with increasing trepidation. An address which was delivered by the Virginia Council in March, 1768, had included the statement: "The horrid barbarities and unheard of cruelties that were committed upon many of the frontier inhabitants, in the course of the last Indian war, are so recent in our memories, that we shall be ready to adopt every proper measure to avert the like calamities for the future. . . ."[68] It can be seen that the superintendent's proposed boundary was acceptable as a "proper measure" insuring peace.

THE DELINEATION OF THE LOCHABER LINE

On June 21, 1770, the governor of Virginia informed the superintendent of Indian affairs that his colony would co-operate in an effort to secure an alteration and extension of the Hard Labour Line of 1768. The colony provided a fund of £2,500, which was raised by an additional £400, to cover the cost of gifts required for the Indians at a congress which would be convened with the Cherokee.[69] Virginia also agreed to bear the expense of the survey and demarcation of the boundary to be delineated at the congress. Colonel John Donelson, a member of the House of Burgesses, was appointed to represent the colony at the congress, which the superintendent was arranging to hold in October at Lochaber, the South Carolina frontier plantation in his deputy, Alexander Cameron.

The Cherokee chief, Oconostota, had indicated in March, 1769, that the tribe expected a sizable compensation for any additional

67. *Ibid.*, p. xiii.
68. *Ibid., 1766-1769*, p. xxvii.
69. *Ibid.*, pp. 116, 118, 133, 135.

land surrendered. He stated: "We shall give no part of our land away unless we are paid for it and indeed we want to keep the Virginians at as great a distance as possible, as they are generally bad men and love to steal horses and hunt for deer. . . . but what are a few goods in comparison onto good land. The land will last forever and will yearly produce corn and raise cattle."[70]

During the autumn of 1770, John Donelson, the Virginia representative, made his way southward to meet over one thousand members of the Cherokee tribe led by Oconostota at Lochaber, South Carolina. His passage was noted by the North Carolina Moravians, whose diarist reported on September 20, 1770: "A Col. Donaldson, of Virginia, and his party, spent the night here. He has been ordered to take a present worth £2500 sterling to the Indians in South Carolina, according to treaty, and then to run the new line between them and the Province of Virginia. According to this agreement the whole of New River and half of Holston River will belong to Virginia."[71] On the following day the same diarist added another observation to his frontier chronicle which gave an indication of the character of at least one band of pioneers heading for the soon to be ceded Holston valley. He wrote, "there were unusually many strangers in our town today, especially a number who do not wish to be under the law, and are moving to Holston River."[72]

The congress at Lochaber convened on October 18, 1770, and proceeded smoothly until the Cherokee expressed the resolve to retain the Long Island of the Holston. They professed a fear that a fort might be erected there to jeopardise their towns. This was a repetition of earlier refusals to allow the Virginians to establish a position at this strategic site.[73] A compromise on this point was soon reached however, and a boundary line was described which satisfied all parties concerned. The new boundary, which came to be called the Lochaber Line, was to begin where the Virginia–North Carolina boundary terminated and continued west to a point on the Holston River six miles upstream of the Long Island. From this point on the Holston's south fork the boundary was to be carried northward to the north fork of the same river and then directly northeastward in a straight line to the mouth of the Kana-

70. C. O. 5-70, p. 246.
71. Fries, *Records of the Moravians in North Carolina*, I, 415.
72. *Ibid.*
73. C. O. 5-1349, p. 20. The Long Island is incorporated in the present-day city of Kingsport, Tenn.

wha River at the Ohio. This is the boundary identified as "The New Line Settled In 1770" on Figure 6. Figure 7 shows this as the Lochaber Line which, along with the earlier Hard Labour Line, is transposed on to a modern map of the area concerned. During the compromise discussions at Lochaber it came to be generally accepted that the Indian retention of the Long Island had diminished the area included in the cession which Virginia was to receive.

Significantly, the Cherokee offered to allow the boundary to be shifted from the mouth of the Kanawha River to some unspecified point farther west to compensate for the retained Holston lands. The superintendent observed that this westward shift "would have thrown in a great tract of country" for Virginia. He felt, however, that his instructions precluded the acceptance of such a departure from the boundary desired by the Board of Trade, so it was refused.[74]

Although it was not accepted at Lochaber, the Indian's willingness to allow a more westerly termination of the boundary at the Ohio River end should be kept in mind. It indicated that the Cherokee were not overly tenacious of lands located in the Ohio valley far to the north. This is an important point in understanding what transpired while the Lochaber Line was being surveyed during the following spring.

Donelson returned to Williamsburg with the deed of cession signed by the Indians at Lochaber and informed the Virginians of the proceedings there.[75] In his dispatch to London, the acting governor of Virginia reported that:

The Indians have cut us short in the line, about six miles to the eastward of Long Island on Holston River; an equivalent for which they offered to give at the farther end of the line; but the Superintendent thought himself so restricted by his instructions that he declined accepting it . . . it is a pity that this addition to His Majesty's territory, which is so easy to be obtained should be refused.[76]

In the opinions of land speculators, pioneers, and other expansionists, the refusal was more a calamity than a pity. The untimely death of Governor Botetourt had temporarily thrown the administration of Virginia to William Nelson, who failed to urge vigorously an acceptance of the Cherokee offer. The Indian superin-

74. C. O. 5-1349, p. 20.
75. *Ibid.*, p. 17.
76. *Ibid.*

tendent had earlier advised that Virginia should seek permission for acceptance from the Crown prior to the boundary survey which was scheduled for the spring of 1771.[77]

In the light of the absence of a stronger argument by Virginia it is not surprising that the Indian superintendent received notice that the king had greatly approved of "the final conclusion of the boundary line between Virginia and the Cherokee country" which he had negotiated at Lochaber. The retention of the Long Island and refusal of a compensatory cession were also approved. Although the dispatch which contained this information had been dated February 11, 1771, the slowness of transatlantic communications worked a serious delay and it did not reach the superintendent until after July 29, 1771, while he was in Pensacola, West Florida. Thus it was not until the mid-summer of 1771 that the Crown's official attitude, which was opposed to any further extension of the Lochaber Line, became known.

This date is very significant because the survey of the boundary had begun two months before on May 26, 1771. John Donelson, representing Virginia, and the deputy Indian superintendent, Alexander Cameron, were already many hundreds of miles away in the transfrontier wilderness between the Holston and Ohio rivers with a party of Cherokee; they were blazing a line of boundary trees which came to be called the Donelson Line and which marked the westernmost limit of Virginia. Donelson's party could not have known that the Crown was firmly opposed to the acceptance of what had been termed a "great tract of country" in return for the Long Island.[78]

THE DEMARCATION OF THE DONELSON LINE

The section of the Southern Indian Boundary Line demarcated by Donelson, Cameron, and the Cherokee, Chief Attakullakulla, was depicted and described by the Virginia boundary commissioner on an original manuscript map. The large size of this little-known map precluded the use of a photographic copy here, but Figure 9 is an overlay of the original at a reduced scale. Included with the original map in the Public Record Office, London, is a description of the Indian boundary in Donelson's hand. This description is transcribed here in full:

77. *Ibid.,* p. 20.
78. Alden, *John Stuart,* p. 283.

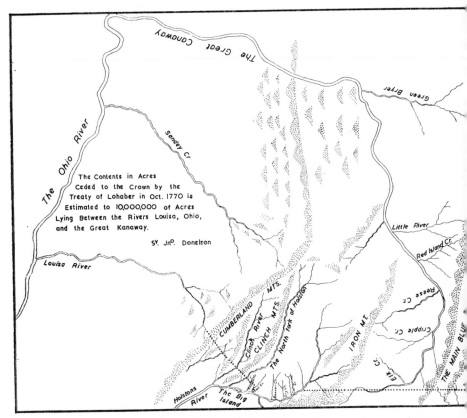

The Contents in Acres
Ceded to the Crown by the
Treaty of Lohaber in Oct. 1770 is
Estimated to 10,000,000 of Acres
Lying Between the Rivers Louisa, Ohio,
and the Great Kanaway.

S.ʸ Jnᵒ. Donelson

Fig. 9.   Tracing from John Donelson's map of 1771. (P.R.O.,
C. O. 700, Maps, Virginia/19.)

Virginia Sv.
In obedience to an Order of His Majs Honble Council on the 26th
day of May 1771 did proceed to Run and mark the Boundary Line
Between the Colony of Virginia and the Cherokee hunting grounds in
conjunction with Alexander Cameron Esq. His Majs. Superintendent
and the Cherokee Chiefs Commissioned by their Nation for that purpose, Ran and Mark the Same as hereafter mentioned Viz.
Beginning at the Steep Rock on the Waters of the Great Canaway
River, to which place Messrs Fry and Jefferson Extend the Colony
Line & thence Extending the Same in its due west Direction—24½
miles and 50 poles crossing the Iron Mountain To several marked trees
on the South fork of Holston's River near several small islands in the
same. Thence down the Stream thereof as it meanders. 30 miles to
a point 6 miles above the Long Island The[nce] N5°W 4.¾ miles

to a Red Oak markt on the top of a Ridge on Col. Byrds Road. The[nce] N36°½ W7¾ miles Crossing the No. fork of Holston's River to a point of Rocks on the top Clinch Mountain. The[nce] N.45°W 20½ miles and 32 poles crossing Clinch River the maney Sink Mountain and Powells River to the top of Powels (or the Rockey) Mountain, Thence N33°W 15½ miles crossing Cumberland Mountain to 3 Sycamore Trees Issuing from one root and several other markt trees on a Creek of Louisa River and thence down the same as it meanders to its confluence with the Ohio and thence up the said Ohio River as it meanders to the mouth of the Great Canaway Rr–

By Jno Donelson Survr–[79]

It can be seen from both Donelson's map and description that the Indian boundary line demarcated by his party during the summer of 1771 was not the Lochaber Line. To more fully appreciate the Donelson Line, it should be studied on Figure 10, which shows this eighteenth-century boundary line translated onto a modern topographic map of the area involved. The Virginia-Cherokee boundary of 1771 or Donelson Line commenced, according to the terms of the Lochaber agreement, at what was understood to be the termination of the Virginia-North Carolina boundary. From

79. C. O. Maps, 700 Virginia/19.
It would appear that Donelson was somewhat confused about the location of the termination of the Fry-Jefferson survey of the North Carolina-Virginia boundary. The Fry-Jefferson maps of 1751 [1753] and 1755 western sections reprinted in Cumming, *The Southeast In Early Maps,* plates 57 and 58, clearly show the line terminating on a branch of "Tooleys River" which flows into the Holston. Williams in his "Stephen Holston and Holston River," *East Tennessee Historical Society's Publications,* VIII (1936), 26, stated "Tooleys River or Creek is now known as Laurel Fork of South Fork of Holston."

Daniel Smith, who surveyed the boundary between "North Carolina and Virginia-Tennessee and Kentucky" in 1779 and 1780, made an attempt to find and follow Donelson's line west from Steep Rock Creek. In his journal he wrote:

August 23, 1779. . . . moved to a camp on Col. Donelson's Line about 7 miles west of the white Top'd mountain.

August 24—Having from some accounts of late together with Col. Fry's and Jefferson's map of the line got an opinion that Col. Donelson did not begin where Fry and Jefferson left off today I went backwards to Donelson's beginning to endeavor to trace up the old line taking with me Jas. Michie one of the surveyors. When I got within about a mile of the same found old line and began to trace it up. It lay in the mountain which divides New River waters from Holston.

August 26. This morning the distance Col. Donelson's line was south of the old one was measured along a line making a right angle with the old one—52 poles. The course of the old line by compass not allowing for variation was N88°30'W. The distance was measured along a course S1°30'W. This day we moved to Tooleys River and encamp'd just above the little flag meadow, south of the line about a mile.

From "Journal of Daniel Smith," introduction by St. George L. Sioussat, *Tennessee Historical Magazine,* I (March, 1915) 48.

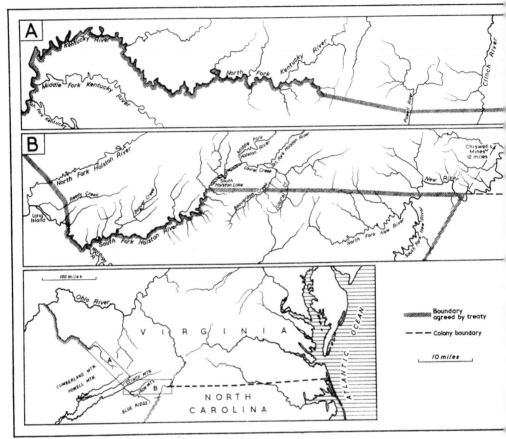

Fig. 10. The Virginia-Cherokee section of the Southern Indian Boundary Line.

this point the surveying party blazed a line of trees "in a due west direction" to the bank of the Holston River's south fork. At this point the surveyors decided to follow the course of the Holston "as it meanders" rather than to continue their due west line to the stipulated point on the river six miles upstream of the Long Island. The deviation can be followed on panel B of Figure 10. It can also be observed that the due west line as originally stipulated at Lochaber would have struck the North Fork of the Holston, if continued, rather than the South Fork upstream of the Long Island. It could have been that the Cherokee's superior knowledge of the local geography had prompted them to make this alteration in order to keep the Virginia boundary at the Holston's south fork and east of the Long Island. In his talk delivered to Donelson at the conclusion of the survey, Attakullakulla chose to explain the alteration in terms of Indian generosity to the whites who were already settled along the Holston in the area effected. He stated:

Brother

As we are now going to part and have finished the line I hope agreeable to both parties I beg that you will carry a short talk from me to the new governor and beloved men of Virginia. When you met us with our father [Stuart] at Long Cane [Lochaber] it was then agreed that the line should run to the mouth of New River [Kanawha] but we have altered that course a little and I hope my father [Stuart] as well as my people will approve of it. I have likewise given away some land by the river side (meaning Holston) as my brothers were settled upon it and I pittied them.[80]

It seems very probable that the rapid advance of pioneers down the Holston River valley in the two years preceding the survey was a factor in the determination of the Southern Indian Boundary Line in this area.

From the Holston a few miles upstream of the Long Island the boundary was demarcated across the hills to the North Fork of the Holston, as the Lochaber agreement had stipulated. At this point, probably close to the present-day city of Kingsport, Tennessee, a decision was made that resulted in a major change in the course of the Virginia-Cherokee boundary line. This decision was to abandon the course of the Lochaber boundary and probably resulted from a bargain struck between Donelson and Attakullakulla. Although the record is not entirely clear on the terms of this bargain, the evidence indicates that Donelson agreed to pay the Cherokee an additional £500 in return for a change in the course of the boundary line which would carry its termination farther to the west than the mouth of the Kanawha as originally stipulated.[81] While the terms of the bargain are not altogether clear, the results are. The Donelson Line was demarcated along a northwesterly course to the Louisa River and followed that stream to its confluence with the Ohio rather than on a northeasterly

80. C. O. 5-1350, p. 27.
81. William P. Palmer (ed.), *Calendar of Virginia State Papers and Other Manuscripts, 1652-1781, Preserved In the Capitol at Richmond* (Richmond, 1875), I, 291.

course to the mouth of the Kanawha River over 150 miles to the east. The river named Louisa in Donelson's map and statement is the present-day Kentucky River.[82]

An examination of Figure 7 will indicate that this abandonment of the Lochaber agreement gave to Virginia what is today the eastern one-quarter of Kentucky plus a large section of western-most West Virginia. Even on Donelson's inaccurate map, Figure 9, this can be seen as an immense area, which he estimated at 10,000,000 acres.

In examining the motives which probably led Donelson and Attakullakulla to make their momentous decision, certain factors must be reviewed. In Donelson's case it should be recalled that he was aware of the Cherokee's willingness to compensate Virginia for the Long Island concession that was included in the Lochaber agreement. As a Virginian, he doubtlessly felt an obligation to further his colony's legitimate ends to the maximum. In this case the acquisition of 10,000,000 acres of virgin land in return for £500 could hardly have been criticized. As stated earlier Donelson had no way of knowing that such an acquisition was opposed by the Crown when he began the boundary demarcation. Donelson's motive was clearly to obtain as much non-contested land as possible for Virginia.

On the other hand, Attakullakulla's motive is more difficult to comprehend. It should be stated initially that it is extremely unlikely that he was duped or working in ignorance of the consequence of his decision to alter the line. It is safe to say that Attakullakulla was one of the most sagacious and best informed Indian leaders of his day. It is not unlikely that he had a hand in the drafting of Donelson's map. Why then did the tribal leader, with his wide experience of the white man's wiles and knowledge of the geography of the country south of the Ohio River, enter into an agreement which gave to Virginia such a vast tract of country which the Crown was willing to reserve as a hunting ground for his people?

Since his ignorance of the consequences is an unlikely explanation, the answer to this question probably lies in one or more of the following motives which can be suggested to account for Attakullakulla's decision. These are: (1) The desire to establish a "natural" boundary rather than to undertake the laborious task of an overland survey to the mouth of the Kanawha River agreed

82. *Infra,* p. 86.

upon at Lochaber.[83] (2) The realization that white population was rapidly expanding and that the cession of lands to the northeast of the Kentucky would act as a "safety valve" and divert their settlements away from the Cherokee coreland farther south. (3) The realization that the Cherokee claim to the lands south of the Ohio River was at best tenuous and subject to serious challenge by Indian enemies.[84] (4) The desire to encourage white settlements in the area to protect the Cherokee flank from northern enemies. (5) The desire for personal gain from the sale of lands to which his tribe held only a tenuous and debatable claim.

Whichever of these motives inspired the Cherokee leader, Attakullakulla, the result of his decision is clear. He entered into an agreement with Donelson that resulted in a westward shift of Virginia's boundary line from the mouth of the Kanawha to the mouth of the Kentucky River far down the Ohio River. This alteration in the previously delineated Lochaber Line, which came to be called the Donelson Line, was reluctantly ratified by the British Crown as a *fait accompli*. It opened a huge area for white settlement during the years just preceding the American Revolution.

AN EVALUATION OF THE DONELSON LINE

No other section of the Southern Indian Boundary Line has been so seriously and frequently misunderstood as that demarcated through the transfrontier wilderness of Virginia by Donelson and Attakullakulla during the summer of 1771. Misunderstanding and confusion concerning the location of the Donelson Line plagued interested officials and private citizens alike

83. Reuben Gold Thwaites, quoting from the unpublished notes of Lyman C. Draper, wrote: "when Col. Donelson ran the line the following year, the boundary was fixed at the suggestion of the Cherokee deputies on the Kentucky River as the southwestern line, as they delighted, they said, in natural landmarks. This considerably enlarged the cession for which they received an additional compensation." Cited in Alexander Scott Withers, *Chronicles of Border Warfare* (Cincinnati, 1915), p. 195.

84. On this point Thwaites quoted Draper's notes and stated: "for some of the visiting Cherokees while on their route to attend the Fort Stanwix Treaty, killed game for their subsistence, and on their arrival at Fort Stanwix, tendered the skins to the Six Nations, saying, They are yours, we killed them after passing the Big River, the name by which they always designated the Tennessee. But probably discovering the other Indian Nations were driving good business by disposing of their distant land rights the Cherokees managed to hatch up some sort of a claim, which they, in part, relinquished to Virginia at the Treaty of Lochaber in 1770." *Ibid.*

during the revolutionary era. Similar misunderstanding and confusion has continued to plague scholars and students of the present century. For this reason clarification is necessary and should result from an evaluation of the Donelson Line in its contemporary and present day conceptual and geographic contexts.

Certainly much of the contemporaneous misunderstanding of the Donelson Line is understandable and easily explicable. It represented a major alteration on the conceptual image of a Virginia-Cherokee boundary line which was framed and frequently endorsed by the British Crown after lengthy investigations and deliberations devoted to the problem. This fact alone, when considered in the light of the slow communications and vast distances involved, was sufficient to create a predictably large degree of confusion and misunderstanding among Donelson's contemporaries in both Virginia and England. An additional factor, the lack of accurate geographical knowledge about the transmontane country, added to the confusion and misunderstanding and delayed the appreciation and acceptance of Donelson's laboriously demarcated boundary line.

Perhaps the most striking facet of this factor of geographical ignorance is to be seen in Donelson's choice of the name Louisa to designate the river that he followed northwest from its headwaters near the eastern edge of the Cumberland Plateau to its confluence with the Ohio River near the present-day Carrollton, Kentucky. This river is now commonly known as the Kentucky River, but in Donelson's day it enjoyed (or suffered) toponymic plurality. Brown wrote, "this simple place name is a classic example of the confusion which can be caused by place names on maps of any age. It was called the Kentucky and the Catawba as well as the Louisa."[85] While such toponymic pluralism alone could have easily given rise to a considerable degree of confusion and misunderstanding among Donelson's contemporaries, the problem was even further complicated by the fact that a river other than the Kentucky of today bore the name Louisa. The second Louisa River is located to the east of the Kentucky and is commonly identified on present-day maps by the name Louisa or Levisa Fork

85. Lloyd A. Brown, *Early Maps of the Ohio Valley* (Pittsburgh, Pa. 1959), pp. 119-20. On the comprehensive Brown-Purcell Map of 1781 (C. O. Maps 700, North America General 15.) the river is indicated by three names: "Cuttawa, Kentuck or Louisa River." Johnston, *First Explorations of Kentucky,* p. 63 stated: "Other names by which the Kentucky River was known were Cuttawa, Catawba, Chenoka and Chenoa."

of the Big Sandy River (see Fig. 7). The Louisa Fork joins the Tug to form the Big Sandy, which with the Tug serves as the boundary between the states of Kentucky and West Virginia. In the vicinity of the Donelson Line, the headwaters of the Kentucky and Louisa Fork nearly interlock. This adjacency at the head-waters of the two similarly named streams, coupled with the fact that the Louisa Fork–Big Sandy River course was more nearly an approximation of the boundary line which had been delineated at Lochaber, added greatly to both the contemporaneous and present-day misunderstandings of the Donelson Line.[86]

It is probable, however, that anyone who had enjoyed access to Donelson's map and description would have been able to form a fairly accurate impression of the new boundary line and the immense tract of Indian hunting ground which it embraced. Donelson's contemporaries, so privileged, could not have failed to appreciate that John Donelson had been instrumental in moving Virginia's boundary far to the west of the line which had been delineated at Lochaber the year before.

Donelson returned to Williamsburg following his arduous demarcation, and on January 17, 1772, he "Attended [the Virginia Council] with a plat of the land by him lately surveyed according to a line agreed upon for the western Boundary of this Colony and run by him with the consent of the Cherokee Indians, whose hunting grounds lie on the other side thereof."[87] He also presented a claim amounting to £1163-14-10 for expenses incurred on the survey. This and a claim for 100 guineas from the deputy Indian superintendent for services rendered was favorably received by the council.[88]

Governor Dunmore of Virginia forwarded Donelson's map and report to London with the observation that:

. . . this line is not exactly run according to the instructions sent by your lordship to Mr. Stuart the superintendent of Indian Affairs, but that it takes in a larger tract of country than by those instructions they

86. Johnston, *First Explorations of Kentucky,* p. 67 n., stated: "The west or Louisa Fork of the Big Sandy River . . . was named Louisa, after the sister of the Duke of Cumberland. . . . The stream is known as the Louisa or Levisa Fork of the Big Sandy and is joined by the Tug Fork, the northeast boundary between West Virginia and Kentucky, at Louisa, countyseat of Lawrence County. . . . The Indian name of the Big Sandy was Chattaroi or Chattarawha. It was also called Totteroi."

87. C. O. 5-1350, p. 34.

88. *Ibid.*

had permission to include, though greatly short of what the Colony, by their memorial to Lord Botetourt which has been transmitted to your Lordship, were desirous of obtaining.

The commissioners upon their entering on this business, found the country thro' which the proposed line was to run, so mountainous rugged and difficult of access, that they could not have accomplished it in many months, nor without an expense that would have been enormous; but they have nevertheless, conducted it as nearly as possible, conformable to their orders, having only deviated from them as your Lordship will see by the map by continuing from the point on Holstein's river where it is intersected by the division line of this colony and North Carolina, down that river a small distance, to a place from whence they had an easier access, than was any where else to be found, to the head of Louisa river, which they followed to its conflux with the Ohio.[89]

In the light of the considerable confusion, contemporary and present day, which has surrounded Donelson's Line the governor's further remark takes on a note of unintended irony: "Thus except where they cross from Holstein's to Louisa river, which being no great distance and the country passable, they have been able to be particularly careful in marking, they have established a natural boundary, that can never be mistaken, and must forever banish all dispute and contention about it. . . ."[90] The governor continued with an illuminating comment regarding the state of settlement in the area near the new boundary: "and by this line are taken in a great number of families who had settled without the intended line, and who, if that had been adopted, would be excluded from the government and protection of the colony, to their great detriment if not utter ruin." In his concluding paragraphs the governor urged strongly the ratification of Donelson's *fait accompli* which he defended as serving the best interests of his colony and also because it was the Indian's "earnest desire."[91]

The secretary of state replied to Governor Dunmore's informative letter by expressing great concern over, "the deviation of the Indian Boundary Line made by the commissioners." He termed this "a matter of very great moment" and stated that it would require the Crown's "most serious attention."[92] The governor was directed to follow the precepts of the Proclamation of 1763 and on

89. *Ibid.*, p. 19.
90. *Ibid.*
91. *Ibid.*
92. *Ibid.*, p. 44.

no account to make any grants of land beyond its limits until a decision was forthcoming on the Donelson Line.[93]

Alden drew attention to the struggle involving the secretary of state and a powerful group of land speculators known as the Grand Ohio Company which was in progress when news of Donelson's Line reached London. This group was petitioning the Crown for a huge grant of land partially included within the area ceded by the Cherokee to Donelson. The maneuverings of the Grand Ohio Company as well as those of two other groups of speculators, one led by Thomas Walpole and Benjamin Franklin and the other by George Washington, doubtlessly had an influence on the secretary of state's strongly worded directive to the governor of Virginia. Ratification of the Donelson Line was of course forthcoming at a later date.

Washington's group of French and Indian War veterans were desirous of claiming their military bounty lands in the west. To this group fell the task of clearing the air of confusion concerning the true location of the Donelson Line three years after its demarcation. This was found necessary so that land surveys could be made and recorded with no doubt or uncertainty in the area ceded by the Cherokee. In 1774 a party of frontiersmen were commissioned to retrace Donelson's survey and verify its location. The affidavit signed by members of this party dispelled all doubts about the location of the Donelson Line and the true identity of the Louisa River. It stated:

. . . the line struck a fork of Louisa River, which Col. Donelson's Company had marke[d] about ten miles down the same creek to where it emptied into the main North fork of Louisa which is the longest of any of the branches of said river; your deponents farther marched down the river till they came to such hunters camps which from the letters of their names on trees fully satisfied your deponents

93. Alden, *John Stuart*, pp. 286-87 suggested that Donelson's map was drawn in a manner calculated to minimize the magnitude of the "deviation" in the boundary line and that Hillsborough had probably not been taken in by the attempt. Certainly the map is far from accurate in scale and direction but Donelson did add an explanatory note to the map which Dunmore forwarded to London. He noted: "The contents in acres ceded to the Crown by the treaty of Lochaber in Oct. 1770 is estimated to 10,000,000 of acres lying between the Rivers Louisa, Ohio and the Great Kanaway. Sv. Jno. Donelson."

If the Virginians were deliberately attempting to employ Donelson's map as Alden suggested it seems doubtful that they would have called attention to the great area of the cession, which Donelson estimated at more than 15,000 square miles.

it is the very river called by the hunters Louisa since called Kentucky which empties about seventy-five miles above the falls into Ohio. . . .[94]

Frequent reference was made to the Donelson Line during Judge Richard B. Henderson's purchase of "Transilvania" from the Cherokees at Watauga in 1775 and it was mentioned by name in the treaty signed at the Long Island in 1779.[95] It can be concluded that in the few years preceding the American Revolution all doubt concerning the location of the Donelson Line had been dispelled and it was generally accepted as marking the western boundary of Virginia.

The contemporary misunderstanding concerning the Donelson Line seems understandable in the context of eighteenth-century conditions. The confusion which has plagued scholars of the past and present century is, however, far less understandable. Farrand omitted entirely any mention of the Donelson Line in his paper and map devoted to the Indian Boundary Line and showed only the Hard Labour and Lochaber lines behind Virginia.[96] Derthick and Henderson both showed an incorrect version of the Donelson Line on sketch maps accompanying their historical studies.[97]

Even more widely known and quoted have been the works of Alvord and Abernethy.[98] Both of these frequently cited experts labored without any knowledge of the contents of Donelson's map and as a consequence presented erroneous interpretations of his important survey and boundary demarcation. Although Abernethy did correct many of Alvord's mistakes, his own study was not without errors which would have doubtlessly been removed had he consulted Donelson's map.[99]

94. Included in a letter from Colonel William Preston to George Washington, May 27, 1774. Reprinted in Stanislaus Murray Hamilton (ed.), *Letters to Washington and Other Papers* (Boston and New York, 1898-1902), V *(1774-1775)*, 1-2. See also Palmer, *Calendar of Virginia State Papers* I, 310, for a deposition by John Floyd which supports this affidavit.

95. *Ibid.*, pp. 282, 283, 284, 286, and 291. Archibald Henderson, "The Treaty of Long Island of Holston, July, 1779," *North Carolina Historical Review*, VIII (Jan., 1931), 55-116.

96. Max Farrand, "The Indian Boundary Line," *The American Historical Review*, X (July, 1905), 782-91.

97. Lawrence G. Derthick, "The Indian Boundary Line In the Southern District of British North America, 1763-1779," (Master's thesis, University of Tennessee, 1930). Archibald Henderson, *The Conquest of the Old Southwest* (New York, 1920), map opposite p. 192.

98. Alvord, *The Mississippi Valley in British Politics*, II, 85-89. Thomas Perkins Abernethy, *Western Lands and the American Revolution* (New York, 1937), pp. 63-78.

99. Both Alvord and Abernethy realized that Donelson's map had existed and

Another frequently cited source of information on the subject of the Virginia-Cherokee section of the Southern Indian Boundary Line is Royce's map showing Cherokee land cessions.[100] The Lochaber Line was illustrated and indicated as the actual boundary between the Cherokee and Virginia during the period 1770 to 1772. The area between the Lochaber Line and Kentucky River was shown incorrectly as being ceded to Virginia as a result of a treaty made with the governor in 1772. Royce's map should not be accepted as a source without careful checking and the addition of much supporting evidence.

Alden was the first scholar to employ Donelson's map in an interpretation of the events pertaining to the establishment of the Virginia-Cherokee section of the Southern Indian Boundary Line.[101] Although his excellent work received wide circulation, scholars have repeated some of the mistakes of the earlier experts since its publication in 1944.[102] Part of the reason for this may have been owing to the fact that Alden was unable to include a copy of Donelson's map in his book. It was not until 1961 that a published version of this map became available to scholars and general readers alike.[103] It is to be hoped that the boundary line which Donelson demarcated in 1771 will now be included as an element in the history and political geography of the Virginia frontier during the second half of the eighteenth century.

This boundary evolved in response to a recognized need—that of separating the white pioneers of the bourgeoning colony of

would have been a vital piece of evidence but both stated that they were unable to uncover it in their research and so presumed it to be lost or destroyed. Earl G. Swem, *Maps Relating to Virginia in the Virginia State Library and Other Departments of the Commonwealth* (Bulletins of the Virginia State Library, VII, Nos. 2 & 3 [Richmond, Va., 1914]) p. 227, Appendix A, "A List of Maps of Virginia and Maryland Copied from the M.S. Catalogue of the State Paper Office, London," includes the following reference: "19 Virginia. Plan of the Boundary between Virga. & the Cherokee Indians. J. Donelson 1771 transmitted by Lord Dunmore March 1772, No. 7. Book 12. page 11." This map was located in the British Public Record Office under this heading by Alden in the course of his research on his study, *John Stuart and the Southern Colonial Frontier*, which appeared in 1944, and by the author in the preparation of this study twenty years later. The map is now available in photo copy at the Library of Congress and several other United States archives.

100. Charles C. Royce, *The Cherokee Nation of Indians (Fifth Annual Report of the Bureau of American Ethnology to the Secretary of the Smithsonian Institution, 1883-84* [Washington, D.C., 1887]), Plate VIII.

101. Alden, *John Stuart. See especially* "Appendix B: The Donelson Line."

102. See for example Billington, *Westward Expansion*, p. 149.

103. Louis De Vorsey, Jr., "The Virginia-Cherokee Boundary of 1771," *East Tennessee Historical Society's Publications*, XXXIII (1961), 9.

Virginia from their Indian neighbors of the interior. The rapid increase in Virginia's white population and concomitant demand for cultivable land made such an evolution extremely difficult since, as has been shown, the settlement of Virginians frequently proceeded in contravention of the imperial edicts and programs. In a word, the frontier of white settlement advanced into the areas which are now West Virginia, Kentucky, and Tennessee more rapidly than George III's governmental machinery could react. As a result, a study of the evolution of this section of the Southern Indian Boundary Line exhibits a series of stages or steps by which Virginia's interior boundary was carried westward from the Proclamation Line, along the crest of the Blue Ridge, to the Kanawha River, the Hard Labour and Lochaber Lines, and finally to the Kentucky River when Donelson demarcated it in 1771. Much had changed since the first delineation of a Virginia-Cherokee boundary at Hard Labour in 1768, when Chief Oconostota concluded: "The land is now divided for the use of the red and white people and I hope the white inhabitants of the Frontiers will pay great attention to the line marked and agreed upon."[104]

104. C. O. 5-70, p. 77.

V · *The North Carolina-Cherokee Boundary*

Although extensive in area, including as it did present-day Tennessee, North Carolina played a relatively small role in colonial relations with the Indian tribes of the interior during the period preceding 1763.

The lack of good harbors, capital accumulation, and general commercial development retarded the colony's growth as an Indian trade center. In this risky but lucrative activity, North Carolina was eclipsed by neighboring South Carolina and Virginia. Significantly, the "answer of the several governors and the superintendent" to the Cherokees, delivered at the important Augusta Indian congress in 1763, included the statement that, "in North Carolina there are no Indian traders at all, either to your nation or any other."[1] This may have been an exaggeration but it seems safe to conclude that any trading done between North Carolinians and the interior tribes was sporadic and on a small scale.[2]

This economic immaturity did not, however, preclude a rapid growth of population and spread of settlement in the colony. Indeed, in the period preceding the Revolution, North Carolina was the fourth most populous colony. White settlers were found living on the North Carolina side of the Reedy River, to the west of where the South Carolina-Cherokee boundary line was terminated in 1766. It is important to realize that the Reedy River was generally accepted as the boundary between the colonies of North and South Carolina at that early date. The present-day boundary which divides the states of North and South Carolina is some fifty odd

1. *Journal of the Congress* . . . , p. 36.
2. Paul Chrisler Phillips, in his two-volume work, *The Fur Trade* (Norman, Okla., 1961), 413, provides an interesting statement on the relative unimportance of North Carolina trade with the interior Indians.

miles farther north and results from a survey which was not completed until 1772, or well after the demarcation of the Indian boundary line by the colonies.[3] The white settlers warned to evacuate
their Reedy River site in 1766 were identified as North Carolinians.[4] Their location is shown on Figure 12.

During the negotiations preceding the delineation of a South
Carolina-Cherokee boundary, held at Fort Prince George in 1765,
the Indians had complained of encroachments being made by
North Carolinians and Virginians on their hunting grounds. They
requested that the boundary, then being negotiated with South
Carolina, be extended to the north to separate the offending colonies from their hunting grounds. The Superintendent of Indian
Affairs was extremely sympathetic to such a request, since it coin-
cided with the already mentioned "Plan for the Future Management
of Indian Affairs" which the Board of Trade had promulgated in
1764.

The Indian point of view on an extension of the boundary line
north to include the colonies of North Carolina and Virginia was
stated in a talk which they delivered to the governor of South
Carolina on October 20, 1765. The Cherokee stated: "That they
expect the Line on the North Carolina side shall Commence,
where that of the South Carolina side terminates, and be run a
north course into the mountains whence a straight line to the Lead
Mines of Col. Chiswell should fix the boundary on the Virginia
side."[5]

Discussion of this important suggestion was resumed by the
Indians in May of the following year when they completed the
demarcation of the South Carolina boundary line. In another talk
the Cherokee stated: "At our meeting with you here in October
last we proposed also a boundary line on the North Carolina and
Virginia side. We repeat it once more, and desire to have it extended from where that of South Carolina terminates upon Reedy

3. The boundary between North and South Carolina was the subject of debate
which lasted several decades. Marvin L. Skaggs, *North Carolina Boundary Disputes Involving Her Southern Line* (Chapel Hill, 1941), and A. L. Salley, *The
Boundary Line Between North Carolina and South Carolina* (Bulletin of the Historical Commission of South Carolina, No. 10 [Charleston, 1929]), present an
exhaustive review of the problem. For a map illustrating the various North
Carolina-South Carolina boundary lines see Charles O. Paullin, *Atlas of the
Historical Geography of the United States* (Washington, 1932), Plate 100A.
4. C. O. 5-66, p. 398. The deputy Indian superintendent wrote of three or
four families settled "on the North Carolina side of Reedy River."
5. C. O. 5-66, p. 417.

River, a streight [*sic*] course to Colonel Chiswell's Mines, which will be a just boundary and the only one we can allow of."[6] It should be noted that this second suggested boundary was not identical to the first. Rather than a boundary following "a north course into the mountains" the Cherokee were now suggesting a line which would extend from Reedy River directly to Chiswell's Mines in Virginia. The significance of this is immediately apparent when the two lines are plotted on a map. Figure 11 shows the first suggestion as "N.C.1767 (Surveyed)" and the second as "(Second Cherokee Proposal)." Clearly the Cherokee were moving the boundary farther to the east, a fact which had significance as the negotiations for a boundary line with North Carolina progressed.

The Cherokee justified their demand for a boundary by calling attention to the advancing tide of white settlement, which they viewed with obvious disapproval. They stated in 1766:

The number of families that have come from North Carolina and Virginia and settled upon a great part of our best lands and within an easy days march of some of our towns, are circumstances very alarming to us; therefore we shall be ready at the end of the 5th moon (September) from this time to attend at the marking of a line: our minds will not be easy till it is completed; and if our brothers will not be assisting we must then effect it ourselves.[7]

Clearly, the Cherokee were recognizing the establishment of a boundary as a matter of urgency and vital concern to the tribe's welfare that would brook no delay.

To lend further weight to their arguments the Indians invoked the provisions of the Proclamation of 1763. They stated:

. . . when the Great Kings Proclamation relative to his red children was read to us and we were promised quiet possession of our lands and redress of our grievances, that we might claim the land a great way beyond where we propose the line to be run but chuse much rather to part with it than have any disputes concerning it . . . we are poor people depending on the woods for our support and without the means of redressing ourselves but by violence which we do not chuse to exercise against our brothers.[8]

6. C. O. 5-67, p. 5.
7. *Ibid*.
8. *Ibid*. The allusion to a Cherokee claim "a great way beyond where we propose the line to be run" is probably a reference to the area between the Broad River and the Blue Ridge. This area was recognized as Cherokee territory as the result of an earlier victory over the Catawba. The Broad River was frequently

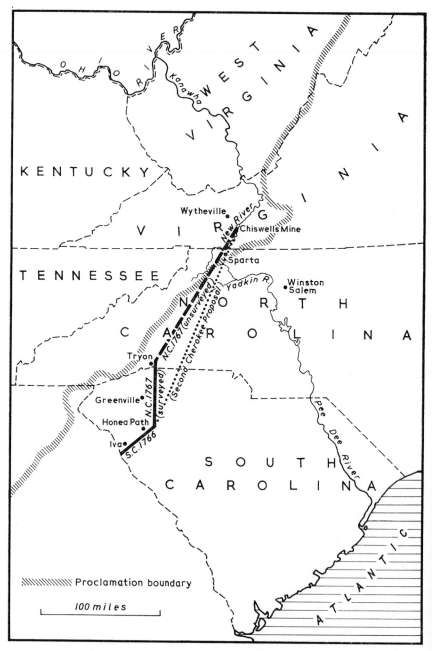

Fig. 11. Reference map showing North and South Carolina Indian boundary lines.

The Proclamation of 1763 had indeed stipulated that those lands to which the Indians had a valid claim should be exclusively theirs even though located to the east of the divide of the Appalachians. It can be seen on Figure 11 that the Southern Indian Boundary Line in South Carolina and North Carolina was in fact well to the east of the water parting mentioned in the proclamation.

NEGOTIATIONS FOR A BOUNDARY BEGIN

John Stuart, the superintendent of Indian affairs, informed the governor of North Carolina of the successful agreement on a boundary line which had been concluded between the Cherokee and South Carolina on February 5, 1766.[9] With his letter was enclosed a copy of the talk in which the Indians had suggested the continuation of this boundary line to separate their hunting grounds from North Carolina and Virginia, as well as from South Carolina. The superintendent suggested that the governor designate a commissioner who would work with his deputy superintendent, Alexander Cameron, to negotiate the details of the boundary extension.

In replying to this suggestion, the North Carolina governor claimed that such an action was not within his power and that orders from "home" would be required before he could act. He further stated that the Indians had never complained to him of encroachments.[10]

The superintendent answered these objections by sending the governor a copy of an official circular letter which had been directed to the southern governors and Indian superintendent in 1763, admonishing them to win the confidence of the Indians by assuring them that they would be protected in the retention of their tribal lands.[11] It would appear that this document was order enough from home for the governor, who began to consider seriously the problem of fixing an Indian boundary line for his colony.

Whether it was another obstruction or an honest admission of geographic ignorance is difficult to determine, but the governor next complained that he was unable to proceed because he could

understood to be the boundary between these tribes. Kenneth B. Pomeroy and James G. Yoho, *North Carolina Lands* (Washington, D.C., 1964), p. 69.

9. C. O. 5-66, p. 376.

10. *Ibid.,* p. 380.

11. *Ibid.,* p. 207.

find no one who knew where Dewises Corner, South Carolina, lay.[12] The superintendent assured the governor that the termination of the South Carolina boundary would be easily found, since the Indians had taken pains to clearly mark the trees along it.[13]

Governor Tryon, the vigorous chief executive of North Carolina, was concerned about the possible adverse effect which an Indian boundary might have upon the growth and development of his colony. He exerted his efforts toward gaining information about the geography and extent of settlements, as well as the location of such frontier landmarks as Dewises Corner and Chiswell's Mines. In mid-June, 1766, he wrote to the superintendent and stated:

> If the line the Cherokees proposed to be run is continued in a straight course from Reedy River to Chiswell's Lead Mines, I am informed, that a considerable part of Mecklenburg, and a great part of Rowan Counties, will be left to the westward of the said line, and consequently a large body of inhabitants will be shut out of this province; I therefore think the first proposition of the Indians, the most easy to be effected, vide: A north course to be run from Reedy River to the mountains and from thence a straight course to the mines; but this you will be a better judge of, when I have the pleasure of shewing you the rough sketch I have obtained of our western frontier counties.[14]

The governor was forwarding the interests of his colony in holding the Cherokee to their first suggested boundary, which can be seen on Figure 11. To what extent his remarks on the degree of settlement in the area between the two proposed boundaries can be accepted is problematical. It should be realized that North Carolina's frontier counties were unbounded on the west at this period.[15] Further, it should be borne in mind that any settlements located in the present-day counties of Spartanburg and Cherokee, South Carolina, would have been considered as North Carolina's by the governor before 1772. The "rough sketch" which Governor Tryon had obtained of the western frontier counties would be very valuable in judging his remarks.[16] Although neither the Cherokee nor the Indian superintendent challenged the governor's

12. *Ibid.*

13. *Ibid.*, p. 213.

14. *Ibid.*, p. 220. Unfortunately, no sketch or map has been found to illustrate Governor Tryon's proposal.

15. David L. Corbitt, *The Formation of the North Carolina Counties, 1663-1943* (Raleigh, 1950), especially the maps drawn by L. Polk Denmark.

16. A search in Raleigh and London archives has not located any map fitting Governor Tryon's description.

claim that, "a large body of inhabitants" would have been cut off by the Cherokee's second boundary proposal, it would be misleading to accept it without further support. It is advisable to conclude that the settlers located to the west of the "Second Cherokee Proposal" line were probably those already mentioned along the Reedy and other rivers located in what are now known as Spartanburg and Greenville counties, in the present state of South Carolina.

In late July of 1766 the governor of North Carolina informed the superintendent that his colony was ready to delineate a boundary patterned along the lines first proposed by the Cherokee, i.e., north from the Reedy River to the mountains and thence in a straight line to Chiswell's Mines. He stated that this boundary would satisfy the inhabitants of North Carolina's frontier settlements and that the colony would provide 1,000 pounds to buy gifts to compensate the Indians.[17] The North Carolina executive concluded: "If the above line could be run by the end of September and you could accompany me, I should not dislike to be present as it might not only prevent any little jealousies that might arise between the settlers and the Indians, but give me an opportunity to take a view of the back country."[18]

Governor Tryon's change of attitude from his uncooperative stance of a few months before was dramatic and might have had a variety of causes. Doubtlessly important among these was his growing knowledge and awareness of his colony's advancing frontier. Evidence of this is found in a letter to the Board of Trade dated August 2, 1766, in which the governor wrote:

I am of the opinion this province is settling faster than any on the continent, last autumn and winter, upwards of one thousand wagons passed thro' Salisbury with families from the northward, to settle in this province chiefly; some few went to Georgia and Florida, but liked it so indifferently, that some of them have since returned.

The dispatch containing the patents I have granted since my administration will show to your Lordships the great increase of settlers in the western or back counties. These inhabitants are a race of people differing in health and complexion from the natives in the maritime parts of the province, as much as a sturdy Briton differs from a puny Spaniard. . . .[19]

17. Saunders, *The Colonial Records of North Carolina*, VII, 245.
18. *Ibid.*
19. *Ibid.*, p. 248.

The governor's remarks are somewhat amusing and fanciful in the light of present day knowledge about the link between the swamps of the coastal plain and malaria, but they do indicate the importance which he attached to the advancing frontier in his colony.

THE DELINEATION OF THE NORTH CAROLINA-CHEROKEE BOUNDARY

Any hesitation the governor might have evidenced about the boundary when it was first suggested was completely dispelled by a strongly worded dispatch on the subject that arrived from the secretary of state on September 13, 1766. The secretary noted that lack of obedience to the provisions of the Proclamation of 1763 had caused frequent controversies between the Indians and white colonists over land matters, with serious consequences. He continued:

His Majesty's Commander-in-Chief has received express orders to cooperate with the civil government for the enforcing a due obedience to the Proclamation and His Majesty requires and expects every measure to be taken which prudence can dictate for the removing of such settlers [and] preventing in future any such settlements as are contrary to the intentions of the proclamation and for apprehending such offenders whose daring crimes have so direct a tendency to involve the whole of His Majesty's provinces in America in an Indian war.[20]

Governor Tryon began preparations for a meeting with the Indians in the frontier, where he would personally attend to the delineation of a boundary line with them late in 1766. However, unforeseen calamity among the Indians made such a meeting impossible at that time. The Cherokee explained their predicament in a talk sent in late September. They stated:

But altho we came yesterday to a resolution to set out with our brother [the deputy superintendent] on the 10th of next moon for that service the dismal scenes about us this morning weakened our resolutions. . . . When [we] got up this morning [we] could hear nothing but the cries of women and children for the loss of their relations, in the evenings there are nothing to be seen but smoak and houses on fire, the dwellings of the deceased; [We] never remember to see any sickness like the present, except the smallpox, and if we should attempt to go to run the line we might have been taken sick in the woods and die, as several . . . who attempted to escape this devil of a disorder.[21]

20. *Ibid.*, pp. 254-55.
21. C. O. 5-67, p. 240.

In addition to this excellent excuse, the Cherokee stated further that Virginia had not yet agreed to a boundary. They complained that negotiations and meetings were "troublesome" to them and required much of their time and energy. Although not stated by the Indians, it is likely that they felt such time and energy could be better spent in hunting game or engaging in the "honorable" sport of tribal warfare.

speculation

The Cherokee did, however, keep their promise to meet with the governor during the following spring, after some misunderstanding and delay. The meeting was held on the banks of the Tiger River, in what is today the northern part of South Carolina. The negotiations which led to the delineation of a boundary line, "between the western frontiers of North Carolina and the Cherokee Indian hunting grounds," began on June 1, 1767.[22]

In his formal address to the meeting the North Carolina governor stated:

I have it in command from his most gracious Majesty King George to inform you of his steady purposes to support you in your just rights and claims, and he had given me directions to make use of all necessary means to remove and prosecute every white person who shall settle upon your lands or unjustly molest you. These my royal master's commands I shall most faithfully adhere to and when the boundary line is ascertained pursue every measure that may strengthen and brighten the chain which holds fast that peace and harmony which at present happily subjects between us.[23]

As was customary at such gatherings, the Indians retired to consider and discuss the governor's talk and then to prepare a reply to be delivered by a selected chief on the following day. The reply was delivered by the chief known as Jud's Friend or Ustenaka, who had been one of a small group of Cherokee who visited England in 1761.[24] He began by pointing out the similarity between the governor's address and those which the Indians had heard at Augusta in 1763. After reminding his audience of his first-hand knowledge of England, he stated:

The man above is he who made the land and His Majesty over the water desires that the white people and [ourselves] should mutually possess it. As I said before the man above is head of all, he made the land

22. Saunders, *Colonial Records of North Carolina*, VII, 462-64.
23. *Ibid.*
24. Lt. Henry Timberlake, *Memoirs* (London, 1765), includes an account of the journey to London made by several Cherokees in 1761.

and none other, and he told me the land I stand on is mine and all that is on it. True it is the deer, the buffaloe and the Turkeys are almost gone . . . the white people eat hogs, cattle and other things which they have here, but our food is farther off, the land here is very good land, it affords good water, good timber and other good things but I will not love [covet] it . . . as we are going to make a division, I want to do what is fair and right.

. . . There are rogues among your people and among my people, but I will give my people a good and strong talk to be so no more and I hope your excellency will also give your people a talk to be honest. . . . The price the white people give for land when they buy it is very small, they give a shirt, a match coat and the like which soon wears out but the land lasts always. I am now done talking, the land is given when the line is run and I quit all pretensions to it. (Lays down a string of beads on the course the line was to run)[25]

THE NORTH CAROLINA-CHEROKEE BOUNDARY DEMARCATED

Demarcation of the boundary line along the course marked by Ustenaka's symbolic string of beads began on an auspicious date —June 4, 1767, George III's birthday. The party which undertook the task was composed of John Rutherford, Robert Palmer, and John Frohock, commissioners for North Carolina; Alexander Cameron, deputy Indian superintendent and a party of Cherokees led by Ustenaka. They began their demarcation at the Reedy River, where the South Carolina boundary had been terminated the year before. From this point they marked a line of boundary trees which followed:

a north course about fifty-three miles into the mountains to a spanish oak marked with the initial letters of the commissioners names and several other trees with the names and marks of Judd's Friend, Sallowee Ecoy and others standing on the top of a mountain called by us Tryon Mountain on the head waters of White Oak and Packet [Pacolet] Creeks, White Oak running into Green River and Packet running into Broad River and as it was found impracticable that a line should be run and marked through the mountains to Colo. Chiswell's Mines it is further agreed . . . that the line between the frontiers of the Province of North Carolina and the Cherokee hunting grounds be continued as . . . a direct line to Chiswell's Mines in Virginia. . . .[26]

This boundary can be followed on Figure 12, which shows the demarcated section from the Reedy River to Tryon Mountain on

25. Saunders, *Colonial Records of North Carolina*, VII, 464-66.
26. *Ibid.*, pp. 469-71.

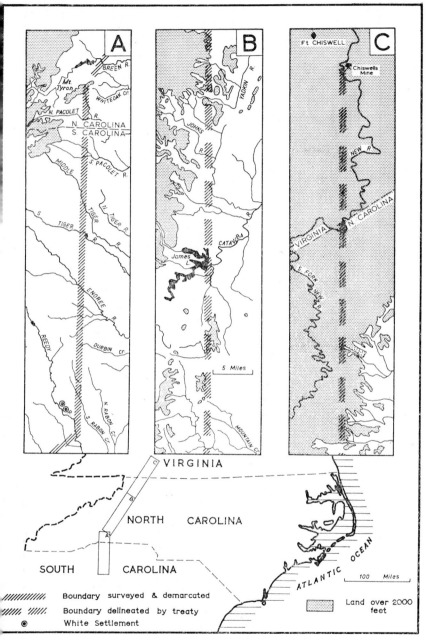

Fig. 12.   The North Carolina-Cherokee section of the Southern
Indian Boundary Line.

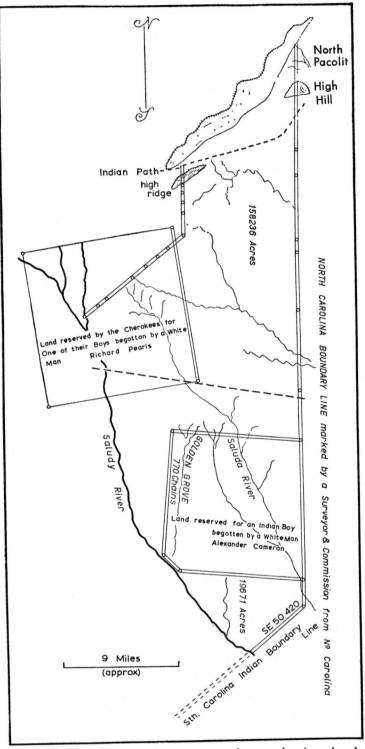

Fig. 13. Tracing from a map of 1770 showing the demarcated portion of the North Carolina-Cherokee boundary. (P.R.O., M.P.G. 338.)

panel A. The remainder of the undemarcated boundary, from Tryon Mountain to Chiswell's Mines in Virginia, is shown in panels B and C as a broken line.

No map of the boundary line prepared by the North Carolina commissioners has been found, but its location can be fixed on the present-day map by employing other eighteenth-century sources. Figure 13 is based on a map drawn by Patrick Calhoun, a deputy surveyor, in 1770 to show certain tracts of land which an Indian trader had received from the Cherokee in payment of the tribe's debts.[27] Clearly shown is the, "North Carolina Boundary Line marked by a Surveyor & Commission from No. Carolina." The Reedy River is incorrectly identified as the Saluda River, but in other respects this map corresponds closely to panel A of Figure 12 which depicts this boundary on a modern base map of the area.

On the present-day political map of South Carolina, sections of this north-south boundary line are still incorporated in the county boundaries which divide Greenville and Laurens, as well as Greenville and Spartanburg counties.[28] The county boundary which separates the last two terminates at a boundary stone placed earlier to mark the end of the 1772 boundary between the colonies of North and South Carolina. This stone is still visible and marks the position of a "Red Oak Corner Tree" which stood at the intersection of the Indian and colonial boundaries in 1772.

The party of Carolinians and Indians who demarcated the north-south boundary from the Reedy River to the mountains in 1767 did not, of course, end their efforts at this boundary tree. They continued blazing trees along the North Carolina-Cherokee boundary until they gained the summit of Tryon Mountain some six miles farther north.[29] From this hard-won vantage point of more than 3,000 feet above sea level they were treated to a splendid view of the incredibly rugged mountain landscape which stretches away in a seemingly endless panorama to the north and northeast. It is not difficult to accept the opinion of the demarcation party who found the mountainous landscape between Tryon Mountain

27. M.P.G. 338, P.R.O.

28. John B. O. Landrum, *History of Spartanburg County* (Atlanta, 1900), p. 3, quoted a 1785 act of the legislature which stated: "One other county bounded by Laurens County on the South, the Indian line on the west, the North Carolina Line and Broad River to Tales Ferry, thence along the road by John Ford's plantation and the Enoree now including the same, and shall be called by the name of Spartanburg."

29. Tryon Mountain is an outlier of the Blue Ridge mountain system located in Polk County, North Carolina.

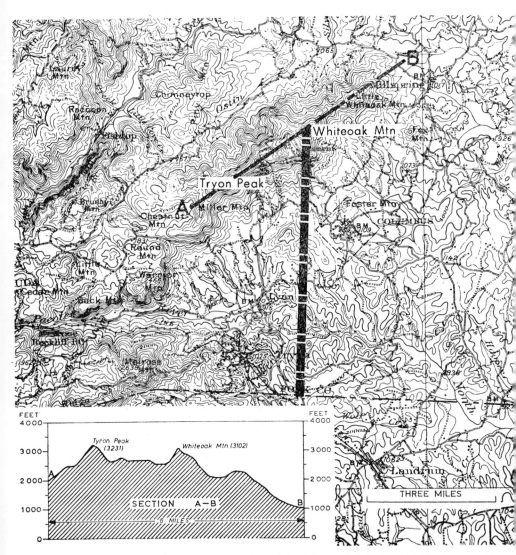

Fig. 14.   Map and profile of Mount Tryon, Polk County, North Carolina. The demarcated portion of the North Carolina-Cherokee boundary of 1767, within the present state of North Carolina, is shown as a heavy broken line. (Drawn on U.S.G.S. Saluda Quadrangle, 1:125,000.)

and Chiswell's Mines in distant Virginia "impervious" and concluded that it was "impracticable to continue to mark the said line."[30] Even with the all-weather highways and conveniences of the present day, a boundary demarcation through this area would be very difficult and expensive—in 1767 it was deemed impossible.

Only one serious problem is encountered in attempting to depict the demarcated section of the North Carolina-Cherokee boundary on a present-day map of the area. This is the spot which was identified in 1767 as, "the top of a mountain called by us Tryon Mountain." As can be seen on Figure 14, Tryon Mountain has a marked northeast-southwest orientation and is approximately six miles long by two miles broad. It rises dramatically above the rolling piedmont of the surrounding countryside to the south and east in two summits, which are separated by a lower saddle. Both of these summits are named on the present-day map—the eastern, Whiteoak Mountain and the western, Tryon Peak. Tryon is the highest at 3,231 feet above sea level; Whiteoak Mountain is slightly lower at 3,102 feet above sea level. If the phrase, "the top of a mountain" is interpreted literally it would seem that the present-day Tryon Peak was meant. This seems very doubtful, however, since both the extended Greenville-Spartanburg County boundary line, shown on Figure 14, and the "North Carolina Boundary Line marked by a Surveyor and Commission from No. Carolina" surveyed in 1770 and shown on Figure 13, would mark the more easterly or Whiteoak summit as the place where the marked Spanish oak stood in 1767. The ravages of weather, disease, and the woodman's blade have, of course, removed this as well as the other trees which originally bore the initials and marks of the white and Indian boundary surveyors of over two centuries ago. Unless evidence to the contrary can be adduced, it should be concluded that the Whiteoak Mountain of the present-day map was the terminal point of the demarcated section of the North Carolina-Cherokee boundary line. From this point northeastward to Chiswell's Mines on the east bank of the present-day New River in Virginia the boundary was agreed upon as an undemarcated straight line, as shown on Figure 12.

THE NORTH CAROLINA-CHEROKEE BOUNDARY PROCLAIMED

On July 16, 1767, the governor of North Carolina announced the establishment of the new boundary, which separated his colony

30. Saunders, *Colonial Records of North Carolina*, VII, 852.

from the hunting grounds of the Cherokee tribe in the west. This announcement took the form of two strongly worded proclamations, one signed by the king, and the other by himself. The royal proclamation took the form of an instruction to the colonial government to secure the peace with the neighboring Indian tribes by keeping the treaties and agreements made with them and protecting their lands from encroachments. The governor was instructed that his own proclamation should be one, "strictly enjoining and requiring all persons whatever who may either willfully or inadvertently have seated themselves on any lands so reserved to or claimed by the said Indians, without any lawful authority for so doing, forthwith to remove there from."[31]

Following these royal instructions the North Carolina governor issued the following proclamation:

Whereas a partition Line has been run between the Western Frontiers of this Province and the Cherokee Hunting Grounds beginning at Reedy River where the South Carolina and Cherokee dividing Line terminates, running a north course, to Tryon Mountain of the Blue Ridge of Mountains, supposed to be sixty miles from the said River, and from the top of Tryon Mountain Aforesaid, beginning at the marked trees thereon, a direct Line to Chiswell's Mines, which said Line is established and confirmed as a dividing Line between the Cherokee Indians and this Province (until his Majestys Pleasure be further known thereon) by an instrument of writing executed between the Commissioners appointed for this Province, and the Cherokee Chiefs, on the thirteenth day of June last past.

I have therefore thought proper by and with the advice and consent of his Majestys council, to issue this Proclamation, strictly requiring all Persons settled within the Indian Lands to remove from thence by the first day of January next: that no persons on any pretence whatsoever may disturb the said Indians in the quiet and peaceable possession of the lands to the westward of the aforesaid Line, or presume to Hunt thereon, or any other way or means to give them cause for uneasiness. And all persons who regardless of their own interest and disobedient to His Majestys Commands shall neglect to remove from off the Indian Lands as required, or shall at any time hereafter settle thereon, will not only expose their Families and Effects to the depredations of the Indians, but also deprive themselves of the protection of this Government. And as no land will be granted within one mile of the aforesaid Line, the Surveyor General or his Deputys are forbid making Surveys of the said dividing Line. Any of the Inhabitants of this Province who desire to Trade with the said Indians are

31. *Ibid.*, pp. 504-5.

required to take out a Licence from the Governor or Commander in Chief for the time being, and subject themselves to such general regulations as may be required by the Superintendent of Indian Affairs.

And as the peace and security of the Western Frontiers of this Province greatly depend upon cultivating the Harmony and Friendship that at present subsists between the several Nations of the Indians and Inhabitants thereof I recommend that all Indians who may have business within the settlements may be received in the most friendly and amicable manner and assisted with any necessaries agreeable to humanity and hospitality; as all injuries and violence offered them will be prosecuted with the utmost vigour of the Law; the Indian having promised a kind and friendly treatment to all white persons that may have occasion to go into their Nation.

Given under my hand and the Great Seal of the Province at Brunswick, the 16th day of July 1767, and in the Seventh year of His Majesty's Reign.

WILLIAM TRYON.

By his Excellency Command
   Benjamin Heron.
     God save the King.[32]

It is obvious that Governor Tryon had clearly described the North Carolina-Cherokee Boundary Line in this important proclamation. He also made the unique provision of a mile-wide "no man's land" along its eastern side, where no land surveys would be allowed. It has not been determined to what extent this provision was carried out or effective in limiting settlement near the boundary line. It would seem probable that such a provision could only have had meaning where the boundary had been demarcated, i.e., from the Reedy River to Tryon Mountain. Merrens, in his recently published volume devoted to the geography of pre-revolutionary North Carolina, unfortunately does little more than mention the fact that a boundary was delineated and partially demarcated between the colony and the Cherokee hunting grounds.[33]

Thus, during the summer of 1767, the North Carolina-Cherokee segment was added to the Southern Indian Boundary Line. In a letter to London dated November 14, 1767, Governor Tryon wrote, "I shall use every means in my power to prevent any encroachments being made on the Indian Lands by the Inhabitants of this province should any be attempted."[34] There is every evidence that

32. *Ibid.,* pp. 502-3.
33. Harry Roy Merrens, *Colonial North Carolina in the Eighteenth Century: A Study in Historical Geography* (Chapel Hill, 1964), p. 31.
34. C. O. 5-311, p. 99.

he carried out this promise; but in spite of the vigorous efforts of the superintendent of Indian affairs and the colonial administration of North Carolina to publicize its location and enforce its effectiveness as a barrier to white expansion, it was soon breached by the advancing pioneer tide.

In late 1768 or early 1769 white pioneers began to cross the Indian boundary line and establish settlements in what is today the northeastern corner of Tennessee along tributaries of the Holston River.[35] Probably the earliest and most well known of these illegal settlements were those established along the Watauga River.

These and adjoining settlements are eloquently described by Hamer:

Not many more than a hundred miles to the northeast of the Overhill Cherokee Towns on the Little Tennessee were several hundred frontiersmen who had settled in the fertile valleys of the Holston, Watauga, and Nollichucky Rivers. The first to come to the Watauga had erected their cabins as early as 1769, and the Nollichucky region had been settled by 1772. They were the advance guard of those restless, land-hungry frontiersmen who could not be restrained by Proclamations of the British king and royal governors or later by Congress, taking from the Indians the lands that they desired.[36]

The available evidence would seem to indicate that the Wataugans and their fellows settled beyond the Indian boundary line had not originally realized that their establishments were within the area reserved for the Indians. Rather, it seems certain that they felt they were settled in the Virginia frontier zone. It was not until 1771 when John Donelson surveyed the North Carolina-Virginia boundary from the point where Fry and Jefferson had ended in 1749, due west to the Holston River, that the Watauga settlements were found to be within the charter limits of North Carolina but beyond the boundary line in Indian territory.[37] It is, however, possible that at least some of the Wataugans were aware of their trespass. A Moravian diarist mentioned "a party of men from Orange County [North Carolina] passed through our village.

35. Samuel A'Court Ashe, *History of North Carolina* (Greensboro, N. C., 1908), I, 333; and Philip M. Hamer, "The Wataugans and The Cherokee Indians In 1776," *East Tennessee Historical Society's Publications*, III (Jan., 1931), 111.
36. Hamer, "Wataugans and Cherokee Indians," *East Tenn. Hist. Soc. Pub.*, p. 111.
37. Saunders, *Colonial Records of North Carolina*, X, 885.

They were Regulators and said they were going to Holston River to look for land."[38]

Whatever the reason, geographical ignorance or disregard for royal edict, it was in the frontier zone behind North Carolina that the most serious encroachments on the Indian territory beyond the Southern Indian Boundary Line took place in the years imme- diately preceding the American Revolution. The Watauga viola- tions were followed by the adventuresome Judge Richard Hen- derson's grandiose establishment of "Transylvania" to the west of the Indian boundary line.

Unfortunately, space does not allow an extended examination of these transboundary settlements in this study. It can be ob- served in conclusion, however, that here in the frontier beyond the North Carolina-Cherokee segment of the Southern Indian Bound- ary Line more than anywhere else along its great length that the presence of such a boundary line seemed to play a crucial role in determining the allegiance of a large group of frontiersmen in the Revolution. Hamer states that the frontiersmen, in their desire to retain their land within the Indian reserve, actively supported the revolutionary cause. They went so far as to make it appear that an impending Cherokee attack resulted from British incitement rather than because they were encroaching on the tribe's land.[39]

MacLeod stated that "the Indian policy of the Crown did more than anything to alienate the borderers from loyalty to the Crown and led the frontiersmen to throw their weight on the side of sedition in the forthcoming struggle against constituted govern- ment and rebellion."[40] This statement might be made even more meaningful in the case of the North Carolina frontier by substi- tuting "the North Carolina-Cherokee boundary line" for "the Indian policy."

38. Quoted by Williams, *Dawn of Tennessee Valley*, p. 337.

39. Hamer, "The Wataugans and the Cherokee Indians In 1776," p. 122-23. There is ample corroboration to this view found in a letter from the North Caro- lina Council of Safety to Samuel Johnston dated July 22, 1776, published in Walter Clark (ed.), *The State Records of North Carolina* (Goldsboro, N. C., 1895-1905), XI, 320. In this letter the following statement appeared: "the council had determined to adjourn to Salisbury to prevent if possible an Indian war think- ing perhaps that many of our people who had settled on the Cherokee side of the line might have been desirous of precipitating the Southern Colonies into war in order that they might have it in their power to cut off the Indians and possess themselves of their land."

40. William C. MacLeod, *The American Indian Frontier* (London, 1928), p. 423.

VI · *The South Carolina-Cherokee Boundary*

There were probably earlier land cessions made to South Carolina by the Cherokee Indians, but the one concluded in 1747 marked the beginning of a series of negotiations which ended in the demarcation of the South Carolina-Cherokee section of the Southern Indian Boundary Line almost twenty years later.[1] The cession of 1747 involved the area located to the east of Long Canes Creek, a north-south stream between the present-day cities of Greenwood and Abbeville, in western South Carolina. The cession resulted from a purchase agreed upon between the colony and tribe and was described at the time as:

all that tract or parcel of land lying and being south and easterly of a certain branch or stream of water commonly called Long Canes, within about 60 miles more or less our towns on the path [from] 96 that is from the head of said branch and down it until it falls into the Savannah River, and then again from the head of said branch and over to the head of the next nearest branch that falls into Santee (otherwise Saluda) River and from whence a direct north course to the path that leads from our town Kewohee [Keowee] to the present Catawba Towns. . . .[2]

1. Grace Steele Woodward, *The Cherokees* (Norman, Okla., 1963), p. 59. Woodward here mentions a cession made in 1721 and states that it was "the Cherokees' first land cession to white men in the history of the tribe." As an authority for this assertion Woodward cites C. C. Royce, who showed such a cession on his "Map of the Former Territorial Limits of the Cherokee 'Nation' of Indians, Exhibiting the Boundaries of the Various Cessions . . . ," in *The Cherokee Nation of Indians*, Plate VIII. Royce's map contains several errors and should not be accepted as authoritative. A better documented account of an early Cherokee cession is found in Mabel L. Webber, "An Indian Land Grant In 1734," *The South Carolina Historical and Genealogical Magazine*, XIX (Oct., 1918), 157-61. This cession included a large area between the Tugaloo and Seneca rivers in the present Anderson and Oconee counties, South Carolina. It is not shown on Royce's map.

2. C. O. 5-373, p. 200.

No contemporary map showing this Long Canes boundary line has been found. This is not surprising since there is no indication that it was ever surveyed or demarcated. An attempt is made here, however, to locate and illustrate it on Figure 15, where it can be traced northward from the Savannah River to the Catawba Path.

Perhaps even more important than the precise location of this early boundary separating the Indian hunting grounds from the area open to white occupation and settlement in South Carolina, were the factors leading to its establishment. Chief among these seemed to be the increased demand for productive land which was being felt in South Carolina during the middle and late 1740's.[3] Evidence of this growing demand for land by potential home-steaders along the outermost fringe of the South Carolina frontier is found in the petition of two pioneers "from the northern parts of America."[4] These petitioners, John Turk and Michael Taylor, had located several hundred acres of vacant land which they wished to occupy and farm. Pioneers settled farther to the east, in the area around Ninety-Six, informed them that the desired land was claimed by the Cherokee, who customarily hunted on it. These informants felt, however, that the Indians could be persuaded to give up their claim for a modest price.

Direct purchase of land from the Indians had been declared illegal by a South Carolina statute passed in 1739.[5] Rather than flaunt the law of their newly adopted colony, Turk and Taylor petitioned the governor and his council to make the necessary arrangements to purchase the land from the Indians. The lands petitioned for were described as being in the vicinity of the Indian trading path seven miles west of Ninety-Six, "near N. side of Coronaka Creek." The present-day map of this area shows the name Coronaca for a small community about seven miles west-northwest of Ninety-Six which probably corresponds to the area petitioned for in 1746.[6] The James Cook "Map of the Province

3. Governor James Glen, *A Description of South Carolina* . . . (London, 1761), p. 81, estimated that the colony had about 14,000 white inhabitants and 32,000 slaves in 1724. In his report of 1749 he estimated the whites to have increased by 80 per cent to a total of 25,000 and the slaves only 20 per cent to a total of 39,000. (Report in British Museum Kings MSS. 205.)

4. C. O. 5-455, p. 3.

5. J. H. Easterly (ed.), *The Journal of the Commons House of Assembly September 12, 1739-March 26, 1741: The Colonial Records of South Carolina* (Columbia, 1952), p. 141. G. Thomas Cooper and David J. McCord (eds.), *Statutes at Large of South Carolina* (Columbia, S. C., 1836-41), III, 525-26.

6. U.S. Geological Survey, Eastern United States 1:250,000, NI 17-4, Greenville Sheet.

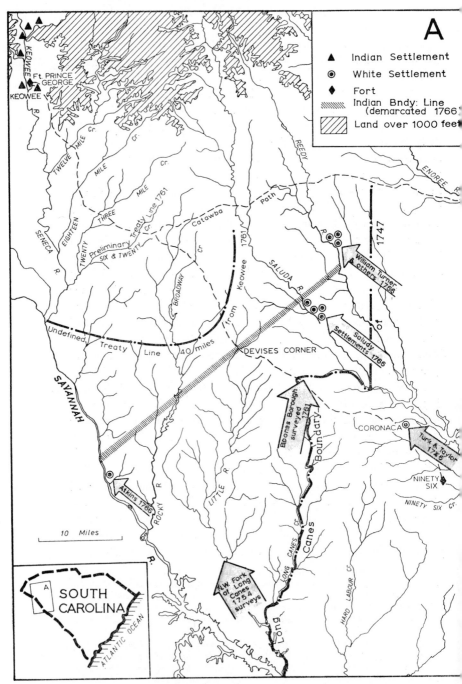

Fig. 15.   The South Carolina-Cherokee section of the Southern
Indian Boundary Line.

of South Carolina" of 1773 and the Stuart-Purcell "Map of the Southern Indian District" of 1775 both show a creek named "Coronacre" and "Corn Acre" as a tributary to the Saluda River in this area.[7]

In describing their "area pitched upon" Turk and Taylor provided an informative glimpse of the frontier zone where contact with the Indian hunters of the interior was common. They wrote of an "Indian hunting camp, where the Indians have a few houses that they resort to in hunting time, about 200 miles from Charles Town."[8] Thus it can be seen that in 1746 white pioneers were actively petitioning to be allowed to settle on the Cherokee hunting grounds closest to South Carolina. By employing eighteenth-century and present-day maps, it is possible to fix the place of this action in the area between the city of Greenwood, South Carolina, and nearby Lake Greenwood. The proximity of other white settlers near Ninety-Six with their grazing stock had probably caused a diminishment of game in the area and lessened its attractiveness to the Indians. This would account for their willingness to abandon their claim to it for "some small acknowledgment."

The government of South Carolina acceded to the desires of the petitioning pioneers and undertook to extend the colony's limits at the Cherokee's expense. On February 12, 1747, the tribe ceded all of their lands located to the east of the already described Long Canes boundary line. Governor Glen, in an official report made sometime later, commented: "I lately made a considerable purchase from this Nation [Cherokee] for His Majesty's use of some of their hunting grounds at the expense of the Province, and had the Deeds formally executed in their own country, by their head men in the name of the whole people and with their universal approbation and good will."[9] There can be little doubt that South Carolina's purchase of the area hastened its settlement. Meriwether stated, "the effect of this purchase was to hasten settlement on the Cherokee path, but the early settlers were the hunters and squatters of Ninety-Six rather than farmers or planters like the clients of the Turks."[10] The Taylors and Turks did not take up

7. James Cook, "A Map of the Province of South Carolina, 1773," Plate 67 in Cumming, *The Southeast In Early Maps,* and C. O. Maps 700, North America General/12.

8. C. O. 5-455, p. 5.

9. British Museum, King's MSS. 205, fol. 573.

10. Robert L. Meriwether, *The Expansion of South Carolina, 1729-1765,* (Kingsport, Tenn., 1940), p. 125. Wallace, *The History of South Carolina* (New York,

the land they originally desired. After becoming alarmed by Indian disputes they sought less exposed quarters for their establishments.

Before concluding this discussion of the Long Cane cession, attention should be called to the frequency of references to Indian trading paths which occurred in the literature illustrating it. These crude horse trails through the wilderness were, in Meriwether's words, "a channel along which came a trickle of the ebb and flow of the commerce and civilization of the distant little city, and the early settler sought a place upon it where he could fancy himself a part of it or at least in touch with the life."[11] In view of the attractiveness of the trading paths, they should be considered in the preparation of population maps of the frontier zone. Friis pointed out that the riverine pattern of settlement in the colonial South was descriptive of the coastal plain.[12] It is suggested that the pattern of settlement in the Piedmont was frequently tied to the pattern of trading paths found there during the early decades of the eighteenth century.

Cherokee involvements with their French and Indian enemies, plus an intermittent war with the Creeks, distracted the tribe during the late 1740's and early 1750's. These distractions on other fronts were not ignored by the South Carolinians who were occupying the area of the Long Canes Purchase during this period. It appeared that the productive bottom lands located along the creeks which laced the area were most in demand by the pioneer settlers. It was not long before the desire for such productive land resulted in the establishment of settlements to the west of the Long Canes boundary along the Little River. In what was probably a thinly veiled attempt to obscure this violation, the Little River was referred to as the "Northwest Fork of Long Cane."[13] Surveys of land were made along the lower Little River between 1754 and 1756 and it would seem likely that actual settlement of the area by the whites either preceded or followed shortly after these surveys on the Indian land.

The Cherokee became alarmed by the advancing tide of white

1934), II, 29, was less sanguine in his view of the boundary and stated only that "The Long Canes Line of 1747 was in effect a mere truce at the point then of greatest danger."

11. Meriwether, *The Expansion of South Carolina*, p. 162.
12. Friis, *A Series of Population Maps of the Colonies and the United States, 1625-1790*, p. 20.
13. Meriwether, *The Expansion of South Carolina*, p. 134.

settlers which flowed up the courses of the creeks and rivers and along the trading paths toward their Lower Towns. On April 29, 1752, one of the leading Cherokee chiefs, Caneecatee, or as he was known because of lameness, Old Hop, sent the following talk to the governor of South Carolina in Charleston:

Says he looks every Day to the Rising Sun where his Brother lives close by the Great Water Side, and that when he was a little Boy the white People began to settle thick in the country and that all the Ground [then?] from that to this was theirs till the King their Father told them to live together as Brothers upon one land, but now he says he finds they are debarred from it, his people being not suffered to go farther than the dividing waters commonly called the Long Canes. Says that the Lower Town People received some presents or consideration for it, but that neither he nor his people in the Mother Town of all got any thing for it.[14]

In August, 1758, the Lower Cherokee, whom Old Hop had identified as having been compensated for the Long Cane cession, requested the governor of Georgia to exert his influence to have the illegal settlements west of Long Cane Creek removed. The Indians of the Lower Towns stated that these South Carolinians should be removed because, "they have settled so near that the deer have become so scarce we can hardly feed or clothe our wives and children."[15] In spite of compensation received earlier, the Lower Cherokee were feeling the pinch of white encroachment on their hunting grounds.

It can be seen that the Indian resistance to the advancing white frontier was feeble and could have hardly been considered an effective protest against the violation of the Long Cane boundary. As stated above, Indian warfare and French machinations among the Cherokee were effective distractions which often drew their attention from the Long Cane encroachments. The aggressive governor of South Carolina took advantage of this troubled time to extend his colony's influence with the Cherokee. Included in his program was a tour of the colony with a strong show of military force in the frontier to awe the Indians.

Meeting at Saluda Old Town, the governor and a large party of Cherokee renewed the "chain of friendship" which existed between the tribe and colony. During the proceedings at Saluda,

14. McDowell, *Documents Relating to Indian Affairs, May 21, 1750-August 7, 1754,* p. 258.
15. Wallace, *History of South Carolina,* II, 29.

the governor suggested the possibility of the construction of an English fort among the Cherokee's Overhill towns, ostensibly to protect them from their French and Indian neighbors. The immediate reaction to such a fort was unfavorable, but continued pressure by Indian traders and other South Carolina agents among the Indians caused the Cherokee to request such a fort in 1747.[16] In reporting this Indian request for a fort on April 28, 1747, the governor observed: "They are not so ignorant not to know that this will be a restraint on their natural liberty, but that they may have a pretext of keeping the French from amongst them. . . ."[17] This is one of several instances which clearly indicated the Cherokee preference for the English and their cheaper trade goods over the French in America. The governor also reported that the Indians had proposed (1) to give the land on which the fort was to stand freely, (2) to assist in the fort's construction, and (3) to provision the garrison stationed there with food for two years. It would appear in the light of these proposals that the Indians were making certain there could be no doubt as to the co-operative nature of the undertaking to build an Overhill fort. Such proposals, if accepted, would clearly define a partnership of equals between the Cherokee and South Carolina and not, as the governor erroneously concluded, indicate an Indian surrender of "their natural liberty." As the tragic surrender of Fort Loudon proved thirteen years later, such an advanced outpost could not possibly have been maintained without the sufferance of the Cherokee. From the Indian point of view, detached military outposts within their coreland were probably less a threat to "their natural liberty" than the advancing frontier settlements that were steadily encroaching their hunting grounds on the eastern extremities.

A series of Anglo-Cherokee crises led to a serious deterioration in the relationship existing between South Carolina and her Indian neighbors to the west. The year 1748 saw preparations for war underway in the colony and the requested fort among the Overhill Towns was not undertaken. All trade to the Cherokee towns was stopped by the government of South Carolina in 1751 in an effort to bring the Indians to terms. Throughout this period of tension, the South Carolinians continued to press the Cherokee for permission to erect a fort. South Carolina's ambition was realized in 1753 when a delegation of friendly Cherokee visited Charleston

16. Alden, *John Stuart,* p. 32.
17. C. O. 5-371, p. 133.

and chided the governor for breaking his earlier promise to build a fort which would help to protect their towns.[18]

The governor, taking advantage of this opportunity, mustered a large force and proceeded to the frontier post of Ninety-Six in order to complete the negotiations. The fort which was agreed upon, was to be located among the Cherokee Lower Towns, i.e., those nearest to the South Carolina frontier, rather than among the distant Overhill Towns. This doubtlessly pleased the South Carolinians, who saw the Cherokee as a very real potential danger to their exposed settlements in the frontier. The Lower Cherokee were also pleased with the prospect of a supply of trade goods on their very door step. The proposed fort hardly satisfied the Indians' original request for protection from their French and Indian enemies. It was, however, admirably located to protect the South Carolina frontier from all enemies, were they French, northern Indians, or Cherokee.

At Ninety-Six the governor, with some difficulty, recruited a labor force to undertake the construction of the fort. Perhaps a popular indication of the potential danger of the expedition was the refusal of the recruited pioneer laborers to proceed into the Indian territory unless led by no less a figure than the governor himself. The governor complied and in late October, 1753, led his army and labor batallion into the Lower Cherokee country on the eastern slopes of the Blue Ridge mountains. Construction of the fort, named Prince George, was begun across the Keowee River from the principal Cherokee town in the area, also named Keowee. This area can be seen in relation to the South Carolina frontier of the period on Figure 15.

Governor Glen described the area which he purchased for the fort site in the passage which follows:

I desired to purchase a spot of ground for it [the fort], not barely what might be sufficient to contain it, but a tract where the warriors who were to garrison it might plant corn and potatoes and what they should have occasion for not to be burthensome to them [the Indians] where they might have range for horses, good pasturage for cattle and plenty of timber for fire wood and other uses of the fort and that there must be a road to it from the land that I last purchased from them [Long Canes Creek Cession].[19]

18. McDowell, *Documents Relating to Indian Affairs*, pp. 519-21.
19. C. O. 5-375, p. 7.
   McDowell, *Documents Relating to Indian Affairs*, pp. 519-21, includes the "Deed For Fort Prince George Tract."

Although the Cherokee offered to give the land freely, the experienced governor insisted on a purchase *quid pro quo*. He did, however, promise to protect the Indian burial mounds in the area and ordered railings built around them.

Later statements made by Governor Glen and others in reference to the Fort Prince George purchase have led many to conclude that a vast tract, composing "half the up-country of South Carolina," was acquired from the Indians. That such was not the case can be easily appreciated from the governor's description quoted above. South Carolina acquired a generous plot on which to locate the fort, farm and grazing land around it to provide for the wants of the garrison and the right to a road to provide a communication with Ninety-Six and the other frontier settlements.[20]

No time was lost in the construction of Fort Prince George on the east side of the Keowee River within a "gun shot" of the Cherokee town on the opposite side.[21] A contemporary reporter described it as being: "a square of about a quarter of an acre, flanked with four bastions, the rampart of earth about six feet high, surrounded with a ditch five feet deep and twelve broad, covered with Pallisados in front of each curtain, and in which a sergeant and fourteen men were left as a garrison."[22] Although this reporter was not greatly impressed by the fort, which had been completed in only twenty-two days, it should be concluded that its presence did give to South Carolina a military position on the very flank of the Cherokee coreland. The cession and construction of Fort Prince George marked a significant step in the advance of white settlement across the upper Piedmont in South Carolina.

South Carolina efforts to exert an influence over the Cherokee were stimulated by the French threat which was becoming a major consideration during the middle years of the eighteenth century. Following the construction of Fort Prince George, the effort to secure the Cherokee allegiance to the English king led to an important meeting at Saluda Old Town during June, 1755. Here the Cherokee, in exchange for gifts worth £1,100 gave their solemn pledge of allegiance to the English cause in the growing Anglo-French conflict. The governor of South Carolina renewed

20. For an excellent review of the misunderstandings concerning the area of the Fort Prince George purchase, see David D. Wallace, *The Life of Henry Laurens* (New York, 1915), pp. 503-10.

21. For a photograph of the site see Francis Harper, *Bartram's Travels*, photo 24.

22. Jacobs, *Indians of the Southern Colonial Frontier*, p. 54.

his earlier promise to construct a fort amid the Overhill Towns to insure their security against the French. While certain scholars have viewed this pledge of allegiance by the Cherokee as a total surrender of their lands to the English, this was clearly not the case. In Governor Glen's words the agreement at Saluda Old Town was, "an acknowledgement of [the English King] as their Superior and Lord."[23] It seems certain that the Cherokee had no intention of permitting the advance of white settlements beyond the Long Canes line in making this pledge of loyalty. As one authority stated, "thus in the later course of events the cession of 1755 amounted to nothing."[24]

The South Carolinians did not lose this opportunity to establish a fort amidst the Overhill Cherokee, however, and by the close of 1756 had troops quartered in it. The new fort was located a short distance above the juncture of the Little Tennessee and Tellico rivers, in the area which is now Monroe County, Tennessee. This transmontane outpost of English military power was named Fort Loudon, which is familiar in the area still, being attached to a dam and reservoir of the Tennessee Valley Authority.

Several factors, including the encroachment of Indian land, contributed to the rupture in Anglo-Cherokee relations that developed into the Cherokee War in 1760.[25] This war was a violent and bloody episode in frontier history, frequently punctuated by the massacre of red and white groups alike. Significantly, one of the first attacks directed at white civilians was aimed at the settlers in the Long Canes area. While crossing Long Canes Creek in flight to Ninety-Six, about one hundred and fifty men, women, and children were attacked by a large Cherokee war party. In the

23. McDowell, *Documents Relating to Indian Affairs*, p. 537. Probably the major source of misunderstanding on this as well as several other important points is the discussion included in the introduction to Royce, *Indian Land Cessions In the United States*, p. 633. This source, although frequently cited, omits entirely any mention of the South Carolina section of the Southern Indian Boundary Line which resulted from the cession of 1765 and was demarcated during the following year. Omissions such as this one and a conspicuous lack of documentation seriously detracts from the value of Royce's work on the subject of Indian land cessions.

24. Wallace, *The History of South Carolina*, II, 2. Alden, *John Stuart*, p. 46, stated: "The Cherokee on this occasion undoubtedly knew what they were doing and were properly authorized to do it. In reality, however, the treaty which they signed meant little, since the English did not immediately follow up the agreement by occupying the Cherokee country."

25. Wallace, *History of South Carolina*, II, 28.

melee that followed few of the pioneers had even an opportunity to put up a defense.[26]

In an effort to reduce the Cherokee, Lieutenant Colonel James Grant (later the royal governor of East Florida) led a force of 2,250 troops on a punitive expedition into their towns. Grant's troops caused large-scale destruction of Cherokee villages and crops in the Middle Towns division during the early summer of 1761. Tiring of the war and faced with an impending food shortage, the Indians sued for peace at Fort Prince George in August of that year.

Prominent in a list of peace conditions to be required from the Indians, which had been drawn up earlier by the embittered South Carolina government, was an article which stated: "The Cherokees must accept a line twenty six miles east of Keowee to be their boundary toward Carolina."[27]

It is apparent that the South Carolinians were determined to secure an additional land cession as a result of the military effort which had reduced the Cherokee to submission. The Cherokee were to be required to accept the new boundary line, which was to be only twenty-six miles from their Lower Towns. This stipulation, as well as others, calling for the execution of one leading chief from each of the tribe's four divisions, was unacceptable to the Cherokee peace delegation that met with Grant at Fort Prince George. Grant was probably anxious to conclude a preliminary peace settlement before he lost the whole of his South Carolina infantry, already disbanding for lack of pay, and so agreed to a compromise settlement with the Cherokee.[28] He sent the Cherokee delegation under the leadership of Attakullakulla to Charleston to consult with the governor and work out an acceptable peace treaty.

At the conference which resulted, the Commons House of Assembly reversed the conciliatory policies toward the Indians begun by Grant and continued by the governor. They demanded that the Cherokee agree to a boundary to be drawn at Twenty-Six Mile Creek where it was crossed by the trading path from Keowee to Ninety-Six.[29] This was in effect, a return to the

26. Meriwether, *The Expansion of South Carolina*, p. 222.

27. South Carolina Commons House Journals, Sept. 17, 1761, quoted by David H. Corkran, *The Cherokee Frontier: Conflict and Survival, 1740-62* (Norman, Okla., 1962), p. 259.

28. Alden, *John Stuart*, p. 130.

29. James Mooney, *Myths of the Cherokee*, p. 412, stated: "In Pickens and Anderson counties, in the northwest corner of the state, is a series of creeks joining Keowee River and named, respectively in order, from above downward,

demand which the Cherokee had already refused. Attakullakulla reluctantly bent to the will of the bellicose assembly and signed the preliminary treaty so severely limiting the Cherokee Lower Towns' hunting grounds.

Although this boundary line was never surveyed or demarcated, its probable location is indicated on Figure 15 as the "Preliminary Treaty Line 1761." The Cherokee protested this restrictive boundary to a well-respected Indian trader and stated that they had to insist on at least forty miles to separate their villages from the whites. The governor of South Carolina, eager to pacify the Indians and aware of the Crown's desire to avoid conflict with them over land, acceded to the proposed forty-mile boundary.

A definitive treaty of peace was signed during December, 1761, fixing the undelineated boundary between the Cherokee and South Carolina at an undefined point forty miles from Keowee.[30] No landmarks or specific directions regarding the boundary were provided to assist in accurately fixing its location. An attempt has been made to indicate this vague boundary on Figure 15 where it is marked "Undefined Treaty Line 40 Miles from Keowee 1761." It can be seen that the Cherokee had made a significant retreat from the Long Canes boundary of 1747. The South Carolina settlements established along Long Canes Creek and the Little River were unquestionably included in the area ceded late in 1761, but the further advance of the South Carolina frontier was in doubt. The ephemeral forty-mile boundary line could hardly serve as a viable boundary until it was demarcated and clearly recognized by both interested parties.

Although the boundary of 1761 was far from clearly defined, it is clear that the pioneers in the South Carolina frontier interpreted it as having freed the area beyond the Long Canes Creek Line for settlement. Among the South Carolinians it came to be

---

Mile, Six-Mile, Twelve-Mile, Eighteen Mile, Twenty-Three-Mile, and Twenty-Six-Mile. According to the local story they were thus christened by a young woman, in one of the early Indian wars, as she crossed each ford on a rapid horseback flight to the lower settlement to secure help for the beleaguered garrison of Fort Prince George. The names really date back almost to the first establishment of the colony, and were intended to indicate roughly the distances along the old trading path from Fort Ninety-Six on Henleys Creek of Saluda River to Keowee, at that time the frontier town of the Cherokee Nation, the two points being considered 96 miles apart as the trail ran. Fort Prince George was on the east bank of Keowee river, near the entrance of Crow Creek, and directly opposite the Indian Town."

30. Meriwether, *The Expansion of South Carolina*, p. 240.

understood that the boundary of 1761 was a line reaching from the mouth of the Keowee River to the trading path at a point which was computed to be forty miles miles from Keowee and then as a straight line north to the mountains.[31] The new governor of the colony, Thomas Boone, authorized surveys beyond the Long Canes Line, including the new township which bore his name. The general location of this 20,500 acre township at the head of Long Canes Creek and athwart the trading path is shown on Figure 15.[32]

The rapidity with which the debatable area between the Long Canes and forty-mile boundaries was occupied by white pioneers following the settlement of the Cherokee peace in 1761 was nothing short of astounding. On April 2, 1763, the *South Carolina Gazette* reported that over 1,000 families from colonies to the north had settled in the region of Long Canes during 1762 and that 400 additional families were expected.[33] The Commons House of Assembly took note of these frontier additions to the colony and referred to them as "flourishing new settlements near the Long Canes."[34] In a Schedule of Charges included in the commons *Journal* was "A muster Roll for Six months pay of the men commanded by Patrick Calhoun, for the protection of Long Cane Settlement £2,058."[35] This was a considerable sum, indicating to some degree the extent and significance of the "flourishing new settlements near the Long Canes."

Clearly, the South Carolinians were actively occupying the area beyond the Long Canes Line. What, however, was the Cherokee attitude toward this advancing frontier? The Indians took advantage of the important Indian congress held at Augusta in 1763 to air their views and complaints relative to this question. Attakullakulla, the Cherokee leader, stated, "white people are settled beyond the Long-Canes, they may stay there but must proceed no farther."[36] Another chief from the Cherokee Lower Towns, Sallouih, stated: "The lines run out between the English and them he is satisfied with, though they are small for his people; the white people settled at or near Long-Canes he desires not to remove, but

31. Alden, *John Stuart*, pp. 216-17.
32. Meriwether, *The Expansion of South Carolina*, p. 251 and map on p. 116.
33. *The South Carolina Gazette*, April 2, 1763.
34. A. S. Salley (ed.), *Journal of the Commons House of Assembly of South Carolina January 8, 1765-August 9, 1765: The Colonial Records of South Carolina* (Columbia, S. C., 1949), p. 10.
35. *Ibid.*, p. 170.
36. *Journal of the Congress* . . . , p. 31.

none more to settle nearer the Cherokees."[37] It is significant to note that although the Cherokee leaders drew attention to the Long Canes settlers, both grudgingly stated that they would be allowed to remain but no further advance would be tolerated. In their official reply to the Indians at Augusta, the southern governors stated: "In relation to the settlements above Long Canes in South Carolina, those settlements were allowed and agreed to in the treaty of peace signed at the close of the last war, by lieutenant-governor Bull and Attakullakulla between the white people and your nation."[38]

Although it was not included in the official journal of the congress, there is evidence that further debate on the topic of a boundary line between the Cherokee and South Carolina took place at Augusta in 1763.[39] Alden suggested that a serious misunderstanding arose on this vital issue which remained unresolved, possibly due to difficulties in communicating through interpreters.[40] Whatever the cause might have been, no decision was reached on the problem of establishing a boundary line between the tribe and the colony at that time. *speculation*

The congress at Augusta had provided an excellent forum in which to discuss the issues threatening the Anglo-Indian peace in the Southeast. Several matters remained unresolved, however, and potentially very dangerous. Not the least of these was the Cherokee-South Carolina boundary problem. The pioneers forming the vanguard of the advancing frontier in that colony had not halted as the Indians had demanded. On August 20, 1764, the governor of the colony reported a complaint from Sallouih, who had spoken at Augusta, about some "straggling Englishmen" who had begun to settle within twelve or fifteen miles of the Cherokee Lower Towns.[41] The governor issued orders to have the "trespassers" driven off and their huts "burned."[42]

The officer in command of Fort Prince George received frequent complaints from the Indians protesting the activities of the undisciplined "crackers" (as the frontiersmen were called), who were creating a serious problem and threat to the peace by poaching

37. *Ibid.*, p. 32. "Sallouih" is another spelling of "Saluy." Saluy played a leading role in the attempted surprise massacre of Fort Loudon in January of 1760.
38. *Ibid.*, p. 37.
39. C. O. 5-66, p. 412.
40. Alden, *John Stuart*, p. 184.
41. C. O. 5-378, p. 1.
42. *Ibid.*

and hunting on the Cherokee lands. The commander obviously recognized the Cherokee as the rightful owners of the area and urged them to seize the poachers' traps and pelts and drive them off the Indian land. When the affair became inflammatory the fort commander arrested and detained three of the offending "crackers." Informed of this action, the governor denied having any authority to punish the culprits and they were set free after severe warnings from the not-so-cautious military commander.[43]

These encroachments were creating an explosive situation which could easily have once again embroiled South Carolina and the neighboring colonies in a repetition of the costly and bloody Cherokee War of a few years before. While addressing the Commons House of Assembly on January 8, 1765, the governor of South Carolina stated that he had received a request from the Cherokee to have a commissioner designated who would, with their chiefs, "mark out the boundaries between the English and them, to prevent disputes and jealousies of incroachments."[44] The governor stressed, "this is become the more necessary from the vicinity of our settlers attracted thither by the richness of those lands."[45]

The assembly responded to this information by allowing a sum "not to exceed £500" to be granted in order to "defray the expense of marking out the boundaries between the English and Cherokee." They went on to stipulate "that His Hono'r be requested to direct a natural boundary, (if possible) be fixed on."[46] Thus during the opening weeks of 1765, South Carolina, at the request of the Cherokee, took the preliminary steps toward establishing a viable boundary with the tribe somewhere west of Long Cane Creek. Significantly, the colonial leaders expressed the desire for such an important boundary to be a "natural" one.

THE DELINEATION OF THE SOUTH CAROLINA-CHEROKEE BOUNDARY

The governor informed the Cherokee of his colony's readiness to join them in the effort to establish a boundary. The reply the Indians sent to his message is a valuable source of information relating to the state of the frontier settlements west of the Long

43. Alden, *John Stuart*, pp. 215-16.
44. Salley, *Journal of The Commons House of Assembly, 1765*, p. 6.
45. *Ibid.*
46. *Ibid.*, p. 38.

Canes Line and the background of the whole boundary line negotiations. They wrote:

Brother—We received your talk where you desire that some of our warriours be present at the running out of the boundary line . . . but we are informed . . . that the white people would have it that the boundary line was Broadies Plantation; We remember very well that no Cherokee was to go lower than Broadies Plantation without a white man in company by the articles of peace, but no boundary was settled at that time . . . when . . . Captain Stuart read the Great Kings talk to us at Augusta in the hearing of four governors, it was then stipulated that Swearingham across to Templeton on the Road should be our bounds. We might then claim below that, but as the white people were settled, we did not choose they they should be removed; We know that the white people are very troublesome to you for land & that they tell you that their boundary is Broadies Plantation; and if it [the boundary] is not soon run out, the white people will say next that twelve Mile River is the boundary. We desire therefore since you was not at the Treaty at Augusta that you will stop your white people from settling on our ground until our beloved brother [Stuart] comes home.[47]

The Indians' request that nothing further be done until their "beloved brother" returned to the area was significant and indicated the high regard in which they held John Stuart, the superintendent of Indian affairs for the Southern District. Stuart expressed strong criticism of the manner in which the governor of South Carolina was proceeding in the boundary negotiations. In a letter to the secretary of the Board of Trade dated August 24, 1765, he stated:

I cannot inform you particularly of Mr. Bull's Negotiations with the Cherokee Indians relative to a Boundary Line, as they have all been carried on entirely independant of me, my having any concern in that Matter being thought quite unnecessary by the Lieutenant Governor.

I humbly offer it as my opinion, that it cannot be done properly but with the consent of all the Nation, any grant from a Part will be productive of perpetual Grumbling and Disputes; and I humbly submit to their Lordships, if such matters should not be transacted with the Participation of the Superintendent, or some Person acting for him, as he will be applied to by the Indians in case of any Dispute,

47. C. O. 5-66, p. 412.

and therefore it seems proper that he should be acquainted with the circumstances of the transactions.[48]

The superintendent followed this passage with an interesting and informative comment which succinctly summarized his attitude on the subject of an Indian boundary line in South Carolina. He stated:

> I beg leave to observe, that the far Extension of our Boundaries backwards, by approaching too near the Indian Nations, will expose us to perpetual Broils. The Inhabitants of those back Countries are in general the lowest and worst Part of the People, and as they and the Indians live in perpetual Jealousy and Dread of each other, so their rooted Hatred for each other is reciprocal.
>
> The Laws in the American Provinces are not strong enough to operate with necessary Vigor amongst People living so remote, and who require to have the Hand of Justice perpetually stretched over them, and I submit to their Lordships how far such People so situated answer the intent of Colonists. Their Distance from Commerce lays them under the Necessity of making cloths and other stuffs for themselves, and the Productions of the Back Countries, especially more Northerly, are similar to those of the Mother Country.[49]

This, it should be noted, was voiced by one intimately concerned with the problem and not merely the doctrinaire utterance of yet another mercantilist.

Stuart urged the Cherokee to co-operate with South Carolina in fixing a boundary line. Although other duties prevented his personal supervision in the matter, he delegated his deputy, Alexander Cameron, to act for the Indian Department. At Fort Prince George on October 19, 1765, the Cherokee ceded to the English: "that tract of Land (which previous to this time we deemed our own) lying between a Brook known to the White People by the Name of Dewises Corner, and to us by the Yellow Water, and another Brook distant from the former about ten miles, and known to both White and Red People by the Name of Long Canes."[50] The brook referred to as Dewises Corner was known by a number of variants and is identified as Corner Creek on present-day maps of the area.[51] It can be seen on Figure 15 that Dewises or Devises Corner Brook is one of the head streams forming the Little River.

48. *Ibid.*, p. 369.
49. *Ibid.*
50. *Ibid.*, p. 372.
51. Some of the variants were Devises, Dewitt's, and Duet's.

It will be recalled that it was on the Little River that settlements were being made a decade before under the guise of referring to the stream as the Northwest Fork of Long Canes. These and other settlements made in the area to the west of the Long Canes boundary of 1747 were at last legally included in South Carolina.

Although the deed of cession signed at Fort Prince George delineated only the single stream, Dewises Corner Brook, provisions were made for the demarcation of the boundary line to be completed during the following spring after the Indians' hunting season had ended.[52] One of the Cherokee described the cession to South Carolina in the following terms: "The Land we gave the other day we wish may be fruitful of grain; we gave with it to Our Brothers the game that is upon it, the grass for their cattle to feed upon, the Running Waters and Springs that are upon it for their drinking, the Wood for their burning & hereafter shall never make any claim to any thing belonging to it." Following this statement, the Indian spokesman went on to remind the whites of their responsibility in the matter: "I desire all our Brothers to remember all our dependence for the necessaries of life is upon Hunting—that we shall Hunt nowhere but on our own land, and that we expect to reserve it for ourselves unfrequented by white hunters." In conclusion, he admonished his own tribesmen to

Build good Houses and think of living amicably & peaceably, nor say hereafter you know not where the Line is to be run. I tell you all it is at the Yellow Water, and is to be done in the Spring, so don't shame your warriors any more with being told that you went below it, stole horses, burnt the Woods and committed other disorders; but when you buy a Horse or a gun take care that you get a Bill of Sale with it.[53]

This cession was accepted and ratified by the governor of South Carolina on December 10, 1765, and endorsed by the superintendent of Indian affairs during the next month.[54] Clearly, all that remained to be accomplished was the demarcation of the new boundary line by blazing the trees along its course during the spring of 1766.

52. C. O. 5-66, p. 416.
53. *Ibid.*, p. 418.
54. *Ibid.*, pp. 372-373.

THE DEMARCATION OF THE SOUTH CAROLINA-CHEROKEE BOUNDARY

The demarcation of the new boundary began on April 24, 1766, at Devises Corner with Edward Wilkinson, boundary commissioner, and John Pickins, surveyor, representing South Carolina. Alexander Cameron, representing the Indian superintendent, with six important Cherokee chiefs and thirty warriors completed the party. In Cameron's words:

We began the Line at Dewise's Corner and proceeded Southwest 50 Miles [degrees] to Savannah River; The Indians blazed the Trees as we went and made the Boundary very clear and strong as they term it. . . . The distance from Dewis's [*sic*] Corner to the River (as near as we could make it) is 27 miles; The Course of the Line from Dewis's Corner to Reedy River, where the Line terminates, is N.E. 50 miles [degrees], and the distance 18 miles.[55]

This description can be followed on the tracing of John Pickins' manuscript map of the original survey forming the right-hand panel of Figure 16.[56] Cameron was guilty of carelessly interchanging directions and distances in his statement. These interchanges have caused some confusion in the past, but are easily corrected in the presence of Pickins' map of the boundary line.[57] The correct location of the South Carolina-Cherokee section of the Southern Indian Boundary Line demarcated in 1766 is shown on Figure 15 as the "Indian Boundary" and on Figure 11 as "S.C. 1766."

The governor of South Carolina was pleased by the completion of the boundary demarcation which promised to stabilize conditions in the colony's frontier and put an end to Indian disputes arising from land encroachment. He expeditiously made the new boundary line known to the citizenry of his colony by the means of a clearly worded proclamation published on June 2, 1766. In this official announcement of the establishment of the new Indian boundary line he described its location and stated:

And I do hereby in His Majesty's name strictly enjoin and require all persons whatever, who have either willfully or inadvertently seated themselves upon any lands in this province northwestward of the

55. *Ibid.*, p. 398.
56. C. O. Maps 700 Carolina/26, P.R.O.
57. "Map of the Former Territorial Limits of the Cherokee 'Nation' of Indians," in Royce's *The Cherokee Nation of Indians*, Plate VIII, incorrectly showed the boundary of 1766 as terminated at the Saluda River some miles short of its correct termination on the Reedy River.

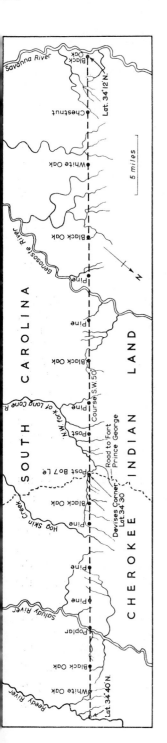

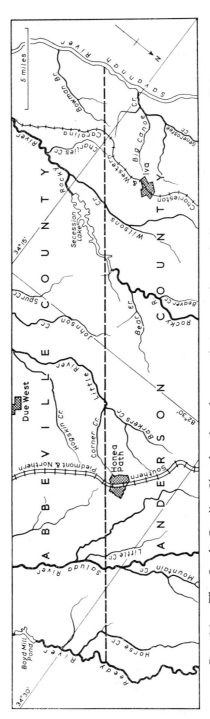

Fig. 16. The South Carolina-Cherokee boundary on the present-day and the contemporary map. (P.R.O., C. O. 700, Maps, Carolina/26.)

boundary line . . . reserved to the Indians, to remove themselves from such settlement: and all surveyors, hunters and other [of] His Majesty's subjects are hereby forbidden to pass beyond said boundary line except on their lawful occasions, as they shall answer the same at their peril.[58]

To what extent the boundary line could be policed to insure it was crossed only by those who were on "their lawful occasions" was, of course, problematical. The line was, however, visible and well publicized and could be expected to eliminate accidental encroachments of the Indian hunting grounds beyond it.

In his report of the successful demarcation of the new boundary line, the deputy Indian superintendent, Cameron, provided a commentary on the state of white settlement in the immediate vicinity of the line. He mentioned:

About Saludy, there are several Houses within four miles of the line, and one house within one mile of it. On the North Carolina side of Reedy River, there are three or four families settled; and even if the Indian Boundary be run a North Course, these settlements will fall five or six miles above it. One William Turner on Saludy below Ninety Six, has settled a Cowpen and Plantation on the above Indian Lands, altho' he very well knew, that Mr. Wilkinson by Governor Bull's orders, removed a settlement off the same tract of land last year: I have sent a warning to remove without loss of Time, otherwise, I should take upon me to drive them off, and distribute part of their cattle among the Indians, as a tax belonging to them etc.[59]

In another section of this valuable report he noted: "I could not learn that we took in any land, that had been surveyed by any White man before; but there is one Atkins, settled within four Miles of the Line, near to Savannah."[60] An attempt has been made to show the locations of these white settlements in relation to the boundary line on Figure 15. They probably represent the vanguard of the South Carolina settlement frontier during the spring of 1766.

These few pioneers were soon joined by many new settlers who took up land in the newly ceded territory. The superintendent of Indian affairs described a visit to the South Carolina-Cherokee Boundary Line he made two years after its demarcation. His description of this excursion provides a valuable commentary on

58. *The South Carolina Gazette,* June 2, 1766, bound with C. O. 5-378, p. 126.
59. C. O. 5-66, p. 398.
60. *Ibid.*

the appearance of the boundary line and on the condition of settle-ment in its vicinity. He wrote:

I set out upon that Service accompanyed by some Indians and rode along that part of it [the boundary] which divided this Province [South Carolina] from the Lands reserved by the Indians it is marked at least 50 feet wide the trees within which space are blazed on both sides.

The country near the Line is very full of Inhabitants mostly emi-grants from the Northern Colonies it is remarkable that in going hence to the Frontiers I rode at times 30 & 40 miles without seeing any house or hut yet near the Boundary that Country is full of In-habitants which in my memory was considered by the Indians as their best hunting grounds; such is their rage for settling far back.

The people Inhabiting the Frontiers of this Province carry on a trade with the Indians by bartering rum for Horses, the Chiefs com-plained of this as the source of many disorders their young men being thereby encouraged to steal horses from the neighbouring Provinces besides the danger of committing outrages when intoxicated which may involve their Nation in trouble. These back settlers pay little or no regard to Law or Government. . . . The Indians detest the back Inhabitants of these provinces which will account for the reluctancy with which they give up any part of their lands being anxious to keep such neighbors at a distance.[61]

This boundary was ratified in the treaty signed at Hard Labour on October 14, 1768, and remained South Carolina's west-ern boundary until 1772, when it was determined that the area to the north of Reedy River was also within the limits of that colony and not North Carolina, as had been assumed in 1766. After 1772 and into the revolutionary era the colony's western boundary was formed by the Indian boundary demarcated in 1766 and the north-south North Carolina Indian boundary which had been demar-cated in 1767. Figure 11 shows these lines on a present-day base map and clearly illustrates South Carolina's westernmost boundary on the eve of the American Revolution.

THE SOUTH CAROLINA-CHEROKEE BOUNDARY ON THE PRESENT-DAY MAP

Few if any of the countless travelers who daily move across the rolling Piedmont of the present-day state of South Carolina realize the earlier significance of what is now the boundary

61. C. O. 5-70, p. 105.

dividing Abbeville and Anderson Counties. This county boundary is illustrated in the left-hand panel of Figure 16. It can be seen that this is the same boundary line demarcated almost two centuries ago to separate colony from Indian tribe in an effort to maintain peace between the competing white and red residents in this corner of the British Empire.

Figure 16 places the Abbeville-Anderson County boundary in juxtaposition with the original eighteenth-century map of the South Carolina Indian boundary line to facilitate comparison. It is easily seen that the boundary cut across the "grain" of the landscape and presents none of those characteristics usually associated with so-called natural boundaries, i.e., boundaries which coincide with marked terrain features such as mountain ranges or large rivers. It might even be remarked that a less "natural" boundary could hardly have been demarcated in this area, in spite of the exhortations in favor of such a boundary voiced during the months prior to its demarcation. Clearly, this boundary was determined less by considerations of physical geography than by those of human geography in its most simple terms, i.e., where the contestants for the land were living at the time.

As in the case of the North Carolina segment, the South Carolina-Cherokee segment of the Southern Indian Boundary Line was crossed by land-seeking pioneers in the period following its demarcation. One of the most flagrant instances of private citizens' defying the authority of the Crown in attempting to acquire land from the Indians beyond the boundary line occurred in the South Carolina frontier.

Richard Pearis, in 1769, "secretly and fraudulently secured the consent of a number of Lower Cherokees to a cession twelve miles square in the alley of the upper Saluda for his half-breed Cherokee son."[62] The location of this cession is shown on Figure 13. Although Pearis and his cohort Jacob Hite knew full well that their claim to this Indian land was in direct disobedience to stated Crown policy and provincial law they proceeded to settle in the area and sell land to "emigrants from the northern colonies."[63] John Stuart recognized the great threat that Pearis' precedent represented and was vigorous in bringing him to task. Stuart undertook a legal action against Pearis in the court at Ninety Six in the autumn of 1773. He was obviously pleased when he re-

62. Alden, *John Stuart,* p. 299.
63. C. O. 5-74, p. 69.

ported the successful outcome of this prosecution to his superior, General Haldimand. In his report Stuart pointed out that Pearis was required to relinquish his claim to the Indian land, pay the costs of the court, and pay a fine for his infraction of the provincial statute forbidding the acquisition of Indian land by individuals, "which will I hope deter other people from such attempts."[64] Unfortunately this was not to be the case. In an amplifying report to Haldimand in 1774 Stuart stressed the serious lack of legal sanctions which could be employed to restrain settlement west of the Indian boundary line. On this subject he observed, "in provinces where there are not any such municipal laws [as those in South Carolina] I should cautiously undertake such an action, as I am afraid little regard would be paid by the courts and juries to His Majesties Proclamation especially in the present times of licentiousness."[65] It can be seen that disregard for the Indian boundary line was not limited to the land-hungry frontiersmen alone in 1774.

It should be added that a disturbingly large number of Cherokee showed an unusual willingness to part with tribal lands facing South Carolina as Pearis and Hite were pressing for their cession. The Indians claimed that they wished to employ the profits gained in the disposal of these lands in educating future leaders for the tribe. In any event, such private cessions for whatever purpose were contrary to royal edict and colonial statute alike. The Indians proved reluctant to sacrifice their freedom of action in return for the protection which the boundary line was intended to provide. This discordant note in Anglo-Indian affairs was to expand and have great significance in frontier Georgia to the south and will be discussed at greater length in the next chapter.

64. British Museum, Additional MSS. 21,672, fol. 156. For the South Carolina statute see Easterly, *Journal of the Commons House of Assembly 1739-1741*, p. 141.

65. British Museum, Additional MSS. 21,672, fol. 257. As a postscript to this mention of Richard Pearis it is necessary to add that he was ultimately successful in his attempt to secure land from the Cherokee. Through legal manipulation Pearis was able to have his title made over to his son. Eventually, as a loyalist, he was to receive a very handsome compensation for the loss of this property from the Loyalist Claim Commission in England.

VII · *The Georgia-Indian Boundary Lines*

Prior to the arrival of James Oglethorpe and his band of colonists on the Savannah River in 1733, the area known as Georgia had been the scene of a long series of Anglo-Indian confrontations. The territory had been included in the original and generous limits of the earlier Carolina charter and had for several decades been within South Carolina's sphere of influence. The remains of several forts and trading posts, some of which were reoccupied by the followers of Oglethorpe, gave mute testimony to South Carolina's earlier activities in the area. The Carolina tenure in Georgia had not gone unchallenged. The Spanish, for example, had located a series of early missions to form the vanguard in the march of empire northward from their base at St. Augustine. Nor, it should be added, were the French oblivious to the lure of Georgia during the early decades of the eighteenth century.

In 1715, the Yamassee Indians led most of the southern tribes in a general uprising against South Carolina which has been referred to as the Yamassee War. As a result of British victory in this conflict, a number of the southern tribes undertook rather far-reaching migrations in an attempt to escape Carolina revenge and influence. These migrations brought about significant changes in the population distribution map of the Southeast. The Creek Confederation, long a numerous and influential group of Indians, for example, withdrew from their village sites in what is today central Georgia to more remote areas to the west. Although physically far removed from the centers of South Carolina strength, the Creeks did not abandon their long-standing claim to suzerainty over the whole of southern Georgia. It is clear that the smaller tribes and bands of Indians residing in the area evidenced a recognition of Creek suzerainty when Oglethorpe and the original Georgia colonists began to establish their own settlements there.

It was doubtlessly fortunate for the new colony and its founders that the main Creek villages and leaders were several hundred exhausting miles to the west as they began to clear the forest on the bluff site which became Savannah, the new colony's metropolis. This geographic separation provided valuable living space within which the nascent colony could be established before it directly impinged on Creek interests and attracted their attention. It should be stated that the Trustees for Establishing the Colony of Georgia showed an early recognition of the significant part which the Indians were destined to play in the development of the colony.

The trustees made the Indians the subject of their first law passed for the administration of the new colony of Georgia. It was titled "An Act for Maintaining the Peace with the Indians in the Province of Georgia . . ." and was passed at a meeting held in the Vestry Room of St. Brides Church in Fleet Street on March 21 1733.[1] In its preamble, the act revealingly stated that, "the safety, welfare and preservation of the Colony of Georgia doth . . . depend on the maintaining of good correspondence and regulating the trade to be carried on between your Majesty's subjects and the several nations of Indians in amity with the said colony."[2]

The record shows that Oglethorpe, the trustees' "voice in the wilderness," was also possessed of an extraordinarily keen appreciation of the role which the Indians were inevitably to play in Georgia's future. Perhaps even more significant was his rapid appreciation of Indian temperament and ways of life. Oglethorpe indicated his understanding of the aborigines in an interesting simile when he stated that the Indians "have as much right to their woods as an English Gentleman to a forest or a chace, and they are more necessary to them since the venison is the flesh that chiefly feeds them, and the skins of the deer is what enables them to pay the English for their goods. . . ."[3] In a letter to the trustees in London, Oglethorpe took space to explain his reasons for select-

1. Allen D. Candler (ed.), *The Colonial Records of the State of Georgia* (Atlanta, 1904-11), I, 31.
  The act was patterned after one passed in South Carolina in 1731. It was deemed necessary since Georgia was to be an independent colony and would no longer be subject to the laws of the older colony.
2. *Ibid.*
3. *Ibid.*, VI, 148.

ing the site of the colony's metropolis, Savannah. In his concluding remark, he provided a hint to the importance of Indian knowledge and advice which probably helped him and his followers in coping with the problems of an alien environment on many occasions. He wrote, "the last and fullest conviction of the healthfulness of the place [Savannah] was that an Indian nation who knew the nature of this country chose it for their situation."[4]

Perhaps the most significant factor of all underlying the British attitude toward the Indians of Georgia arose from their strategic position in the tripartite struggle for empire which was concerning France, England, and Spain in this corner of North America. The significance of the location of the Indians, vis-à-vis the antagonistic empires of Europe, was summarized as follows:

The Trustees endeavored very early to secure the friendship of the Indians, who by ranging through the woods would be capable of giving constant intelligence to prevent any surprise upon the people and would be a good outguard for the inland parts of the province. for this reason they were treated with all possible candor and gentleness, they were acquainted that the English had no intentions to hurt or distress them, but would be ready to assist and protect them on all occasions.[5]

In the effort to convince the Indians "that the English had no intentions to hurt or distress them" Oglethorpe met with a number of Indians under chief Tomochichi during the spring of the colony's first year, 1733. Tomochichi played a long and important role in Anglo-Indian relations, which included a visit to London where he was received by the king. At the meeting between Oglethorpe and the Creeks a "Treaty of Friendship and Commerce" was signed which allowed the colonists of Georgia to "make use of and possess all those lands, which our nation hath not occasion to use . . . provided always that they upon settling every new town, shall set out for the use of ourselves, and the people of our nation, such lands as shall be agreed upon between their beloved men, and the head men of our nation, and that those lands shall remain to us forever."[6]

4. C. O. 5-711, p. 17. The advice and assistance received from South Carolina should not be overlooked. See Thomas Gamble, "Colonel William Bull—His Part in the Founding of Savannah," *The Georgia Historical Quarterly*, XVII (June, 1933), 111-26.

5. C. O. 5-711, p. 17.

6. Hugh McCall, *The History of Georgia* (Savannah, Ga., 1811), I, 358, Appendix 2. See also "Oglethorpe's Treaty with the Lower Creek Indians," *The Georgia Historical Quarterly*, IV (March, 1920), 12-16.

Hugh McCall, the chronicler of early Georgia, stated in 1811 that:

It was further stipulated that a free and complete right and title was granted to the Trustees for all the lands between Savannah and Altamaha rivers extending west to the extremity of tide water, and including all the islands on the coast from Tybee to St. Simon's inclusively, reserving for themselves the islands of Ossabaw, Sapeloe, and St. Catherines, for the purpose of hunting, bathing and fishing—also the tract of land lying between Pipe-Makers bluff and Pallychuckolo Creek, above Yamachraw bluff, now Savannah; which lands the Indians reserved for themselves for an encampment when they came to visit their beloved friends at Savannah.[7]

From the terms of the treaty and McCall's amplifying commentary, it would seem that the Lower Creeks, locally represented by Tomochichi, ceded an extensive but hazily defined tract of their coastal domain to the English to allow the establishment of a colony south of the Savannah River. While often devious, the Indians were seldom capricious in dealings involving land. In this case, it seems probable that the Creeks were genuinely desirous of the success of the Georgia scheme. They probably saw Georgia as an alternative source of English trade goods which would help to break the near-monopoly enjoyed by South Carolina in supplying essential and attractive manufactured articles in return for their annual harvests of deer skins and peltry. In addition to breaking the Carolina monopoly, Georgia could be expected to make frequent gifts to the Creeks not unlike tribute for their co-operation and favor. As Flippin pointed out, "the Indians were recognized as the rightful owners of the land, for no settlements were made during the proprietary period without the consent of the natives."[8]

During the first five or six years of the proprietary period Georgia developed rapidly, with settlements being established near to Savannah and at greater distances in the south along the Sea Isles and coastal plain, and inland along the Savannah and Ogeechee rivers. In summary, it can be said that these settlements resulted as responses to three principal motives which directed the early course of Georgia's growth. First, there was the strategic need to command routeways and approaches to Savannah as well as to South Carolina. Secondly, there was the great desire to acquire

7. McCall, *The History of Georgia*, I, 37.
8. Percy S. Flippin, "The Royal Government In Georgia, 1752-1776," *Georgia Historical Quarterly*, X (March, 1926), 2.

fertile and productive land natural among individuals who had been carefully selected "both as a planter and as a soldier."[9] Third, there was the desire to profit from trade with the Indians, which led to the establishment of the flourishing fall-zone outpost at Augusta.

During this period of rapid development, relations with the Indians concerning land matters were marked by an apparent lack of formality which left the earliest documentary record of Georgian land acquisition a much-rent fabric. There is reason to believe that during the years immediately following the signing of the treaty of 1733, its terms were obeyed and the Indians consulted as new settlements were established. In a letter dated July 26, 1736, Oglethorpe mentioned the jealousy which his success with the Indians had engendered among many of the South Carolinians and went on to state: "The opposition from Carolina forced me to give the Indians large presents to procure their confirmation of the cession of the islands: and they have refused as yet to give leave to settle the inland parts up the Altamaha."[10]

In another source, it was noted that the Georgians were keeping to their promise "that they upon settling every new town, shall set out for the use of [the Indians] such lands as shall be agreed upon."[11] In a dispatch of December 9, 1737, the officer in charge of the group constructing the outpost at Augusta reported that he had also "run out a little town near him, for the settlement of some of the Chickasaw Indians, which he apprehended would be of great benefit and addition of strength to that part of the province."[12]

Continued attempts by the Carolina traders to turn the Indians against Georgia, coupled with Spanish attempts to subvert the Creeks, caused Oglethorpe to fear an Indian war in 1739. Such a conflict might easily have extinguished the colony at this point, when many other problems were threatening its ruin from within. In an effort to deal with the Indian threat and counter the Spanish intrigues, Oglethorpe led a body of his Scottish Highlanders on the perilous journey to the council fire of the Creek center, Coweta

9. C. O. 5-711, p. 6.

10. *Letters From General Oglethorpe to the Trustees of the Colony and Others, from October, 1735 to August 1744* ("Collections of the Georgia Historical Society," Vol. III [Savannah, 1873]), p. 41.

11. McCall, *The History of Georgia*, I, 358.

12. "Stephens Journal 1737-40," Candler, in *Colonial Records of Georgia*, IV, 47. This band of Chickasaw was mentioned by Edmund Atkin in his report of 1755. See page 9, above.

Town. Coweta Town was located near the present day Phoenix City, Alabama, deep in the Creek coreland.

At Coweta, Oglethorpe had an opportunity to meet and confer with members of the Cherokee, Choctaw, and Chickasaw tribes as well as the Creeks. A formal treaty was signed in August, 1739, unanimously reaffirming the "Treaty of Friendship and Commerce" of six years before. Oglethorpe won the Creek allegiance to the English cause in the gathering conflict with Spain by accepting the tribe's claim to a vast territory in the Southeast. In return for diplomatically supporting the Creeks against the common rival Spain, Oglethorpe obtained confirmation of Georgia's title to (1) all areas which had, by that date, been settled; (2) all of the sea coast "as high as the tide flows;" (3) all of the Sea Isles except "St. Catherine, Osabow and Sapelo," which were retained by the Creeks along with the area known as Pipe Maker's Bluff near Savannah.[13]

At the ceremony held to solemnize the treaty in the Creek town of Cusseta, Oglethorpe added a statement which should be considered as a proclamation addressed to the white citizens of Georgia. He stated:

By James Oglethorpe, Esq., General & Commander in Chief of All His Majesty's Forces in South Carolina & Georgia, Etc.
To All His Majesty's Subjects to whome these Presents shall come. Greeting.
Know Ye that you are not to take up or settle any lands beyond the above limits settled by me with the Creek Nation, at their estates held on Saturday, Eleventh Day of August, Anno Domini, 1739, as you shall at your peril answer.[14]

Thus, by 1739, the colony of Georgia had accepted certain geographical limits beyond which the land was recognized as the property of the Indians and not available to the white pioneers establishing themselves along the coastal plain. Although no attempt will be made here to delineate these limits, an approximation of them is shown on Figure 17, which is derived from an eighteenth-century map. The Georgia-Creek Line of 1739 can be traced from the Alatamaha [Altamaha] River, just upstream of Fort Barrington,

13. McCall, *The History of Georgia*, I, 365, Appendix 3. "Oglethorpe's Treaty with the Lower Creek Indians," *The Georgia Historical Quarterly*, IV (March, 1920), 3-16.
14. "Oglethorpe's Treaty," *Ga. Hist. Quart.*, pp. 3-16.

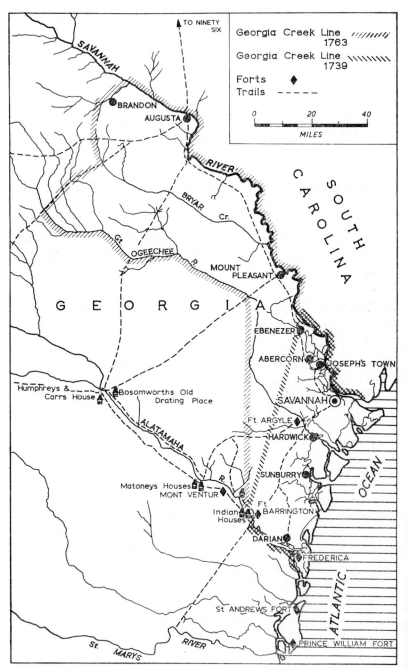

Fig. 17. Georgia-Creek boundary lines shown by Yonge and De Brahm.

to the Savannah River upstream of Ebenezer. Augusta was flourishing at the fall-zone of the Savannah River, but the land above Ebenezer as far as Bryar Creek was occupied by the Indian group known as the Uchee, who peopled the village called Mount Pleasant. There was, however, no formally delineated boundary between the Georgians and Indians at that date. It will be recalled that the original terms of the Creek cession had granted the trustees "all the lands between the Savannah and Altamaha rivers extend-ing west to the extremity of tide water," which was, in 1739, a nebulous boundary at best.

A long series of problems, ranging from a war with the Spanish to disagreements between the trustees and the Georgia settlers over such topics as the use of alcoholic beverages and employment of slaves, disturbed the progress of the colony through the decade of the 1740's. After a stormy period in which the trustees surren-dered on several of their restrictive principles, Georgia became increasingly like its neighboring British colonies. The trans-formation from a somewhat utopian experiment which had at-tempted to combine the ideals of eighteenth-century piety with those of imperial design was completed on June 23, 1752, when the trustees surrendered their charter to the king. Georgia had, by that date, already lost most of those qualities which led Coulter to call it "A Peculiar Colony," and took on the governmental machin-ery common to other royal colonies of the day. In Coulter's words, "the Georgia experiment had failed, but enough had been salvaged to be handed over to the king to make possible a permanent colony."[15]

The growth of Georgia's population and the consequent land encroachment during the 1740's and 1750's led to incidents and tension with the Indians. The Uchee group, which occupied the lands along the Savannah River above Ebenezer Creek, provide an example of Indians disturbed by advancing white settlements. The Uchee had, by 1741, abandoned their village called Mount Pleasant, "chusing to settle farther up; but a few of them frequent it still, with some vagrant Creeks among them, occasionally. . . ."[16] Settled on the Georgia side of Ebenezer Creek, facing these Uchee lands, were the numerous and energetic group known as the Salz-

15. E. Merton Coulter, *Georgia: A Short History* (Chapel Hill, N. C., 1947), p. 78.
16. "Stephens Journal," in Candler, *The Colonial Records of Georgia*, IV, 86.

burgers.[17] The Salzburgers had, as early as 1735, created an incident which was described by a contemporary, Francis Moore, who wrote:

The Uchee Indian king and his people had a conference with Mr. Oglethorpe. They had taken some disgust at this colony, by reason of an indiscreet action of some of the Saltzburghers, who had cleared and planted four acres of land beyond the Ebenezer River, contrary to Mr. Oglethorpe's order and without his knowledge; they had also turned their cattle over the river, some of which had strayed away and eat the Uchee's corn twenty miles above Ebenezer.[18]

Oglethorpe ordered the Salzburgers to withdraw and successfully averted a breach with his Indian neighbors in 1735.

Writing in 1751, the Salzburger pastor and leader Reverend Johann Martin Bolzius observed:

In the area around Ebenezer all good land has been taken up, and so it has around Savannah, particularly large neighboring fertile districts. Neither around Ebenezer nor Savannah is there any lack of land on which the most beautiful, biggest and tallest fir trees grow, but the lack is land on which big oaks, nut and other leaf trees grow which is really the good fertile land which bears without fertilizer. Whoever wants to have good land now would . . . have to . . . move farther up the Savannah River about 30 or 40 miles English Miles.[19]

Bolzius' advice, that new settlers would have to travel thirty or forty miles farther up the Savannah to find fertile land in 1751, would support Callaway's conclusion regarding the Uchee lands at the mid-point of the eighteenth century. Callaway stated, "the English by this time [1750] considered these lands as practically their own."[20] Although being occupied and settled by the Salzburgers, these lands were not formally relinquished by the Indians until 1763. In a flood of land grants issued by the trustees immediately prior to the surrender of their charter was the stipulation that the grants were to take effect "when the Indians shall have ceded the same."[21] It can be seen that the old limits to white

17. Coulter, *Georgia: A Short History*, p. 28, called the Salzburgers "the most numerous single population element in Georgia during the period of the Trustees, which, in fact made Georgia more German than English."

18. Francis Moore, *A Voyage to Georgia, Begun In the Year 1735* . . . ("Collections of the Georgia Historical Society," Vol. I[Savannah, 1840]), p. 145.

19. Klaus G. Leowald, Beverly Starika, and Paul S. Taylor (eds.), "Johann Martin Bolzius Answers A Questionnaire on Carolina and Georgia," *The William and Mary Quarterly*, Third Series, XIV (April, 1957), 228.

20. James E. Callaway, *The Early Settlement of Georgia* (Athens, Ga., 1948), p. 38.

21. *Ibid.*

settlement which had been agreed upon by Oglethorpe and the Creeks were giving way to the relentless demand for land which motivated the majority of newcomers to Georgia. Alden stated that "before 1754 . . . the gravest of the British-Indian disputes over land arose from the growth of Georgia."[22]

In 1757, following an altercation between a band of Creeks and a group of white settlers along the Ogeechee River, a congress was held with the Indians at Savannah. In the terms of the treaty signed, all former agreements "between the Great Squire [Oglethorpe] or any other of the King's Governors, Councillors or Beloved Men & the Head Men of the Creek Nation," were ratified and reaffirmed.[23] In Article IV of the treaty, a further cession was made to Georgia by the Creeks. This included those of the Sea Isles, which had so long been retained by the Indians, "Ossebaw, St. Catherines & Sappalo & the lands from the town of Savannah to Pipe Makers Creek."[24] In a letter to William Pitt concerning the cession, the governor of Georgia stated:

the article respecting lands & islands was inserted at the desire of the Indians themselves, regards certain claims that a man trumped up here by virtue of a marriage with an Indian woman, & a purchase he pretends to have made from some of the principal people of that nation [the Creeks]. This affair which has caused many disputes with the Indians, strong apprehensions in the minds of our people, & a quantity of the best lands on the front of the province to remain waste, lies now before the Board of Trade & it is greatly to be wished may soon be accommodated, as that would accelerate the settlement of the colony & increase our influence with the Savages, whom at present we are on very good terms with.[25]

The governor's allusion to, "a quantity of the best lands on the front of the province," which remained unsettled as late as 1757, indicated that the original Creek claim here had been honored until the cession made in that year.

22. Alden, *John Stuart*, p. 22.
23. C. O. 5-18, pp. 258-59.
24. *Ibid.* This cession is frequently overlooked. Samuel G. McLendon, for example, makes no mention of it in his *History of the Public Domain of Georgia* (Atlanta, 1924).
25. C. O. 5-18, p. 255. The Indian woman and white man referred to in the governor's letter were the Creek known as Coosaponakee and her third husband, the much-discredited Reverend Thomas Bosomworth. They had obtained a questionable title to the islands and lands above Savannah which the Creeks had, until 1757, retained for their own use. They were finally satisfied with a financial settlement, as the governor had hoped.

After his successful Congress with the Creeks in 1757, Governor Ellis in no way lessened his efforts to maintain peace with Georgia's powerful Indian neighbor. Among other dangers, he recognized the hazards of allowing individuals or combinations the freedom of privately purchasing or acquiring land directly from the Indians. During February, 1758, he succeeded in having an act prohibiting private land purchases from the Indians passed by the General Assembly.[26] The efficacy of this act, as well as others of a similar nature, was probably limited by the unregulated character of the frontier, but it may well have reassured the Indians of the sincerity of colonial officials. These officials were careful to assume attitudes which would convince the Indians of their determination to protect the tribal hunting grounds.

If the Indians had cause to be encouraged by this action of the Georgia General Assembly during February, 1758, they would have doubtlessly been quickly discouraged by an act passed during March, the following month. This was "An Act for constituting and dividing the several Districts and Divisions of this Province into Parishes...."[27] As its title suggests, this act provided for the division of Georgia into parishes with delineated limits and boundaries carefully described. Although no discussions had been held, nor any agreement with the Indians sought on the subject, the new parishes were boldly extended toward the interior beyond any possible construction of the long-standing tidal limit boundary. From the wording of the act, as well as a study of a contemporary map showing the newly created parishes, it is obvious that by 1758 the Georgians had ceased to acknowledge their tidal limit boundary with the Creeks. Figure 18, which is based on a tracing of a 1763 map, shows the parishes as they were constituted by the act of 1758. What reaction this territorial aggrandizement elicited from the Indians is difficult to determine. No formal announcement was addressed to them on the subject and it seems unlikely that they were fully aware of the implications of the new internal political geography of Georgia. Indeed, it is safe to assume that the Georgians would have been careful not to risk provocation by bringing the matter to their attention.

Georgia was more fortunate than its neighbor, South Carolina, and remained at peace with its Indian neighbors while the Chero-

26. *Acts Passed By the General Assembly of the Colony of Georgia, 1755 to 1774* (Wormsloe, Ga., 1886), p. 190.
27. Candler, *Colonial Records of Georgia*, XVIII, 258-72.

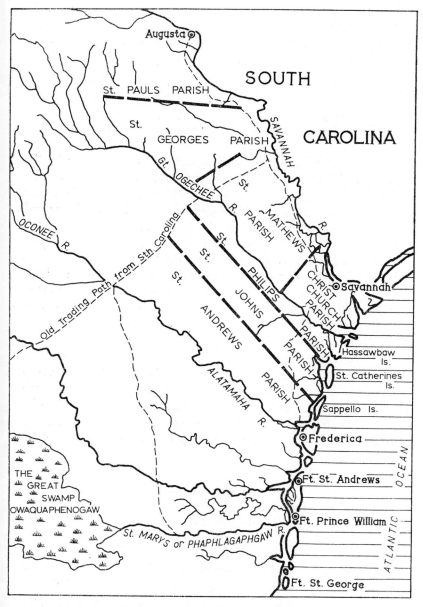

Fig. 18.   Georgia parishes, 1763. (P.R.O., C. O. 700, Maps, Georgia/13.)

kee War raged at the opening of the 1760's. This may explain in part the rapid increase in population which the colony enjoyed during the decade from 1753 to 1762. Governor Wright provided the following estimates of the colony's population:

Year	Negro	White	Total
1753	1,061	2,381	3,442
1761	3,600	6,100	9,700
1762	4,500	6,800	11,300[28]

Concomitant with this population increase was a change in the whole political climate in the New World. The Spanish surrendered their colony of Florida to the British in 1763, and in a trice Georgia was freed of the Damoclean threat which had influenced the colony's development from its inception. A decision by the Crown in 1763 made the St. Mary's River the southern boundary of Georgia and formally allowed the colony to extend its settlements beyond the Altamaha River, which had served as its southern limit for three decades. In 1764, a commission to the governor further defined Georgia's bounds and made the Mississippi River the westernmost limit of the colony.[29] It will be recalled that the French, too, had surrendered their claims to the Southeast in 1763.

Thus, under a royal administration, free of external threat from rival European empires, and with a population which had nearly trebled in a decade, Georgia's leaders were anxious to expand the colony's territorial base. This expansion could only take place by the acquisition of the Indian hunting grounds which restricted white settlement to the relatively infertile outer coastal plain, except where they had encroached farther inland up the Ogeechee and Savannah rivers.

The governor had been empowered to purchase Indian land above the tidal limit boundary in 1761 but chose not to risk such action in fear of alienating the Indians. It will be recalled that Spanish and French propagandists were then attempting to sow seeds of discord among the Indian tribes by telling them that the victorious British intended their extermination to provide land for the avaricious colonists on the seaboard. In recognition of the potential danger of such beliefs, were they accepted by the Indians, the secretary of state for the Southern Department set in motion a

28. British Museum, King's MSS. 205, fol. 626. Callaway, *Early Settlement of Georgia,* pp. 45-46.
29. McLendon, *History of the Public Domain of Georgia,* pp. 32-33.

program aimed at reassuring them of the pacific and benevolent intentions of the English. It was out of these two antithetic aims that a new and formally delineated Georgia-Creek boundary line was to emerge. On the one hand was the colony, anxious to expand by acquiring title to the contiguous Indian hunting grounds, and on the other hand were the officers of the Crown, anxious to cement the Indians to the English cause by removing their apprehensions and guaranteeing the inviolability of their claim to those same hunting grounds.

THE DELINEATION OF THE 1763 GEORGIA-CREEK BOUNDARY

In accordance with the secretary of state's orders to the four southern governors and the superintendent for Indian affairs, a general congress with members and representatives of the major Indian tribes in the Southeast was arranged during the autumn of 1763. Several thousand pounds worth of trade goods were shipped from England for distribution as gifts to the Indians at the congress. Military commanders were informed that many of the forts located in the southern interior were of no further value, in view of the French and Spanish withdrawal from the area, and should be abandoned in a manner which would appear as a sacrifice designed to please and reassure the Indians. The Indians were to be forgiven for past misdeeds, promised a fair and flourishing trade for the future, and convinced that the deceitful French and Spanish had been driven beyond the Mississippi by the paternalistic English king solely for the welfare of the tribes. Lastly, the Indians were to be reassured, in vigorous terms, that their lands were to be in no way jeopardized by their new British "brothers." It will be recalled that the concept of "some line for a western boundary to our ancient provinces beyond which our people should not at present be permitted to settle" was already firmly fixed in the minds of most of the king's advisors.[30]

The Southern Indian District Congress formally opened at Georgia's frontier outpost, Augusta, on November 5, 1763, with the superintendent and four southern governors facing members of the Chickasaw, Choctaw, Creek, Cherokee, and Catawba tribes.[31] A

---

30. *Supra,* chap. 2.

31. *Journal of the Congress. . . .* Alden states that only fifty copies of this *Journal* were printed, one of which he consulted in the William L. Clements Library, Ann Arbor. The author encountered two copies in the Public Record Office, London, in the course of research for this study.

wide range of topics were brought under discussion, with the governors and superintendent constantly endeavoring to assuage the legitimate fears of the Indians without appearing to pander to them. Among the more important problems discussed were those concerning the Creek hunting grounds facing Georgia and the new colonies of East and West Florida. The Creek chief, Telletsher, first broached the topic of a boundary line when he proposed a line to separate the hunting grounds of his tribe from Georgia. Chief Telletsher stated:

> That the red people were formerly ignorant, but God Almighty, and the king of England, had made them otherways; and proposed, that the lands above the rocks should remain unsettled; and that the line, between the white people and the Indians hunting grounds, should run from the rock, down to Savannah river; and the other way from the said rock to Mr. Galphin's cowpen; from thence to the lower ford on Ogeechie river, near the settlement of one Lambert; and from thence to cross to Sancta Sevilla, to the Alatamaha river.
>
> Little River by no means to be settled, but from thence.[32]

In their official reply to the Indian proposal, the four governors and Indian superintendent stated:

> You have proposed enlarging and extending the boundaries or limits of the lands to the westward, which may be settled by the white people; and this you declare to be in gratitude and return for the great clemency and generosity shewn to you by his majesty, and which in his name we agreed to accept of: So that for the future, the settlements of the white people are to extend up Savannah river to Little river, and back to the fork of Little river, and from the fork of Little river to the ends of the south branch of Briar creek, and down that branch to the Lower-Creek path, and along the Lower-Creek path to the main stream of Ogeechie river, and down the main stream of that river just below the path leading from Mount-Pleasant, and from thence in a strait line cross to Sancta Sevilla on the Alatamah river, and from thence to the southward as far as Georgia extends or may be extended. . . .[33]

Following this careful explanation of the boundary line, which was also included in the treaty to be signed, the Indians were asked if they "*clearly* [italics in the original text of the *Journal*] understood it?" The clerk who transcribed the minutes of the Congress

32. *Ibid.*, p. 27. Many of the landmarks mentioned here can be found in Fig. 20.
33. *Ibid.*, pp. 34-35.

noted that all the Creeks "and the Wolf King in particular, answered in the affirmative."[34]

In the "Treaty for the preservation and continuance of a firm and perfect peace and friendship . . . ," signed as the guns of Fort Augusta sounded a salute, Article IV provided for the establishment of a boundary between the Creeks and the colony of Georgia. The preamble of this article clearly stated the reasons why such a boundary was necessary:

Whereas doubts and disputes have frequently happened on account of encroachments or supposed encroachments, committed by the English inhabitants of Georgia, on the lands or hunting grounds reserved and claimed by the Creek Indians for their own use; Wherefore, to prevent any mistakes, doubts, or disputes for the future, and in consideration of the great marks of clemency and friendship extended to us the said Creek Indians, we, . . . have consented and agreed . . . [to] the boundary between the English settlements and our lands and hunting grounds. . . .[35]

Thus the Georgia-Creek boundary line was described and solemnized at Augusta in 1763, becoming the first delineated section of the Southern Indian Boundary Line. The need for the boundary was clearly understood by both the Indians and white pioneers, as was its general location. Figure 1 shows the general location of the new boundary as depicted on a map prepared by the superintendent of Indian affairs after the congress.

THE DEMARCATION OF THE GEORGIA-CREEK BOUNDARY LINE

While the location of the Creek boundary delineated at Augusta was probably understood in a general way by the colonial administrators, military officers, Indian traders, and pioneers who were in attendance at the congress in 1763, there were no provisions made for its demarcation to avoid future misunderstandings. Continued Indian crises, some of which were distant reflections of the general conflagration sparked by Pontiac to the north, made it inexpedient to press the Creeks for a demarcation of the boundary during the years immediately following the congress at Augusta.

Added to the general problem of Anglo-Creek relations was a schism within the tribe, influenced by the land cession made to

34. *Ibid.,* p. 35. Wolf King was a very prominent Creek chief during this period.

35. *Ibid.,* pp. 39-40.

Georgia. The list of gifts distributed to the Indians present at the congress indicated that 305 Creeks attended the ceremonies.[36] This was not a large attendance when it is recalled that the tribe totalled approximately fifty times this number. Notable among the absentees were several of the Upper Creek chiefs who deliberately avoided the congress. It is probably safe to say that the strongest francophile elements were found among the Upper Creeks at that time. Shortly after the congress, Superintendent of Indian Affairs John Stuart, reported:

> I cannot omit acquainting Your Lordship that at the last conference I had with the Creeks, some of the Upper Towns people expressed a dissatisfaction at the cession in favor of Georgia by the Lower Creeks, to which these answered, "The lands we have ceded were our own hunting grounds to which you never had any claim nor can the want of them be any inconveniency to you. We hope your future behavior will be such as may not lay us under the necessity of giving away more land to atone for your crimes."[37]

This report provided a rare insight into the internal organization of the Creeks, who, as it has been shown, were more a confederation than a nation, as many eighteenth-century authorities indicated. It is further clear that an important section of the tribe was opposed to the new boundary line in the months immediately following its delineation. Writing three years later, in 1766, the governor of Georgia observed that the Creeks were "very tenacious of, and at present extremely jealous of our making any encroachments on them."[38]

There were certain alterations made in the boundary line delineated at Augusta in 1763 prior to its demarcation five years later. The most extensive of these involved an area in the southern part of Georgia near the Phenhollaway Swamp, close to the present-day city of Jessup, Georgia. The Georgia-Creek boundary in this area came under discussion at the congress held between the Creeks and the neighboring colony, East Florida, in 1765.[39] The Creek chief known as Captain Aleck was delegated by the tribe to settle the boundary line in this area with Georgia's governor, James Wright.

36. C. O. 5-65, p. 74.
37. *Ibid.*, p. 71.
38. British Museum, King's MSS., fol. 205.
39. C. O. 5-70, p. 100.

In January, 1766, Governor Wright informed the upper house of his legislature that:

Captain Alleck having been fully empowered by the Upper and Lower creek Indians to sell his Plantation at Sta. Sevilla and to agree with me upon an alteration of the line between us and the lands reserved for their hunting grounds, I have settled the same with him, and send you the original agreement for your perussl—The consideration agreed upon with Alleck is a Negro who ran away from Mr. John Calwell and came to the possession of Alleck on the River near the Indian Nation, as he says; for this Negro and the loss of a years work Mr. Calwell asks 60 to which I told him I would lay the matter before you for your consideration and determination thereupon. . . .[40]

The upper house agreed to the unique payment of a negro slave for a cession, which the governor estimated at 20,000 acres.[41] A later reference to this alteration in the boundary line was included in a talk sent from a group of Lower Creeks gathered at "Chehaws Square" on September 18, 1768. In this message, the Creeks stated that they had earlier agreed to a boundary line running . . . "in a straight course to the bend of Phenholoway [Penholloway] Creek, which will just take in the Goose Ponds. . . ."[42] This shift in the line from the mouth to the "bend or elbow" of Penholloway Creek meant that an extensive gore of territory, which contains a large portion of the present-day Fort Stuart Military Reservation, would pass to Georgia in return for a slave.

On the opposite end of the boundary line in the vicinity of the Little River, a tributary which enters the Savannah above Augusta, a very disturbing condition arose in 1767 concerning the location of the yet-undemarcated boundary line. White settlers who had moved into the valley of the Little River following the 1763 congress directed a petition to colonial officials complaining of horse thefts, stock killing, and other disturbances created by Creeks in the neighborhood. In a letter accompanying their petition, they included the ominous observation that "if something is not done . . . the settlement must break up."[43] The situation worsened, with tempers on both sides becoming inflamed.

The governor reacted by sending a message to the Creek leaders on August 5, 1767. This informative document diplomatically

40. Candler, *Colonial Records of Georgia,* XVII, 246-47.
41. C. O. 5-663, p. 10.
42. C. O. 5-70, p. 64.
43. Candler, *Colonial Records of Georgia,* X, 246.

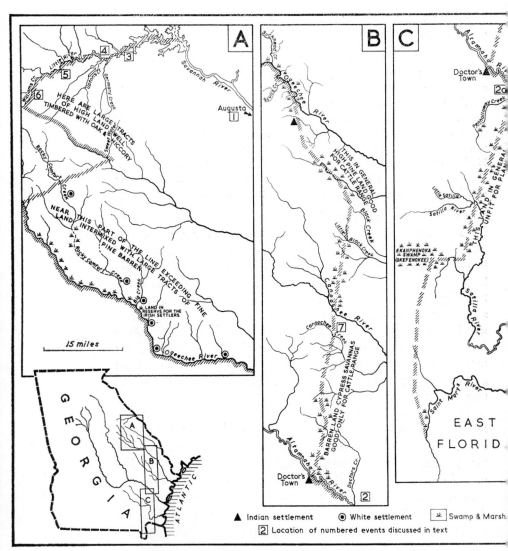

Fig. 19.   The Georgia-Creek section of the Southern Indian
Boundary Line, 1768.

commenced with an apology for the burning and sacking of an
Indian village by the irate pioneers. The governor then cast a part
of the blame on the Indian leaders themselves. He did this by
reminding them of their obligations under the treaty signed at
Augusta four years before. Continuing in this vein, the governor

went so far as to recommend that the Creeks "not . . . suffer any of [their] people to settle on the Oconee River, or in the woods especially near the white people but to keep together in your Towns in the Nation."[44] A wide geographical separation between his unruly frontier dwellers and their Indian neighbors was clearly desired by the governor.

Shortly after the summer clashes along the Little River, the Creeks began to claim that the boundary line in this area was somewhat different from what the whites on the scene had under-

LIST OF EVENTS SIGNIFICANT IN THE EVOLUTION OF THE
GEORGIA-CREEK INDIAN BOUNDARY OF 1768

Place*	Time	Event
[1]	November, 1763	Creeks suggest a boundary at the congress held at Augusta
[2]	November, 1765	Georgia-Creek boundary mentioned in treaty signed at Fort Picolata, East Florida (to run from Ogeechee River to the Altamaha River opposite Penholloway Creek)
[2A]	September, 1768	Creeks agree to further shift of boundary up the Altamaha River to a point opposite the "bend" of Penholloway Creek
[3]	Summer, 1767	Little River settlers complain of Indian horse thefts; Governor Wright suggests a "buffer zone" to Indian leaders
[4]	September, 1767	Creeks declare Upton Creek on Little River to be the boundary
[5]	September, 1767	Governor of Georgia states that land between Upton and Williams creeks has already been granted
[6]	June, 1768	Survey and demarcation of boundary begun with Williams Creek accepted by Indians
[7]	Summer, 1768	Demarcation ceased by Indians at Canoochee River, resumed and completed by Samuel Savery (see Fig. 20)
	November, 1768	Boundary ratified in treaty signed at Augusta

*Numbers in brackets are keyed to Fig. 19.

44. *Ibid.*, p. 277.

stood it to be. This difference of opinion was, of course, a pre-
dictable outcome arising from the fact that the boundary line had
never been demarcated. Whether the Indians, piqued by the
clashes with the pioneers, were attempting to contract the earlier
limits, or the pioneers, eager for more land along the Little River,
were seeking to expand them, is difficult to determine. Whichever
was the case, the result was clear: a serious difference of opinion
as to the location of the boundary line in the Little River valley
was endangering the peace. The Creeks were maintaining that
the boundary ran along the Little River from the Savannah only
as far as Uptons Creek (see Fig. 19, panel A), rather than several miles farther to Williams Creek, as the Georgians maintained.
In Governor Wright's words, this meant that "many of the tracts
of land already granted will be on the Indian side of the line."[45]
The influential Indian trader, George Galphin, was commissioned
to press Georgia's claim in the controversy. His success was apparent in the fact that the demarcation party, which surveyed the
boundary during the following year, selected Williams Creek to
mark this section of the Southern Indian Boundary Line.[46]

It can be seen that the Georgia-Creek segment of the Southern
Indian Boundary Line was very much a live issue in frontier
affairs throughout the five-year period following its delineation
at Augusta in 1763. Demarcation of the boundary began in June,
1768, when a party of Creeks met with Roderick McIntosh, John
Stuart's commissary stationed at Augusta. When the Georgia
boundary commissioners failed to appear as scheduled, McIntosh
and the Creeks began the demarcation of the Georgia-Creek
boundary on Williams Creek. They continued blazing the trees
along the course of the boundary to the head of Briar Creek,
along the Ogeechee River, and into the swamps of central Georgia.
At the Canoochee River: "they [the Creeks] took umbrage at
something and upon pretense that the presents given by this province [Georgia] were of inferior quality they left the work un-
finished and returned home."[47]

The superintendent of Indian affairs succeeded in placating the
Creeks and persuading them to finish demarcating the boundary
line. Samuel Savery, described as a "proper geometer," conducted

45. *Ibid.*, p. 303. Present-day maps of this area show two creeks bearing the
name Upton. There is no doubt that it is the Upton Creek located to the south
of the Little River which was referred to in the 1767 discussions.
46. *Ibid.*
47. British Museum, Additional MSS. 21, 671 (Haldimand Papers), fol. 299.

the final survey of the line and prepared a valuable map which depicted it. Figure 20 is a tracing made from the northern one-half of the original Savery map. To best appreciate this map, it should be compared with panel A of Figure 19, which shows Savery's boundary translated onto the present-day map of the area.

Savery encountered difficulty in collecting compensation for the labor he expended on the boundary demarcation during 1768. In a memorial requesting additional compensation from the Georgia Legislature in 1770, he stated that on June 1, 1768, he had been

employed to run the boundary line . . . from a place called Williams Creek about 50 miles above Augusta to the River Saint Mary the southern extremity of the Province being about 260 miles . . . 3 months on this service . . . exposed to all inclemencies of the season to the great injury of his health . . . given 65 £ in 1769 which was greatly inadequate to the trouble loss of time and health of the memorialist.[48]

The Georgia-Creek segment of the Southern Indian Boundary Line was finally demarcated by late summer of 1768. Formal ratification of the new boundary followed swiftly at a congress held with the Creeks at Augusta on November 12, 1768.[49] It marked a significant stage in the evolution of the Southern Indian Boundary Line, but, as De Brahm pointed out, the 1768 boundary was to mark only a temporary halting place in the advance of white pioneer settlement across the map of Georgia. Pressures and events were already building which would bring about yet another accretion of Indian territory to the burgeoning colony along the Savannah.

THE "NEW PURCHASE" BOUNDARY LINE

The boundary which Joseph Savery so laboriously surveyed and mapped during the summer of 1768 demarcated essentially a territorial agreement which had been made five years before and so was not entirely the reflection of frontier conditions as they were in that year. During the five intervening years, the flow of new settlers into Georgia had in no way abated, nor had the procreative powers of those already there lessened. It will be recalled that Governor Wright had reckoned his colony's total population, white and negro, to number 11,300 souls in 1762. He estimated this total to have increased by over 50 per cent in 1766, when he set

48. Candler, *Colonial Records of Georgia*, XV, 402.
49. C. O. 5-70, p. 101.

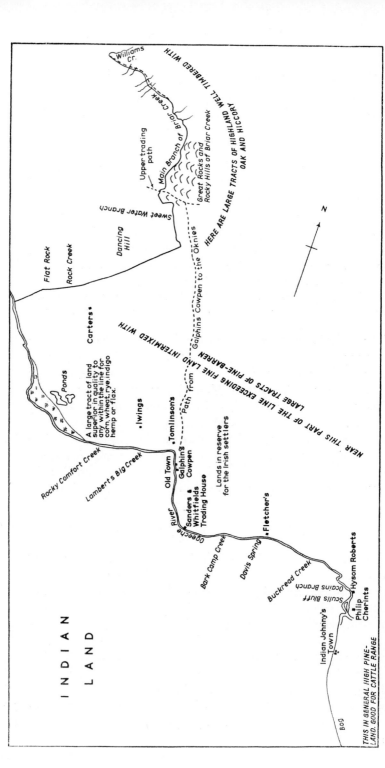

Fig. 20. Tracing from the original map of the Georgia-Creek boundary of 1768. (P.R.O., C. O. 700, Maps, Georgia/14.)

the total at 17,750.[50] While the accuracy of the governor's estimates may be questioned, it seems certain that Georgia was en-
joying a period of rapid population increase and that many of
the colony's new citizens were being attracted to frontier areas
close to the Georgia-Creek boundary line.

Significantly, many of the newcomers were attracted to Georgia
by programs instituted by the colony for this purpose. Perhaps
the best example of such official encouragement to immigration
was the "Act for Encouraging Settlers to Come Into This Province . . . ," passed on March 6, 1766.[51] The act provided a generous
offer to establish townships, for "any number of families, being
protestants, not less than forty . . . ," which would be surveyed and
registered free of charge. As a further enticement, the new
settlers were to enjoy a ten-year exemption from all provincial taxes,
except those on slaves. The Georgia leaders were attempting to
settle the colony's frontier in a manner which was reminiscent
of the policies of the trustees. They sought large groups of families
who could form compact townships more easily defended than dispersed, casual settlements. Further, the tax clause clearly favored
non-slaveholding families over slave holders. Experience in South
Carolina had shown that slaves were often a liability when Indian
war threatened.[52]

Taking advantage of the generous terms of the 1766 act were
two large groups of markedly dissimilar origins. The first was a
congregation of Quakers from North Carolina who occupied a
12,000-acre tract along a tributary of the Little River in 1768. The
second was a group of Scotch-Irish emigrants who took up a large
reserved site on the Ogeechee River late in the same year. The
Quakers established Wrightsborough Township, named in honor
of the governor, in the area drained by Germany and Upton's
Creeks in what are the present-day counties of McDuffie and Warren. The Scotch-Irish settlement was made on a tract along both
sides of "Great Creek," near the present-day city of Louisville, in

50. British Museum, King's MSS. 205, fol. 626. Callaway, *Early Settlement of
Georgia*, pp. 45-46.
51. *A Digest of the Laws of The State of Georgia* (Philadelphia, 1801), p. 125.
52. The continuity of the ideal of frontier settlement in compact units of
non-slaveholding families in Georgia is noteworthy. During the revolutionary period
another act titled "An Act for the More Speedy and Effectually Settling and
Strengthening This State" offered encouragements very similar to those of the
1766 act. The pioneers who settled Wilkes County (the area of the New Purchase) were granted an exemption from militia service, except in defense of their
home county. Candler, *Colonial Records of Georgia*, XIX, 134.

Jefferson County. It can be noted on Figure 20 that land along the Ogeechee River in this area had already been marked as being in reserve for the Scotch-Irish. This reflected the earlier attempts by Lachlan McGillivrary, John Rae, and George Galphin to persuade the Georgia Assembly to assign a tract of 50,000 acres for the use of immigrants expected from Ireland in 1765. These Scotch-Irish immigrants had been described as "oppressed by the rents exacted . . . as also by Taxes and other duties in Ireland."[53] The Irish settlement, as it was referred to, became known as Queensbury or Queensborough. In 1771, De Brahm described both settlements as follows:

1) Wrightsborough [at location of former settlement called Brandon abandoned by Edmond Grey and his renegade band some years before] inhabited by above 60 families, and its township contains about 200 families, all Quakers; they are indulged by the Govr: that no person but such as they approve of, shall be permitted to settle among them.

2) Queensbury is inhabited by about 70 and its environs by above 200 families mostly Irish from which it is generally called the Irish Settlement.[54]

During the period which saw the establishment of these ambitious settlements along the Georgia-Creek boundary line, a less orderly and less well-documented influx of pioneers was affecting Georgia. These newcomers were from the frontiers of Virginia, North Carolina, and South Carolina and were moving into the area west of Augusta. They seemed to have been predominantly small farmers and brought few if any slaves with them to their new Georgia homes. From statements made by the Indians, it would appear that these southward-moving pioneers were the chief source of friction between the two races in frontier Georgia. In 1768 the Creek leader, Captain Aleck, stated: "before these Virginia Men came to settle in the Back Country [of Georgia] the White Men and Red Men lived like brothers. English Men and Scotch Men, I have been long acquainted with, and always

53. Callaway, *Early Settlement of Georgia*, p. 59.
54. John Gerar William De Brahm, *History of the Province of Georgia with Maps of the Original Surveys* (Wormsloe, Ga., 1849). This is a published portion of the manuscript copy of De Brahm's "Report of the General Survey in the Southern District of North America" in the Harvard University Library. The author has a photo copy of the British Museum's complete version of this valuable report by De Brahm. The British Museum version is signed by De Brahm as follows: "William Gerard de Brahm." See British Museum, King's MSS. 210 and 211.

found them to be good men. But these Virginians are very bad people, they pay no regard to your laws. . . ."[55] Another Creek added a revealing commentary regarding the contrast between the Quakers of Wrightsborough and their unruly neighbors in the frontier. He observed:

I was with your Deputy, Mr. McIntosh, when the Line was marked. I then saw a number of people (Quakers) settling near the line, who I liked much. They are good and peaceable, and do not take a pride in riding about with riffle [*sic*] guns in their hands & drinking and swearing like the Virginians. They offend nobody but cultivate their fields. . . . I wish, however, that a great number of them may be encouraged to come and settle near the line, by which means the Virginians may be kept from settling near it.[56]

On yet another occasion, a Creek chief complained of the lawlessness of the Georgia pioneers to the superintendent of Indian affairs. He stated: "Whenever the Virginia people are told by our people that they are over the line & if they don't keep in the bounds they will burn their houses, they make answer they will burn the Governors house over his head. If the Governor cannot keep these Virginia people under how can we keep our people under?"[57]

Clearly, the increasing population in the frontier of Georgia was beginning to spill across the boundary line which had been so recently demarcated with the Creeks. It seems probable that only the fact that the tribe was engaged in a war with their western neighbors, the Choctaw, kept them from expressing their complaints against the encroaching Georgia pioneers more violently.[58]

A fortunate set of circumstances arose along the section of the Southern Indian Boundary Line separating the Cherokee tribe from the colonies of North and South Carolina which was to have a profound influence in the Georgia frontier. Briefly stated, it was that the Cherokee showed an unexpected willingness to part with large tracts of their hunting grounds contiguous to the boundary which had been demarcated between the tribe and North Carolina in 1767. These tracts, which are shown on Figure 13, were intended for two white men who had fathered sons by Cherokee women. Ostensibly, the proceeds from the lands thus acquired would be used to educate their sons to provide future

55. C. O. 5-70, p. 89.
56. *Ibid.*
57. C. O. 5-69, p. 135.
58. C. O. 5-70, p. 55.

leaders for the tribe. Such private cessions were, however, contrary to the spirit and terms of the Proclamation of 1763 as well as several colonial statutes and were not permitted.

An Indian trader who had extended a large amount of credit to the Cherokee followed the lead provided by their apparent willingness to surrender hunting grounds along that part of the boundary line and persuaded them to make a cession of 177,907 acres in return for the £8,000 which they owed him. The Cherokee agreed to this proposition and the trader, Edward Wilkinson, sought to have the cession accepted by the Crown. He intended that he should be repaid his £8,000 from the proceeds of the sale of the land or be allowed free use of it for ten years. None of these schemes to obtain Cherokee land were entirely successful, but they did set into motion other schemes which were to profoundly alter the Georgia-Creek Boundary Line.

Other Indian traders quickly followed Wilkinson in attempting to gain Indian land in payment for debts owed them by the tribes. The traders were not alone in this effort to acquire Indian land beyond the boundary line. In his own words, Governor Wright of Georgia "long had it in view to obtain an extension of the Indian Boundary to the westward and Southwestward."[59] The governor viewed the Wilkinson affair with the Cherokee as a useful precedent and helped to set into motion a similar scheme in Georgia.

On February 22, 1771, the Cherokee ceded the tract described below to their Georgia traders in return for the abandonment of the tribes' debt: "a certain tract of land upon Broad River Georgia side, beginning at the mouth of the Kayugas, extending five measures up Savannah River, and Running five measures extending toward the Oconies, Viz. five measures long and five measures broad or sixty miles square. . . ."[60] The Cherokee motives in making such a cession were explained by chief Oconostota, who stated:

we considered the state of our debts justly due to our traders; & out of consideration of their forwardness to supply us with our necessary goods, we therefore out of gratitude, as we were not able to pay them of all at once, and the Deer growing scarcer every year, considering the danger of our enemies, who are surrounding us every where, we have therefore unanimously agreed with the consent of our young

59. C. O. 5-661, p. 188.
60. *Ibid.*, p. 192.

men to give our traders a tract of land to be enabled to support us further with our necessarys.[61]

In his dispatch reporting the Cherokee cession, the superintendent of Indian affairs stated that he had informed the Indians of the irregularity of their action and that the cession was in no way officially sanctioned or allowed. He observed that the land involved was "of a fine rich soil capable of producing corn, wheat, tobacco, Indigo or hemp," although of decreased value to the white because it was located above the falls of the Savannah.[62] The most important factor of all, however, was the location of the Cherokee's intended cession on the Georgia side of the Savannah River. In the superintendent's words, "the Creek Indians and their traders were not inattentive to these transactions: the former claimed part of the ceded land in right of conquest having obliged the Cherokee during the war between them to abandon it."[63]

The Cherokee ignored the superintendent's objection to the cession and joined with a group of traders in surveying its limits during the summer of 1771. The line which they marked to indicate the northern boundary of the cession appeared on a manuscript map prepared two years later. This line is shown on panel D of Figure 21 as "Old Cherokee Line (July 1771)." For comparison, the South Carolina-Cherokee boundary line has been extended as a broken line across the same area. It can be seen that the line surveyed by the Cherokee and their traders was very nearly a continuation of the South Carolina-Cherokee line which had been demarcated in 1766.

In replying to the superintendent's criticism of their actions, the Cherokee maintained that they were free to make a cession to whomsoever they pleased, in spite of the Proclamation of 1763.[64] In direct reference to the proclamation, the Indians reminded the superintendent of the prohibitions which were intended to bar white hunters from the Indian lands and suggested that they be

61. *Ibid.*
62. C. O. 5-73, pp. 163-64.
63. *Ibid.*
James Mooney, *Myths of the Cherokee*, p. 14, stated that the Cherokee seemed to be pushing the Creeks back in northern Georgia during the later eighteenth century. The Cherokee advance was terminated during the postrevolutionary era at a treaty line determined by the United States, acting as mediator between the contesting tribes. Significantly, the treaty signed recognized the Cherokee claim to all of northern Georgia above a line drawn from the Broad River westward.
64. C. O. 5-661, p. 194.

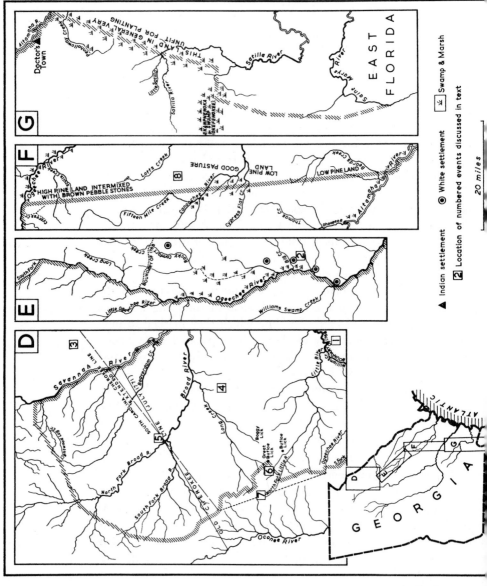

Fig. 21. The Georgia section of the Southern Indian Boundary Line, 1773.

Place*	Time	Event
[1]	December, 1768	North Carolina Quakers arrive on Little River (Wrightsborough)
[2]	December, 1768	Irish Immigrants arrive on Ogeechee River tract (Queensborough)
[3]	Summer, 1768	Cherokee exhibit a willingness to surrender land near the North Carolina Indian boundary
[4]	February, 1771	Cherokee cede 60-mile-square tract to their traders on the Georgia side of the Savannah River
[5]	July, 1771	Cherokee and traders survey and mark limits of the unofficial cession in Georgia
[6]	June, 1773	"New Purchase" boundary demarcation begun after congress with Cherokee and Creeks at Augusta
[7]	Summer, 1773	Governor Wright not entirely satisfied with western boundary of "New Purchase"
[8]	November, 1773	Demarcation of new line between the Ogeechee and Altamaha rivers completed

*Numbers in brackets are keyed to Fig. 21.

more vigorously enforced. The Cherokee concluded their reply by requesting that their wishes on the matter be placed before the king.

Governor Wright of Georgia, long desirous of extending his colony's territorial base at the expense of the Indians, was doubtlessly encouraged in his aspirations by a message from the Cherokee requesting him to use his influence in placing their desire to make a cession before the king. In the talk, which was signed by four of the most influential Cherokee chiefs, the tract to be ceded was described and followed by the statement that "in case any part of this land should be claimed by the Creek Indians, we will use all our endeavours to get them to join with us in consenting to give up their claims; but should we not be able to accomplish this we will engage to make up the full quantity on the frontiers of South Carolina, or elsewhere where we have lands."[65]

65. *Ibid.*, pp. 196-97.

In his reply, the governor indicated that he would argue in favor of the Cherokees' cession, "in this province, but no other," when he arrived in London on his forthcoming leave.[66] He also made a requirement of the Cherokee promise to obtain the Creek agreement to the cession. Governor Wright was careful to keep the Creeks from learning of his interest in the Cherokee cession. He admitted a knowledge of the affair in a message to the Creek leaders, but pointed out that he had informed the Cherokee that "they must settle the right to the land with you and this you must agree upon between yourselves as we have nothing to do with that."[67]

As Governor Wright had intended, the Creeks began to see that the land cession being proposed by the Cherokee might provide a relief for some of their own problems. The Creek traders, too, saw a land cession as a solution to their problems, or as stated in their own terms, "a mode of extricating themselves and their debtor from a burthen . . . intolerable to both parties." They pointed out that the tract to be ceded was "claimed by both nations, not occupied by either of them, as a hunting ground, being so near to our settlements, that the upper line will reach no higher on the south side Savannah River than the Carolina settlements on the north side already do."[68] The traders provided a very favorable description of the land contained in the tract as being "upwards of three millions of acres of as fine land as fit for the culture of Indigo, tobacco, hemp, flax, wheat and other valuable produce as any in America having the advantage of the Savannah, Okony and Great Ogotchy Rivers, bounding or running through it."[69] In an effort to win official support for the cession, the traders included an illuminating commentary on frontier conditions in 1771. They stated:

That the lands to the northward as much worn out and very insufficient for the increase of population in those parts, as appears by the numbers of emigrants that flock from thence to the upper parts of South Carolina and Georgia, where they are obliged to remain being unable through poverty to transport their families by water to the Floridas, and prevented journeying by land by the several Nations of Indians they have to pass through.[70]

66. *Ibid.*, p. 198.
67. *Ibid.*, pp. 208-9.
68. *Ibid.*, pp. 215-16.
69. *Ibid.*, p. 216.
70. *Ibid.* David Taitt mentioned an encounter with one of these hardy south-

Concluding this lengthy memorial to the governor of Georgia, the traders suggested a scheme by which the ceded land might be sold in small tracts at low prices to provide homes for these stranded pioneers. They calculated that the proceeds from such sales would more than equal the Indian's indebtedness to them. The Georgia frontier "would be settled with a great number of industrious poor white families, that would cover the more opulent plantations near the Sea Coast, and prove an acquisition of the utmost importance to His Majesty's Province of Georgia in particular."[71]

Governor Wright sailed for England and upon arrival in London began to petition Crown officers to permit his colony to accept the Indian cession and expand its area beyond the 1768 boundary line. The ambitious governor had set a program in motion before leaving Savannah which was aimed at persuading the Creeks to join with the Cherokee in ceding the already surveyed tract and "also ceding the rest of the land from where the Cherokees claim . . . quite cross to Oconee River, and down that to the Alatamah River and our present boundary line."[72] He estimated the total area of the Indian land to be acquired by Georgia at five million acres, of which two or three million only were included in the original Cherokee cession to the traders.

Governor Wright's well-argued petition for a change in Georgia's Indian boundary line to take in this large area of Indian hunting grounds and allow the colony's expansion was received favorably in London. Before delivering their approbation to his scheme, the Board of Trade expressed concern over the Creek attitude toward the surrender of a part of their hunting grounds. The governor assured the board that "there is no room to doubt that the Creeks will also be readily induced to concur in that cession."[73] The superintendent of Indian affairs was also canvassed for an opinion on the Creek question. He was quoted as stating

ward moving pioneers in the spring of 1772. He wrote: "proceeded to Ogechee where I found a Israel Folesum, with his wife and six children Encamped, he had thirty three head of cattle with him and some horses which he intended going to Pensacola with, but meeting with some traders at the Okono River, they advised him to turn back, telling him that the Indians would kill his cattle and steal his horses etc. upon which information he was returning back and intended to go to Mississippi by the way of Holston River." Quoted from C. O. 5-73, p. 283.

71. C. O. 5-661, p. 216.
72. *Ibid.*, p. 190.
73. *Ibid.*, p. 168.

that, were he authorized to seek a cession from the Creeks, it could "be attempted with great hope of success."[74]

In their representation to the king approving Governor Wright's scheme, the Board of Trade observed: "The confidence we have in the judgement of Governor Wright leave no apprehension . . . and as he is ready to embark for Georgia, . . . we do not hesitate to recommend that the instructions to him should be as general as may be."[75] Thus, Governor Wright returned with a carte blanche from the Crown which would allow him the maximum scope and freedom in negotiating with his Indian neighbors to extend the territorial limits of Georgia.

While it was neither legal nor binding in the absence of royal authorization, the Cherokee survey and cession to their traders did not pass unnoticed by the land-hungry pioneers of the southeastern frontier. A group of North Carolina Presbyterians petitioned the government of Georgia for a twenty-mile-square tract "in the land lately ceded by the Cherokees."[76] This petition was rejected on the grounds that it was premature, coming as it did before any official cession. Others were not so easily forestalled as these 360 North Carolina families, however, and a serious problem was developing in the area of the intended cession. This problem was caused by the large number of squatters who were taking up land beyond the Indian boundary line of 1768. These squatters were described as "persons who have no settled habitation, and live by hunting and plundering the industrious settlers and are by no means the sort of people that should settle those lands . . . idle and disorderly vagrants—you will easily distinguish, that the people I refer to are really what you and I understand by Crackers."[77] Nor were the Crackers the only category of frontier society interested in acquiring portions of the Indian lands. It was reported that, "several persons of apparent repute have been to view them. . . ."[78]

74. *Ibid.*, p. 170. Stuart was not so sanguine in a letter to General Haldimand, dated Sept. 13, 1772, where he stated: "I find the purchase of lands from the Cherokees by their traders which gave such umbrage to the Creeks is likely by Governor Wright's influence to meet the countenance of government, yet I have no hope that the Creeks will acquiesce in the cession, at least I think it will be a very difficult matter to reconcile them to the measure." Quoted from British Museum, Additional MSS. 21, 672.

75. C. O. 5-661, p. 172.

76. Candler, *Colonial Records of Georgia*, XII, 143.

77. *The Letters of Hon. James Habersham, 1756-1775* ("Collections of the Georgia Historical Society," Vol. VI [Savannah, 1904]), p. 204.

78. *Ibid.*, p. 202.

The attempted Cherokee cession to their traders opened the floodgates in front of prospective settlers, many of whom were not content to await the niceties of administrative decisions by Crown officials in distant London and Savannah, not to mention the necessary Indian congress, before they occupied the fertile acres along the Broad and Savannah rivers. To deal with the problem of illegal settlers beyond the 1768 boundary, the acting governor of Georgia issued a proclamation ordering their immediate removal from the Indian hunting grounds.[79]

The superintendent of Indian affairs, too, expressed deep concern over the character of the pioneers who were moving into the Georgia frontier. He felt that these lawless newcomers from North Carolina and Virginia would prove a serious liability by involving the colony in perpetual disputes with the Indians. The superintendent suggested that they be barred from the lands about to be acquired from the Indians, which should, he felt, be settled by "industrious people from Britain and Ireland or . . . German Protestants."[80] He concluded, "for upon the character of the inhabitants its utility to Great Britain as a Colony and to Georgia as an acquisition of strength will entirely depend."[81] The illegal invasion of the Indian lands did not cease, however, and in January, 1773, the Georgia Council was informed "that a number of stragling people were settling on lands proposed to be ceded by the Indians."[82] Even when informed of the proclamation forbidding such settlements, the squatters "paid little or no regard."

Governor Wright returned from England to a hero's welcome from his fellow Georgians, who were greatly encouraged by his news that the Crown had granted permission to proceed with the negotiations for an Indian land purchase. Commenting on the boundary line of 1768, the governor stated, "for by the present boundary line we are so much confined that there is not ungranted lands for any additional number of inhabitants of any consequence."[83] He continued in his efforts to get the Creeks to join with the Cherokee in making a large cession to the colony of Georgia. The colony in turn was to sell the land and repay the Indian traders from the proceeds.

79. C. O. 5-661, p. 161.
80. C. O. 5-73, p. 164.
81. *Ibid.*
82. Candler, *Colonial Records of Georgia*, XII, 347.
83. C. O. 5-662, p. 11.

An Indian congress was held at Augusta on June 1, 1773, where the Creeks somewhat reluctantly joined the Cherokee in making the desired cession of land to Georgia. Perhaps the most lucid and informative account of this congress is the one which was recorded by the famous eighteenth-century naturalist, William Bartram, who attended at the invitation of the superintendent of Indian affairs.[84] Bartram noted how the Creeks, "being a powerful and proud spirited people . . . were unwilling to submit to so large a demand, and their conduct . . . betrayed a disposition to dispute the ground by force of arms." He added that "at length the cool and deliberate counsels of the ancient venerable chiefs, enforced by liberal presents of suitable goods, were too powerful inducements for them any longer to resist."

Although Bartram stated in his *Travels* that the cession was made and treaty signed "in unanimity, peace, and good order" he indicated otherwise in another source. Writing to his patron in England, he candidly observed: "In a few days the business of the Congress was over but not terminating entirely to the satisfaction of the parties, on either side the question, the superintendent told me he thought it not altogether safe to go then into the Indian countries."[85]

Not to be deterred from his original objective of viewing the Indian country, Bartram joined the party formed to undertake the demarcation of the new Georgia-Indian boundary line agreed upon at the congress. Bartram described this party as a:

caravan, consisting of surveyors, astronomers, artisans, chain-carriers, markers, guides, and hunters, besides a very respectable number of gentlemen, who joined us, in order to speculate in the lands, together with ten or twelve Indians, altogether to the number of eighty or ninety men, all or most of us well mounted on horseback, besides twenty or thirty pack-horses loaded with provisions, tents and camp equipage.[86]

The party which Bartram accompanied demarcated the new Georgia-Indian boundary line circumscribing the northern portion of the lands ceded by the Indians. The cession had, however, two parts. The second or southern portion was composed of a broad

84. Harper, *Bartram's Travels*, p. 22.
85. William Bartram, "Travels In Georgia and Florida 1773-74: A Report to Dr. John Fothergill," annotated by Francis Harper, *Transactions of the American Philosophical Society*, n.s. XXXIII, Pt. 2 (Nov., 1943), 138.
86. Harper, *Bartram's Travels*, p. 23.

belt of land between the Ogeechee River and Altamaha River in central Georgia. These two tracts are clearly shown as the "New Purchase" on Figure 29. The name New Purchase was generally applied to the Indian lands acquired by Georgia in 1773. The boundary lines which demarcated the New Purchase are shown on Figure 21 and formed the Georgia section of the Southern Indian Boundary Line in 1773.

Describing the New Purchase after a personal visit, the governor of Georgia wrote: "The quality and proportion of the good and bad lands contained in the late cession from the reports made to me by many and from my own observation on my late tour through the greatest part of it I judge to be at least 2/3 if not three parts of it very fine land."[87] It would appear that the governor was describing only the northern, or Broad River, portion of the New Purchase in these remarks, since the southern portion between the Ogeechee and Altamaha rivers was found to be rather less than "very fine land." In considering petitions for land grants in that tract, the Georgia Council discovered that of a total area estimated at 674,000 acres, only 31,000 were "plantable," with the remaining 643,000 acres pine barren fit only for grazing cattle and horses.[88]

Bartram was favorably impressed with the northern and larger portion of the New Purchase, which he traversed with the demarcation party during the summer of 1773. He described this area, (panel D, Fig. 21) which is located between the present-day cities of Athens and Augusta, Georgia, with characteristic eloquence:

This new ceded country promises plenty & felicity. The lands on the River [probably the Broad River] are generally rich & those of its almost innumerable branches agreeable and healthy situations, especially for small farms, every where little mounts & hills to build on & beneath them rich level land fit for corn & any grain with delightful glittering streams of running water through cain bottoms, proper for meadows, with abundance of water brooks for mills. The hills suit extremely well for vineyards & olives as nature points out by the abundant produce of fruitful grape vine, native mulberry trees of an excellent quality for silk. Any of this land would produce indigo & no country is more proper for the culture of almost all kinds of fruits.[89]

87. C. O. 5-663, p. 9.
88. Lilla M. Hawes (ed.), *The Proceedings and Minutes of the Governor and Council of Georgia, October 4, 1774 through November 7, 1775, and September 6, 1779, through September 20, 1780* ("Collections of the Georgia Historical Society," Vol. X [Savannah, 1952]), p. 6.
89. William Bartram, "Travels . . . A Report to Dr. John Fothergill," p. 144.

These were the acres to be occupied by the pioneer farmers from Virginia and the Carolinas who had moved south through the frontier to settle on the newly acquired Indian land in Georgia. The Southern Indian Boundary Line had been advanced toward the interior to provide new land for these families, which included few, if any, slaves. It seems probable that the process of boundary advance illustrated by the New Purchase would have set a pattern to be followed in other parts of the frontier had not the American Revolution intervened so soon afterward.

THE GEORGIA-INDIAN BOUNDARY LINE ON
EIGHTEENTH-CENTURY MAPS

During the period of the trusteeship, no Georgia-Creek boundary line was formally demarcated or mapped. As discussed above, a number of treaties and less formal agreements delineated those areas which were available for white settlement during the colony's early decades. In attempting to gain a chorographical appreciation of Georgia's division between the Indians and white settlers during that period, two manuscript maps are particularly valuable. Both of these maps were drawn at similar scales in August, 1763, and are signed by the surveyors Yonge and De Brahm.[90] Difference in lettering and style indicate that the respective authors may have been responsible for the separate copies. Figure 17 is a composite based on both of these manuscript maps and shows much of the information pertaining to the Georgia-Creek land division which the originals contain.

In addition to many valuable place names and trail locations, the Yonge-De Brahm map attempted to depict the nebulous tidal limit boundary of the colony which Oglethorpe had obtained from the Creeks in 1739 and which had been reaffirmed in 1757. So far as has been discovered, this was the only eighteenth-century attempt made to depict this boundary. It has been indicated on Figure 17 as the "Georgia Creek Line 1739" for convenience. This

90. Cumming, *The Southeast In Early Maps*, p. 232, discusses both maps. One is found in the British Museum, Additional MSS. 14,036 g, and the other in the William L. Clements Library, Clinton Map 329. Christian Brun, *Guide to the Manuscript Maps in the William L. Clements Library* (Ann Arbor, Mich., 1959), p. 152, incorrectly read a date in one of the captions on the Clements map. He gives 1759 as the date of the Creek cession to Oglethorpe. This should read 1739; it is blurred on the map but correct in view of the fact that 1759 was well into the Royal period of Georgia's history. Also, 1739 was the date of Oglethorpe's treaty with the Creeks, which is discussed above.

line, from the Savannah River near Ebenezer to the Altamaha River, upstream of Fort Barrington, was intended to show the "part of Georgia ceded by the Indians to His Excellency General Oglethorpe in the year 1739." A caption on the original manuscript map states that this cession "contains 1,152,000 acres of land."[91]

It would appear that this line did enclose all of the Georgia settlements made during the colony's period of administration by the trustees, except for the trading posts such as Augusta and military posts located along the Sea Isles south of the Altamaha. To what extent it illustrated the tidal limit boundary which Georgia had agreed upon with the Creeks will only be determined when this part of Georgia is made subject to a study similar to that which Cumming conducted to fix the location of the Florida tidal limit boundary.

While extremely valuable as sources of information on the early geography and Indian boundary lines of Georgia, the Yonge-De Brahm maps contain no mention of the 1757 treaty with the Creeks, which resulted in the cession of the islands of "Ossebaw, St. Catherines & Sappalo & the lands from the town of Savannah to Pipe Makers Creek." This serious omission would appear to have misled a number of scholars who have ignored this significant phase of Georgia's territorial growth.

As noted above, the Yonge-De Brahm maps were prepared during the summer preceding the Indian congress held at Augusta in November, 1763. It is probable that Governor Wright consulted one or both during the congress as the negotiations for a Georgia-Creek boundary delineation proceeded. The 1763 boundary is shown from the confluence of the Little and Savannah rivers to the upper branches of "Bryar" Creek and along the Indian trading path to the "Great Ogeechee River," which it follows as far as the crossing of the Mount Pleasant trail, called the "old Palachocawls Drating [Trading] path," and then as a straight line to the same Indian settlement on the Altamaha, where the line of 1739 terminated. This 1763 boundary can be followed on Figure 19. The area of the cession included in the 1763 line was stated to be 2,408,-800 acres on the Yonge-De Brahm maps.

The Yonge-De Brahm maps are valuable cartographic sources which are almost indispensable in any attempt to appreciate and

91. From Clements Library copy which agrees except in minor respects with the British Muesum copy; cf. Cumming, *The Southeast In Early Maps,* p. 232.

reconstruct the Georgia-Creek boundary line, as it was formally delineated in 1763. They are, however, misleading in that they show the 1739 tidal limit boundary as a straight line. This tends to lend it much more regularity than it probably enjoyed at that time. Also, they omit any mention of the additional cession made by the Creeks to Georgia in 1757.

Clearly, the Yonge-De Brahm maps showed the Georgia-Creek boundary line which was delineated in 1763, but they could hardly be employed to accurately illustrate the boundary as it was demarcated five years later. For a cartographic presentation of this section of the Southern Indian Boundary Line, there is no better source than the original manuscript map of it prepared by Samuel Savery following his boundary demarcation in 1768.[92] Figure 20 is based on the northern one-half of the Savery map and gives some idea of the wealth of first-hand information concerning the frontier landscape and settlements along the boundary line which he gathered. Savery's map, and contemporary copies made from it, provide indispensable sources of information vital in any attempt to appreciate the location and significance of the Georgia-Creek section of the Southern Indian Boundary Line demarcated in 1768.

At least three manuscript maps were prepared to show the area involved in the 1771 Cherokee cession of land to their traders on the Georgia side of the Savannah River. The first of these was prepared by the superintendent of Indian affairs, John Stuart, to illustrate his report of the affair to his superiors in London.[93] This is a very general map and does not provide a great deal of information beyond the location of the tract marked "The Lands Which the Cherokees have Assigned for the payment of their debts."

The other two maps contain much more detail. The first was included with the Board of Trade's representation to the Crown on the subject of the proposed cession of Indian land beyond the

92. C. O. Maps 700 Georgia/14, P.R.O. Cumming, *The Southeast In Early Maps,* p. 240, describes this original Savery map as well as the copy which is located in the Clements Library. (See Brun, *Guide to Manuscript Maps,* p. 154.) He does not, however, mention another valuable copy of this map which was prepared by Bernard Romans. This Romans map is filed as M.P.G. 337, P.R.O., and bears the inscription: "A true copy taken from the original done by Samuel Savery Dept. Survr. for Lands in Georgia certified 31st March 1769. Pr. Bernard Romans Dep. to Survr. General for the Southern District of America.

93. M.R. 18, P.R.O. Cumming, *The Southeast In Early Maps,* p. 251, references this map as "Colonial Office Library. Vol. 73, pp. 321-322." A new system of map cataloguing is being adopted by the Public Record Office which makes the reference M.R. 18 preferable for this map.

1768 boundary.[94] It is a very attractive colored manuscript map showing all of Georgia, from the coastal islands inland to the proposed cession area, on a scale of approximately ten miles to the inch. The second map is very similar to the first, except that the coast line and islands are not included.[95] This omission seems to indicate that the map was intended primarily to illustrate the interior regions which were being discussed relative to the proposed Indian land cession. The three maps together provide an excellent background for an understanding of the negotiations which resulted in the New Purchase and subsequent change in the Georgia section of the Southern Indian Boundary Line during 1773.

The New Purchase and its boundaries are shown on two extremely valuable but little-known manuscript maps.[96] The first of these maps was prepared by Philip Yonge from the survey of the northern or Broad River portion of the New Purchase.[97] Figure 22 has been based on the original manuscript map and gives some indication of the high quality of both the survey and cartography. Any one attempting to reconstruct the frontier landscape of Georgia on the eve of the American Revolution would find Yonge's map an extremely lucid and valuable source. The second map was prepared by Andrew Way from the survey of the southern portion of the New Purchase which lay between the Ogeechee and Altamaha rivers. Figure 23 is based on Way's original map. It can be seen that this map, while informative, is far below the standard of Yonge's. It does, however, represent a valuable source of information which would be of value in a study of the historical geography of this portion of central Georgia.

94. M.P.G. 20, P.R.O. (Removed from C. O. 5-661, p. 437.)

95. British Museum, Additional MSS. 14, 036 f. Cumming, *The Southeast In Early Maps,* p. 230, describes this map and attributes it to De Brahm. He incorrectly assumes that this map showing the intended Cherokee cession pre-dates the Yonge-De Brahm map of 1763. This is not possible, since the British Museum map shows the South Carolina-Cherokee Boundary, which was not demarcated until 1766. It also shows the locations of Wrightsborough and Queensborough townships, which were not established until 1768. The British Museum map is almost certainly a copy made from the Board of Trade Map M.P.G. 20 and should be dated 1771.

96. (1) M.P.G. 2, P.R.O.

(2) Map titled "The Boundary Line Between the Province of Georgia and Nation of Creek Indians from Altamaha to Ogeeche Rivers," bound with C. O. 5-663, p. 113, P.R.O.

Neither of these maps are mentioned by Cumming in his *The Southeast in Early Maps.*

97. This was the survey which William Bartram had taken part in. It was conducted by Edward Barnard, Le Roy Hammond, Philip Yonge, Joseph Purcell, and William Barnard.

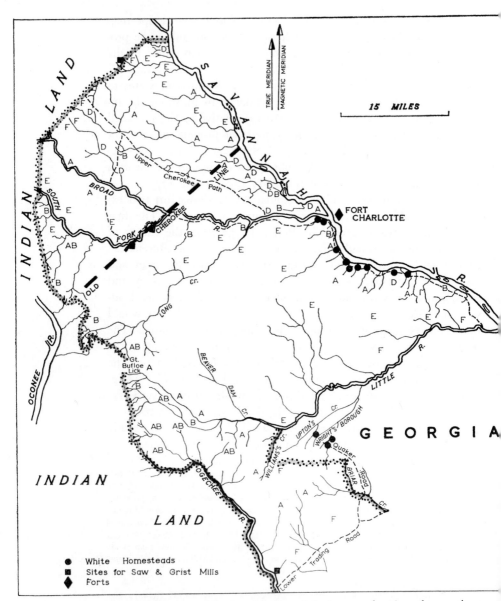

Fig. 22. Tracing of the original map showing the northern portion of the Georgia "New Purchase" of 1773. Letters shown refer to soil quality. (P.R.O., M.P.G. 2.)

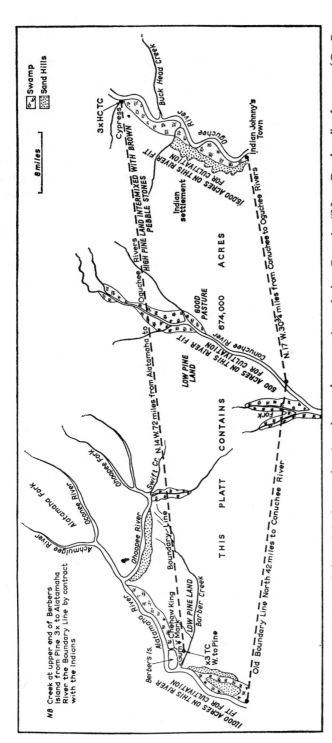

Fig. 23. Tracing of the original map showing the southern portion of the Georgia "New Purchase" of 1773. (C. O. 5-663, p. 113.)

The Georgia-Indian boundary resulted from the New Purchase cession and was correctly shown on the large Stuart-Purcell map of the Southern Indian District, helping to establish the date of this map as post-1773.[98] It is also correctly indicated on the other large wall maps patterned after the Stuart-Purcell, as well as several other late eighteenth-century maps. In conclusion, it can be stated that the Georgia section of the Southern Indian Boundary Line was the subject of several valuable eighteenth-century maps, indispensable in forming an appreciation of both its location and significance.

THE GEORGIA-INDIAN BOUNDARY LINE ON THE PRESENT-DAY MAP

Historians and others have attempted to locate the Georgia section of the Southern Indian Boundary Line on the maps of the current, as well as the past, century. In most cases, these attempts have achieved only partial success at best. In a few the results have been seriously misleading. It seems necessary, for this reason, to point out a few of the errors made in past efforts and then to attempt to translate this significant element of eighteenth-century political geography to a present-day base map.

At the end of the nineteenth century, Charles C. Royce prepared a map of Georgia to show the land cessions which had been made to the United States by the Indians in that state.[99] Unfortunately, Royce was not primarily concerned with the prefederal period of Georgia's growth and so did not present any account or indication of the evolution of the Indian boundary lines during the period which is the major concern of this study. He does, however, indicate the Georgia-Indian boundary line at the close of the colonial period. This boundary corresponds closely to the Georgia section of the Southern Indian Boundary Line shown in Figure 29. The small scale (1 inch: 35 miles) of Royce's map makes detailed comparison and criticism difficult. Perhaps the feature most worthy of comment is the location of the boundary line along the Altamaha River by Royce. The boundary was shifted upstream from Doctor's Town, above Fort Barrington, to the mouth of Beards Creek by the New Purchase of 1773. This was a distance of about twelve miles. Royce seems to have considerably exaggerated this distance on his map and as a result has incorrectly located the sec-

98. C. O. Maps 700 North America General/12. This map is discussed in detail in the concluding chapter.
99. Charles C. Royce, *Indian Land Cessions In the United States*, Plate CXXII.

tion of the boundary which extends from the Ogeechee to the Altamaha River. It has a distinctly northeast-southwest trend on Royce's map, clearly in contradiction with the original map of this boundary, which shows a slight northwest-southeast trend (see Fig. 23).

Farrand showed the Georgia section of the Southern Indian Boundary Line in only the most general way on an extremely small-scale map.[100] Despite the small scale of Farrand's map, it is clear that he did not include the New Purchase boundary of 1773 and showed only an approximation of the 1768 line.

Alden included a map titled "Indian Boundaries of Georgia and East Florida Before 1775" in his extremely valuable study of the southern colonial frontier.[101] Alden's map omits the southern portion of the New Purchase, which reached from the Ogeechee to the Altamaha River, seriously detracting from its value. He does, however, call attention to the islands of Ossabaw, St. Catherine's, and Sapelo, ceded in 1757. This map, too, is very small scale and would be of little aid in any effort to fix the location of the boundary line, except in the most general terms.

Two more recently prepared maps are Fleming's "Georgia- Showing Indian Cession of 1773" and Coleman's "Georgia Indian Cession," which accompany books written by these authorities.[102] On both maps the bounds of Georgia in 1733 are distinctly shown and enclosed by regular and unbroken lines. This is hardly in accordance with the facts of Oglethorpe's early agreements with the Indians and is misleading, to say the least. Neither map indicates the island cession of 1757. Both Fleming and Coleman attempt to show the cessions which were made in 1763 and 1773, but the outlines and areas are only approximate. It should be said, in conclusion, that these maps show that Georgia grew in area through the addition of Indian land cessions during the colonial period. The chronology and chorology of these additions are far from accurate and the maps are of very little real value.

Figures 19 and 21 have been prepared to locate the two de- marcated Georgia-Indian boundary lines on the present-day map of the state. They are composites drawn from the variety of sources,

---

100. Max Farrand, "The Indian Boundary Line," *The American Historical Review*, X (July, 1905), 784.

101. Alden, *John Stuart*, p. 178.

102. Berry Fleming, *Autobiography of a Colony* (Athens, Ga., 1957), p. 111. Kenneth Coleman, *The American Revolution In Georgia, 1763-1789* (Athens, Ga., 1958).

cartographic and documentary, discussed in earlier sections of this chapter. To anyone who has never made the attempt, the translation of data from eighteenth century maps to those of the present day seems a simple and uncomplicated task. Only after making such an attempt and experiencing the frustrations created by inconstant scale, inaccurate azimuth, and contradictory toponymy, would he perhaps concede that he shared an experience not greatly unlike that of Tantalus. The translation is, in general, easiest in areas where such prominent features of the landscape as streams and rivers were noted by the eighteenth-century surveyor, since in broad outline, these features have not greatly altered. Nearly flat marshy areas, where the drainage pattern was almost indistinguishable to the mounted surveyor, impose the greatest difficulties in translation. For this reason, the Indian boundary line has been shown as a broken line on panels B, C, and G of Figures 19 and 21. The captions which relate to the condition and quality of the land contiguous to the boundary lines have been extracted from the original manuscript maps used as sources.

In many respects, the evolution of the Southern Indian Boundary Line in Georgia was the result of the interplay of a more extensive and complex set of factors than found in any of the other southern colonies. For this reason, this chapter is concluded with two lists of events significant in the evolution of the two boundary lines that were demarcated, i.e., 1768 and 1773. These lists of events are keyed to the maps of the boundary lines, Figures 19 and 21, in an attempt to show how the evolution of the elements of chronology and chorology are inextricably interwoven. The reader should locate the number of the listed event on the appropriate map, thereby placing the event or incident in its chronological and chorological framework simultaneously.

VIII · *The East Florida-Creek*
Boundary Line

The British colonies of East and West Florida came into being as a result of the Proclamation of October 7, 1763. They were created to provide governments for the Spanish and French territories of the Florida peninsula and Gulf Coast, added to the American mainland empire of Britain by the terms of the Peace of Paris, which was negotiated earlier in the same year. An emphasis on the "original thirteen" American colonies, which broke away from the empire in 1775, has often led to a lack of appreciation of the significance of the two Floridas to the imperial schemes of Britain in America during the latter eighteenth century.[1] In the case of the evolution of the Southern Indian Boundary Line, however, these colonies played vital roles and carried on extensive programs assisting in its establishment between their white pioneer citizens and neighboring Indian tribes.

Spain, it will be recalled, had belatedly joined France in the war against the British and so was a signatory to the Peace of Paris. Spanish Florida, as well as the French posts and settlements along the Gulf of Mexico, was included in the immense area which the victorious British acquired on the North American continent in 1763. New Orleans, with the other settlements along the eastern bank of the Mississippi River south of the Iberville River, was retained by France and secretly ceded to Spain. Thus, in effect, Britain had title to the whole of the American Southeast from Georgia westward to the Mississippi River after 1763. Along the lower Mississippi, the Spanish controlled the area south of a line following the course of the Iberville River and lakes Maurepas

1. Two excellent monographs have helped to overcome this problem to some extent. They are: Charles L. Mowat, *East Florida As A British Province, 1763-1784* (Berkeley and Los Angeles, 1943), and Cecil B. Johnson, *British West Florida, 1763-1783* (New Haven, Conn., 1943).

and Pontchartrain to the Gulf of Mexico, as well as the remainder of Louisiana west of the Mississippi River.

In large measure, the newly acquired possessions were terrae incognitae to the British. This can be clearly seen in two of the contemporary maps which were prepared to illustrate these new subtropical additions to George III's empire. Perhaps the most striking feature of these maps, which appear here as Figure 3 and Figure 24, is the fragmentation of the Florida peninsula, which is depicted as an archipelago. The eighteenth-century London cartographers were not alone in their ignorance of the true outline and geography of Florida. The Board of Trade itself admitted to a profound ignorance "with regard to the coast, harbours and rivers of Florida, or as to the variety of produce which there is the greatest possibility may be raised in that extended country."[2] To insure the rapid collection of information pertaining to these new territories, the board suggested to the king that an accurate survey be undertaken as soon as some form of government for them be decided upon. The prodigious number of maps and many descriptive accounts which enrich British and American archives in large measure resulted from these surveys which were authorized, financed, and supported by the British during their tenure of two decades in this part of North America.

Included in the Board of Trade's representation to the king dealing with the future disposition of the new territories was the suggestion that two separate provinces, named East Florida and West Florida, be created to provide for the administration of the vast area involved. East Florida would be governed from St. Augustine and would include all of peninsula Florida south of Georgia and west as far as the Flint-Apalachicola River system. West Florida would embrace the Gulf Coast from the west of the Apalachicola River to the boundary with Spanish Louisiana and would be governed from Pensacola. Significantly, the Board of Trade stipulated that West Florida was to "comprehend all the sea coast of the Gulph of Mexico, extending west from the Catahowche [Chattahoochee] River or Flint River towards the Mississippi . . . and stretching up into the land as far as the 31st degree of north latitude."[3] The reason for this limitation to a coastal strip hardly reaching inland to the head of Mobile Bay was explained by the board, who observed that this was "as far north as

2. C. O. 5-65, p. 73.
3. *Ibid.* p. 64.

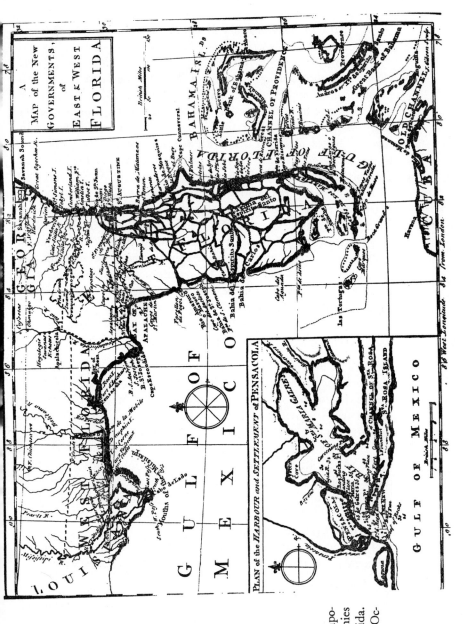

Fig. 24. Contemporary map showing the colonies of East and West Florida. (*Gentleman's Magazine*, October, 1763.)

the settlements can be carried without interfering with lands claimed or occupied by the Indians."[4] Later consideration of this point made it apparent that a viable colony would need a larger area within which to function. A supplementary commission to the first governor of West Florida established a line drawn from the confluence of the Yazoo with the Mississippi River due east to the Chattahoochee River, as shown on the inset to Figure 27, as the northern boundary of West Florida.

East Florida's boundaries were also adjusted so that the St. Marys River rather than the St. Johns would separate the colony from its neighbor, Georgia. Originally, the Board of Trade had suggested the St. Johns, but the newly appointed governor, James Grant, successfully argued against this provision to so limit his "infant colony" on the north. The outlines of East Florida, as it was finally established, can be studied on the contemporary map, Figure 24, and the present-day map, Figure 25.[5]

PRELIMINARIES TO AN EAST FLORIDA-CREEK BOUNDARY

The first mention of an Indian boundary line for the Floridas, like that of several of the other southern colonies, is found in the official journal of the congress held between the colonies and Indian tribes at Augusta, Georgia, in November, 1763.[6] In a talk delivered by a Creek chief named Telletcher is found the following reference to East Florida: "The white people may settle the inside of the River St. Johns to Augustine. St. Johns (a marsh) the Spaniards only possessed, the English must not exceed the same bounds, as from thence is their hunting grounds; he has described the bounds of the lands to the white people, and hopes they will make no encroachments upon them."[7]

In the absence of official representatives from the newly created colonies, the British reply to the Indians on this point stated:

4. *Ibid.*, p. 73.
5. C. O. 5-548, p. 19. In his memorial on the subject of his new colony's boundaries, Governor James Grant gave the following as reasons why the St. Marys and not the St. Johns should form the boundary between Georgia and East Florida: (1) In order to retain for the colony its most valuable area, i.e., that located north of the St. Johns mouth. (2) That the St. Marys River would provide a "natural" boundary much to be desired "in a flat country covered with swamps & full of woods."
6. *Journal of the Congress of the Four Southern Governors, and the Superintendent of that District, with the Five Nations of Indians, At Augusta, 1763* (Charles Town, 1764).
7. *Ibid.*, p. 27.

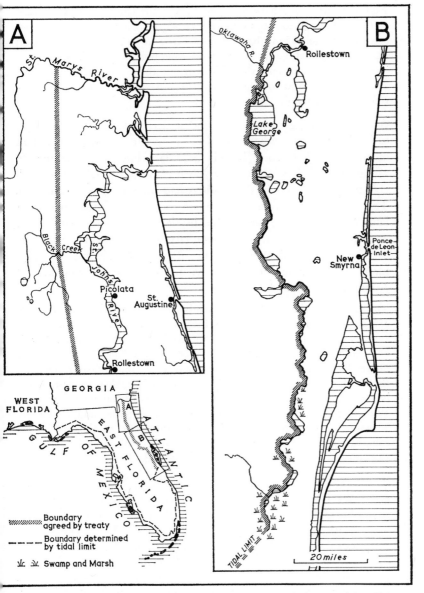

Fig. 25. The East Florida-Creek section of the Southern Indian Boundary Line.

And as to what you have mentioned about the lands to the southward of Georgia, near St. Augustine, Pensacola and Mobile; these are matters that the great king has not impowered us to talk with you about; he has appointed governors to those countries, who will soon come over and be there; and we shall acquaint them with what you have said, and leave you to talk with them and settle that matter, for we cannot do anything in it.[8]

Although this reply seems clear and understandable, there is reason to believe that the Indians failed to appreciate it as a postponment of the discussions on a Florida boundary line. They seemed to assume that their stipulations regarding the territorial limits available to white settlers in the Floridas had been accepted at Augusta. This assumption may in part explain the Indian attitude two years later when congresses were called by the governors of East Florida and West Florida to negotiate boundary line agreements with them.

The superintendent for Indian affairs shed light on this enigmatic state of affairs in a report written after the Congress held at Augusta. He stated:

The Claims of the Creeks to the lands bordering on the Two Floridas are such as must render these Provinces extremely limited, if the Indians cannot be prevailed upon to recede from them. They prevent any settlement being made to the Westward of Saint Johns River or above Fort Picoletta And to the Southward, the Marsh formed by the heads of Mosquito inlet & Saint Johns River, they propose as the boundary. This I understood from them while distributing the presents, altho it be not clearly expressed in the Treaty; the fault of the Interpreters. They do not permit our settling any of the new ceded countries joining their lands above the flowing of the tide, which in the countries to the westward of Cape Florida is not far.[9]

The superintendent continued by stressing: "the necessity of satisfying the Creeks in this matter, before any attempt be made to settle that country beyond the prescribed limits to preserve them in amity with us & confirm them in the Belief of our late solemn Professions which otherwise must be obliterated and their prejudices and jealousies more deeply impressed."[10] If the superintendent's remarks were in need of further emphasis, it was amply provided in his census of the "Gun Men" available to the Creek Nation, which he totalled at 3,588.[11]

8. *Ibid.,* p. 35.
9. C. O. 323-17, p. 234.
10. *Ibid.*
11. *Ibid.,* p. 239.

British military forces took possession of St. Augustine on July 20, 1763, and saw practically all of the Spanish inhabitants of the town and surrounding area depart for Havana or other corners of the empire of Spain.[12] The possession of the province was completed with the occupation of the fort named St. Mark's at Apalache, located some two hundred miles west of St. Augustine at the confluence of the Wakulla and St. Marks rivers, on February 20, 1764. During the period of military occupation preceding the establishment of a civil government in East Florida, a number of events took place which influenced the evolution of the Indian boundary line that came to be established between the colony and its Creek Indian neighbors.

In appreciation of the strength of the Creeks and the other Indian tribes located between Georgia and the Mississippi River, the superintendent of Indian affairs was ordered to resort to the Floridas and take up residence in one of them, "until affairs are settled with the . . . Indians upon a solid foundation."[13] Significantly, the superintendent began his important work in East Florida well in advance of the arrival of the colony's first governor.[14]

On his arrival at St. Augustine, the superintendent met with a group of friendly Creeks led by a chief named Ahoya, or "The Cowkeeper," who had assisted Oglethorpe against the Spanish a quarter of a century before. The Creek leader reaffirmed the allegiance of his band of 130 gun men to the English cause in response to the superintendent's persuasive talks and presents. While experiencing apparent success with Cowkeeper, the British were aware of the potential threat posed by the Creeks living in the interior.

The commander of Fort Apalachie, as the English called the old St. Marks, reported: "there is no place [that] required an interpreter more than this & there is an absolute necessity of making the Indians presents, for they come hungry and ravenous & expect to be supplied now with provisions as they were by the Spaniards. Some of the Indians who lately visited me seem greatly disaffected to the English. . . ."[15] The commander went on to state that he

12. Mowat, *East Florida*, p. 9.
13. C. O. 5-65, p. 85.
14. The first governor was the experienced Indian fighter James Grant, who arrived at his post in St. Augustine on Aug. 29, 1764. He had exhibited considerable skill in negotiating with the Cherokee during South Carolina's war with that tribe a few years before.
15. Mark F. Boyd, "From a Remote Frontier . . . ," *The Florida Historical Quarterly,* XX (July, 1941), 84.

lived in constant fear of an Indian attack and requested an appropriation of funds to allow him to purchase gifts for distribution to the Creeks.

The Indian superintendent proceeded to Apalachie to assist in pacifying the Creeks of the area. In an informative report, he indicated both his *modus operandi* and the principal cause of the Indian disaffection. He stated: "On my arrival I convened the leading men of Five Creek Villages in the neighborhood of this fort . . . during their stay here they drank freely and I endeavored to discover their temper and disposition and I find that their uneasiness and that of their nation proceeds principally from jealousy on account of their land."[16]

At the formal meeting held with the Creeks at Apalachie, the superintendent endeavored to convince the Indians that their fears regarding their lands were groundless. After mentioning the treaty between the English and the Indians which had been signed at Augusta the year before, he stated: "I sent into your nation a copy of the Kings royal instructions to his governors concerning your lands, which you may be assured will be strictly observed, nor shall they any where be settled beyond the limits established at the late Congress without your consent."[17] It will be recalled that the English governors had refused to discuss the Indian suggestions for boundaries with East and West Florida at Augusta. The superintendent would seem, however, to have implied an acceptance of the Indian claims in the direction of these two colonies in his remarks made at Apalachie. He may have felt that this course was necessary and expedient at the time in order to placate the powerful and truculent Creeks.

The Creek spokesman at Apalachie replied to the superintendent's assertion by stating, "The Spaniards are gone and you are now on the ground which we lent them, we approve of it, and shall always hold you fast as brothers."[18] This statement probably referred to only the fort and surrounding areas which had been cultivated by the Spanish.

Indian relations were temporarily improved as a result of the superintendent's activities at Apalachie but hardly settled on a course which could have been expected to endure in peace. The Creeks plainly stated that the Spanish had not owned the land

16. *Ibid.* (Oct., 1941), p. 204.
17. C. O. 5-66, p. 3.
18. Boyd, "From A Remote Frontier," p. 207.

but only occupied it on loan from the tribe. They further implied that the English were now welcome as replacement tenants on the same land vacated by the Spaniards.[19] This was hardly a condition which could have been expected to encourage the settlement of white planters, who, above most considerations, insisted upon clear terms of title and tenure to their land.

The relatively peaceful conditions which existed following the congress at Apalachie may well have resulted from schisms within the Creek federation rather than a diplomatic victory by Superintendent of Indian Affairs John Stuart. The commander of Fort Apalachie undertook the rebuilding and strengthening of his fortress after the superintendent left the area and observed in a report: "as I long ago perceived . . . the Creeks are grown extremely jealous of our proceedings, but cannot as yet bring the nation to be unanimous in breaking with us."[20]

Before leaving East Florida, the superintendent forwarded a large amount of valuable information on Indian affairs to the new governor of East Florida. In Stuart's words, this information was to assist the governor in "whatever he may have to transact with the Creeks . . . amongst which a very material, but I suspect a difficult & delicate point will be the settlement of a Boundary Line to their mutual satisfaction which I sincerely wish may be happily effected."[21]

Upon his arrival at St. Augustine, Governor Grant was immediately concerned by the obvious weakness of his "infant colony" in the face of its powerful Creek neighbors. Shortly after his arrival, he reported finding only 197 men fit to stand duty at St. Augustine and the outposts. Such a small force, he pointed out, was insufficient "to keep our neighbors the Creek Indians, consisting of near four thousand men, in order."[22] The governor stressed the point that, while momentarily at peace, the Indians could not be depended upon to remain so in the absence of English military strength. He concluded by observing that the small garrison then available was "barely sufficient to keep possession of

19. Verne E. Chatelain, in his *The Defenses of Spanish Florida 1565 to 1763* (Carnegie Institution of Washington, Publication 511 [Washington, 1941]), p. 21, suggests that a major element of Spanish policy in Florida was a deliberate restriction against private acquisition of Indian land. The Indian attitude toward the Spanish as "tennants" is understandable when viewed in this light.

20. Boyd, "From A Remote Frontier," p. 295.

21. *Ibid.*, p. 204.

22. C. O. 5-548, p. 30.

[St. Augustine] if the Indians were to differ . . . which of all things I shall endeavor to avoid."[23]

Governor Grant, while advocating the need for military strength in Indian relations, agreed with the Indian superintendent on the importance which the Indian attitude toward their land played. With reference to the Creeks he wrote:

Their good behavior will depend in a great measure upon our force, they can be very troublesome without coming to an open rupture, which does not seem to be their intention at present. I have had some of their head men with me for some days, they have been well treated and are in good humor, but I shall find them very tenacious of their land when they come together at a general meeting which I expect to have here next Spring.[24]

When a crisis between the Creeks and West Florida threatened to precipitate a general war in 1766, Grant wrote: "If there was the least appearance of an Indian War no new settler would desire to attempt fixing their habitations in either of the Floridas, and those which have already formed settlements would immediately abandon them, for the two infant colonys are more exposed than Georgia, they can give no assistance and will want much protection. . . ."[25]

The establishment of a boundary line with the Creeks which would clearly define those areas of the colony where new settlers could fix themselves without controversy was a matter of the highest priority during the early period of East Florida's first civil government. In 1764, settlement seemed free to proceed only in the limited areas immediately surrounding St. Augustine and Apalachie. This situation was in need of remedy if the "infant colony" was ever to grow and prosper.

THE DELINEATION OF THE EAST FLORIDA-CREEK BOUNDARY LINE

Governor Grant requested the superintendent of Indian affairs to call a congress with the Creeks so that he could secure their agreement on a boundary line. The sanguine governor was anxious to clear the air of possible misunderstanding regarding land matters so that he could proceed with his elaborate plans to populate and develop his "infant colony." The congress was called and

23. *Ibid.*
24. *Ibid.,* p. 35.
25. *Ibid.* p. 114.

convened on November 15, 1765, at Fort Picolata, a small post located at a crossing of the St. Johns River west of St. Augustine. The Pennsylvania naturalists John and William Bartram were visiting East Florida and attended the congress at Fort Picolata. The account of the congress written by John Bartram is probably the most colorful and informative description available of any of the Indian congresses held in the Southeast before the Revolutionary War.[26]

In his opening address to the assembled Indians, the governor quickly came to the main cause of discord—the Indian fears concerning their hunting grounds in East Florida. He stated: "You are apprehensive as I have been told that the white people are desirous of getting possession of your hunting grounds. Your fears are very ill founded, for I am ordered by the Great King not to take any lands which are of use to you even if you should agree to give them up. You may judge from that how careful your Father the great king is of your interest and welfare."[27] In an effort to add substance to his remarks, the governor reminded the Creeks of his magnanimous attitude toward the Cherokee, whom he had defeated in war a few years earlier. He continued by emphasizing the degree of interdependence which existed between the Indians and their English neighbors. On this point he stated: "Your profession is hunting, you therefore must have a large tract of country, but it is [in] your interest to have your brothers the English near you, as they only can supply you, in exchange for your skins, with clothes to cover you, your wives & children, with guns, powder & ball for your hunting & a number of other things which you cannot make for yourselves tho' you cannot exist without them."[28]

Although Governor Grant's address was considered "very ingenous" by Bartram, he did not persuade the Creeks to relinquish any of their hunting grounds in the East Florida area. Their tenacity in resisting the governor probably resulted from their experiences with Georgia, where white settlers at that time were steadily encroaching their hunting grounds along the Savannah and Ogeechee rivers. Another important factor which lent added importance to the East Florida hunting grounds was the growing

26. John Bartram, "Diary of a Journey Through the Carolinas, Georgia and Florida from July 1, 1765, to April 10, 1766," ed. Francis Harper, *Transactions of the American Philosophical Society*, n.s. XXXIII, Pt. I (Dec. 1942).
27. C. O. 5-548, p. 66.
28. *Ibid.*

conflict with the Choctaw. This tribe was located to the west of the Creeks, which meant that the Creek hunting grounds toward East Florida were the only areas reasonably free from the danger of Choctaw marauders.

Governor Grant was followed by the Creek chief named Sempoyasse, who said that he was "not the mouth of the nation" and so was not delivering the official Creek reply, which would come on the next day. Sempoyasse did, however, deliver an important speech which could not have been without the endorsement of an important faction of the Creek camp. He began with a complaint of encroachments being made by "Virginians" who were settling on the Indian side of the boundary line in Georgia. Continuing, the Creek stated that game was becoming very scarce and that the rising prices being charged by the traders were creating serious problems for the tribe. In concluding his philippic, Sempoyasse struck a note which doubtlessly caused considerable consternation in the councils of East Florida—the determination not to surrender any land.[29]

The official Creek reply to Governor Grant's address was delivered on the following day by Tallechea, described as "The Head Beloved Man of the Nation," who stated:

I hope the governor and Beloved Man [Stuart] will agree to the limits which were proposed by us at Augusta and that a line from Sta. Sevilla [on the Altamaha River] to Picolata and along the road to St. Augustine will henceforward be the boundary & that you will not allow the white people to settle beyond the road leading from this place to our nation. We have people who will take notice & observe what lands are now settled which we hope will not be beyond the line now mentioned. There is no occasion for a fort on the other side of the river [St. Johns], let the path remain open that our people may go & see the governor when they chuse. You will consider that the presents which are now to be given us may last for a year but will afterwards rot and become of no value but the land which we now give you will last forever.[30]

According to the clerk who transcribed these proceedings, both the governor and superintendent were visibly displeased by the Creek adherence to the bounds first suggested at Augusta. The

29. *Ibid.*, p. 68.
30. *Ibid.* "Tallechea" is probably a variant spelling of the name "Telletsher." Telletsher was one of the Creek spokesmen at Augusta who played a key role in the negotiations for a Georgia-Creek boundary.

anonymous scribe observed that Tallechea "show'd great uneasyness upon seeing very plainly that they were not pleased."[31]

Following this disturbing address by Tallechea came another by the Creek chief called Captain Aleck. His speech seemed to modify certain details of the boundary proposed by his fellow but clearly restricted the whites of East Florida to a narrow coastal belt. He stated:

they [the Creeks] now give from Sta. Sevilla [on the Altamaha] to the Creek above Picolata on the West side of St. Johns River which is more than they agreed to give at Augusta, that he has given to the governor as far as the flowing of the tide and to Picolata, but he only means the Salts & the White People must not settle on the fresh waters, & that the People may be kept within bounds cattle cannot, but the owners must endeavour however to keep them within bounds & the White People are not to settle beyond the road leading from Picolata to their nation.[32]

While difficult to fix with precision, the limits which the Creeks were proposing at Picolata were considerably more generous than the limits described at Augusta two years before. At that time, they had restricted the English to the peninsula of land enclosed by the lower St. Johns River and the Atlantic Ocean as far south as the road between St. Augustine and Fort Picolata. Significantly, however, the Creeks were clinging to their original principle of restricting the English settlements to coastal areas reached by the tide. This was the same principle they had applied in their negotiations with Oglethorpe three decades earlier, when the first Georgia settlements were being established. Tallechea's remarks indicated that the Creeks were proposing to cede to East Florida the area between the St. Marys River and the St. Johns River, inland to a line to be drawn from the St. Marys River, at the head of the tidal reach, to Black Creek on the St. Johns River, in addition to the peninsula described at Augusta. This was a considerable increase in territory and probably amounted to a doubling of the area being ceded to East Florida by the Indians.

This proposal was, however, unacceptable to the governor of the new colony. The formal session of the congress was concluded and the negotiations were continued in a private conference between the governor and superintendent and Tallechea and Cap-

31. *Ibid.*, p. 69.
32. It will be recalled that Captain Aleck too was a central figure in Georgia-Creek boundary negotiations.

tain Aleck. In private, the governor told the Indian leaders that the
cession the Creeks were proposing was unsatisfactory because it
was land fit only for hunters and what he wanted was land for
planters. He went on to state that he had understood from the
Indian's statements made at Augusta, that all of the land to the
east of the St. Johns would be English. The governor concluded
his argument for an enlarged cession by pointing out that the large
and attractive store of presents which he held would only be traded
for land. At the conclusion of the private conference, the Creek
interpreter was directed "to point out to his friends amongst the
Indians the Line which they shou'd offer to draw next day at the
Congress."[33]

On the following day, the Creeks bent to the desire of the
governor of East Florida and ceded an area the executive later
described as, "a sufficient Tract of Country for the White People
to settle upon & would not hurt the Red People."[34] In the treaty
signed at Fort Picolata on November 18, 1765, the East Florida-
Creek section of the southern Indian Boundary Line was delineated
as follows:

To prevent all disputes on account of incroachments or supposed
incroachments made by the English Inhabitants of this his Majestys
said province on the lands or hunting grounds reserved and claimed
by the Upper and Lower Nations of Creek Indians and that no
doubts, mistakes or disputes may for the future arise, in consideration
of the great marks of friendship, benevolence, clemency, generosity &
protection, extended to us . . . by his Majesty King George the Third—
we the chiefs, head warriors & leaders of our respective nations by
virtue & in pursuance of the full right and power which we now have
and are possessed of have agreed . . . that for the future the Boundary
Line of his Majestys said province of East Florida shall be all the sea
coast as far as the tide flows in the manner settled with the English
by the great Tomachiche. With all the country to the eastward of St.
Johns River forming nearly an island from the source to its entrance
into the sea. And to the westward of St. Johns River by a line drawn
from the Creek Achlawaugh into said river above the great lake &
near to Spaldings upper trading store house, to the forks of Black
Creek at Collvills plantation, and from thence to that part of St. Mary's
River which shall be intersected by the continuation of the line to the
entrance of Turkey Creek into the River Altamaha. That no notice
is to be taken of such horses or cattle as shall pass the line.[35]

33. *Ibid.*, p. 71.
34. *Ibid.*, p. 72.
35. *Ibid.*, p. 76. The "great Tomachiche" mentioned was, of course, Tomochichi,

Commenting on the cession described in this treaty article, John Bartram remarked that it "was a fine concession . . . as much or more than ye governor expected."[36] The governor himself described the cession, stating that it "contains many navigable creeks and rivers [and] is advantageously situated for cultivation, and, tho the limits are extensive, the Indians will feel no inconvenience from settlements made within the boundary line, tho tis hoped those settlements will soon increase as many planters waited with impatience for the conclusion of the treaty, which is more advantageous than any of them expected."[37] To appreciate this cession, which formed the areal framework within which the "infant colony" was to burgeon, it is necessary to reconstruct its limits on the contemporary and present-day maps of the area.

Although the British Crown frequently ordered the careful survey and demarcation of the Southern Indian Boundary Line, the East Florida-Creek section of that boundary was never demarcated. In a report forwarded to London during the summer of 1768, the superintendent of Indian affairs explained that the lack of an East Florida demarcation resulted from Governor Grant's wishes. Grant now felt that the territory ceded by the Creeks to his colony in 1765 at Fort Picolata was "too narrow." Stuart reported that the governor was hoping to gain an extension from the Creeks at a later date. He explained the reluctance of the Indians to surrender further territory in East Florida "The Creeks are unwilling to make large concessions on that side [because] they consider East Florida and the country between Augustine and the nation as their most valuable hunting grounds being remote from any enemy and well stocked with game."[38] This was understandable in view of the Choctaw War which was engaging the Creeks to the west and making their hunting grounds in that direction extremely dangerous battle grounds.

During the following year the superintendent again reported that the East Florida governor desired a postponement of a boundary survey until a more favorable period, when he might persuade the Creeks to part with a larger cession. The superintendent noted: "The acquisition he [Gov. Grant] points at, is that part of

who had made the first land cession to Oglethorpe in 1733. The persistence of a tidal limit boundary in the Creek's negotiations is notable.

36. John Bartram, "Diary of A Journey . . . ," p. 51.
37. C. O. 5-548, p. 59.
38. C. O. 5-69, p. 216.

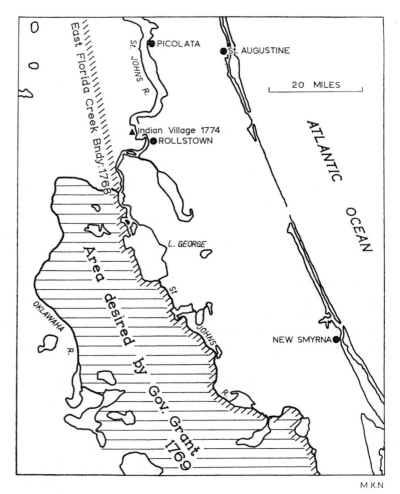

Fig. 26. Map showing the area to the west of the 1768 boundary line which East Florida was trying to gain from the Creeks.

the country situated between the Rivers Saint John's & Acklawaugh which run parallel and form a peninsula; by which the Acklawaugh will form a natural boundary to westward."[39] This area has been shown on Figure 26, which helps give some idea of the area into which East Florida was attempting to expand.

The governor had called a second congress with the Creeks at Fort Picolata on November 21, 1767, but it was attended by only a

39. C. O. 5-70, p. 210.

relatively small number of Indians. Most of the tribe were alarmed by an incident which had taken place between a band of Creeks and pioneers along the Saint Marys River shortly before. During the congress Governor Grant stated:

You gave the land your White Brothers Wanted and as you were convinced that I did not wish to encroach upon your hunting Grounds, your then speakers Tallichea and Captain Aleck left the Boundary Line to my determination; Your White Brothers have begun to cultivate some part of that Land, which was then given up to the Great King, but you will be made Welcome to Hunt upon that ground whenever you chuse to come into the settlements & you shall always be received as Brothers should be.[40]

It is significant that in East Florida the boundary line did not exclude the Indians from the white areas of control, as it did in the older colonies farther north. The small number of Creeks in attendance at this second congress held at Fort Picolata probably discouraged Governor Grant from pressing for a boundary extension and there was no increase to the colony's areal base as an outcome of it.

The East Florida-Creek boundary line was discussed and ratified at the congress held with the whole Creek confederation at Augusta, Georgia, in 1768. Significantly, the treaty article describing the East Florida section of the Southern Indian Boundary Line left blanks where the directions and distances of the various legs of the boundary were to be inserted when it was finally surveyed and demarcated. The verbal description included in the Augusta treaty repeated the Fort Picolata agreement of 1765 without change.

Governor Grant's desire to delay demarcation until a propitious moment, when he might persuade the Creeks to relinquish an even larger tract of territory for his colony, was the major reason why the East Florida-Creek boundary was never demarcated. Another reason that should not be forgotten is that the population of East Florida was never very great. In fact, the total population was extremely small throughout almost all of the period of British control.

In the month of June, 1765, the provincial register reported that there were, as yet, no grants of land registered, but "there are a few made out for lands at a little distance from [St. Augustine]

40. C. O. 5-549, p. 13.

and the River St. Johns."[41] This was before the congress held at Fort Picolata, which resulted in the delineation of the East Florida-Creek Boundary Line. After the successful completion of that congress, Governor Grant worked vigorously to boost the fortunes and population of his "infant colony." Unfortunately, except for a few instances, such as the arrival of 1,400 Greek, Italian, and Minorcan indentured servants transported by Dr. Turnbull, his efforts were not productive of any outstanding success. De Brahm, in his valuable "Report of the General Survey of North America," dated 1771, accounted for a total population of less than 3,000 including Turnbull's immigrants and all slaves reported.[42] Significantly, De Brahm listed only 288 adult white freemen in the whole of East Florida, indicating that peoples of Mediterranean origin associated with Dr. Turnbull's scheme formed the overwhelming bulk of the "infant colony's" population at that time. Mowat estimated that at the outbreak of the American Revolution, East Florida's total population, excluding the troops garrisoned there, was only about 3,000.[43] In the light of this small population and the fact that the East Florida-Creek boundary line was delineated prior to any significant degree of settlement in the colony, it does not seem remarkable or unusual that this section of the Southern Indian Boundary Line was never demarcated.[44]

THE EAST FLORIDA-CREEK BOUNDARY LINE ON
EIGHTEENTH-CENTURY MAPS

Although there is no record that a map was employed to guide the negotiations which led to the delineation of the East Florida-Creek boundary line at Fort Picolata, it is probable that at least two contemporary maps had an influence on the decision reached. The first of these was titled "A Map of the Southern Indian District 1764."[45]

41. C. O. 5-548, p. 53.
42. British Museum, King's MSS. 210, fol. 120. In this amazing document, all white freemen of East Florida are listed by name and profession.
43. Charles L. Mowat, "St. Augustine Under the British Flag, 1763-1775," *The Florida Historical Quarterly*, XX (Oct., 1941), 133.
44. Most of East Florida's modest population was concentrated in a few relatively large settlements, such as St. Augustine and New Smyrna, so that the pressure for an increase in the colony's territorial base was probably even less than might have been expected from 3,000 widely dispersed planters. Mowat, *East Florida*, includes an excellent discussion of the population and settlement of East Florida in his chapter titled "Peopling the Sandy Desert."
45. British Museum, Additional MSS. 14,036, fol. d. This map is described in Cumming, *The Southeast in Early Maps*, p. 234. Not mentioned by Cumming is the

The 1764 map was employed by the superintendent of Indian affairs to illustrate an important report which he had forwarded to London during the same year. A study of this map and report indicates that they summarized the superintendent's ideas concerning the extent of the Indian hunting grounds, following the important Indian Congress at Augusta in 1763. Figure 1 is a simplified tracing of this map and reveals the extent of Creek claims in the area of East Florida. It can be seen that the superintendent indicated the Creek claim only as far south on the Florida peninsula as the Mosquito Inlet. This is the present-day Ponce de Leon Inlet, which is shown on Figure 25. The hydrography of the St. Johns River is vague and fanciful upstream of the large bulge, which was probably meant to indicate Lake George. The positioning of the name "R. St. Juan" seems to suggest that a west fork of the river was being called the upper St. Johns. This "R. St. Juan" could indicate the present-day Oklawaha River, which drains the numerous lakes of Lake County and flows northward parallel to the St. Johns for many miles. In the light of comments made at Picolata in 1765 and afterward, it seems not at all unlikely that a map patterned after the 1764 product was consulted before or during the congress at Fort Picolata.

The second contemporary map which may have had an influence in shaping the boundary delineated at Fort Picolata was a copy of a Spanish map showing the locations of a number of huge land grants, with the names of the grantees.[46] This map was probably presented to Grant soon after his arrival in St. Augustine and may well have played an important part in helping him gain a concept of what he had inherited from the departed Spanish government. If this was the case, it helps to explain his visible dissatisfaction with the Creek's proposed cession of only the narrow coastal strip from

---

fact that this was the map which Superintendent of Indian Affairs John Stuart forwarded to London on March 9, 1764, to illustrate his "A Report on the Indians of the Southern Department" (C. O. 323-17, p. 459). This map was the original on which the endpaper map used in this volume, "A Map of the Indian Nations in the Southern Department, 1766," was based. Both Cumming and Christian Brun, *Guide to Manuscript Maps*, p. 134, suggest that John Gerar William De Brahm was the author of the 1766 map. Cumming states that De Brahm may have been the author of both maps. In any case, it is certain that Stuart employed the 1764 version to illustrate his report of that year and it seems probable that this map and others based on it were employed by him and others in his department.

46. C. O. 700, Maps, Florida/7. Inscribed: "Drawn from the Original Plan of John Gordon Esq. Given to Governor Grant, James Moncrief, Engineer." Of course, this Spanish map does not prove that they at any time occupied the region shown.

the St. Mary's River to the St. Augustine road. The Spanish map suggested that all of the area, from a point below Ponce de Leon Inlet to the mouth of the St. Johns River and inland to the lakes of central Florida, was under their control. The cession finally won at Picolata exceeded the area shown on the Spanish map, a fact which might explain why Grant and the planters gathered there with him had been so pleased at the outcome.

While speculation in this vein is interesting and somewhat informative when it provides some clue to the frame of reference which may have influenced one group of the participants engaged in the boundary line negotiation at Fort Picolata, it is a route of inquiry fraught with danger and intellectual pitfalls. Far safer ground is to be gained in a consideration of the eighteenth-century maps which were used to depict the East Florida-Creek boundary line following its delineation.

One of the most interesting of the contemporary maps depicting this East Florida section of the Southern Indian Boundary Line on a large scale is "A Survey of the Part of the Eastern Coast of East Florida from St. Mary's Inlet to Mount Halifax . . ." by William Gerard De Brahm, surveyor general of lands for East Florida and surveyor general of the Southern District.[47] On this map is shown the East Florida-Creek boundary line which is indicated as "The Ascertained Boundary Between His Majesty's Province of East Florida & the Creek Indian Nation." There is reason to suspect that the boundary was not surveyed by De Brahm, since it is differentiated from the demarcated and surveyed Georgia-Creek boundary. The Georgia boundary is indicated as "The Actually Surveyed Boundary Between the Province of Georgia."[48] In De Brahm's "Report of the General Survey In the Southern District of North America" he stated that the East Florida-Creek boundary "was to begin at the pine stump upon St. Mary's stream where the Georgia boundary line stops, and continue as far as Oklywahaw [Oklawaha] River."[49] Commenting more fully on this

47. C. O., 700 Maps, Florida/53. Although this map is not signed, it resembles closely C. O., 700 Maps, Florida/3 and appears to be the most northerly sheet of an extremely large map of the colony of East Florida which De Brahm completed and signed, [1775].

48. There is reason to suspect that De Brahm drew Florida/53 from surveys which were made by boat along the St. Johns River and Atlantic Coast. The area inland near the "ascertained" East Florida boundary line lacks topographic detail, while areas near the banks of the St. Johns River and sea coasts show a wealth of such detail.

49. British Museum, King's MSS. 210 and 211. Quoted from King's MSS. 210, p. 179.

section of the East Florida-Creek boundary, De Brahm observed: "What is peculiarly admirable in the capacity of the Indians is their natural knowledge of geometry: For in my future surveys their first line, which they joined to that of Georgia, viz. from the pine tree, to the River Ocklywaha [*sic*] proved to be a parallel with the Atlantic Coast."[50] Whether this feature of the East Florida-Creek boundary was a product of design or chance is difficult to determine, but the boundary is nearly a parallel to the fairly regular coastline of northern Florida as shown on Figure 25.

De Brahm was not on good terms with the East Florida administration and was, in fact, suspended from his colonial post as surveyor from 1770 to 1774. This may account for his error in terminating the East Florida-Creek boundary line at Oklawaha River and showing a due east line to the sea as the southern boundary of East Florida. By his own computations based on this truncated boundary line, De Brahm found the area of the Fort Picolata cession to be 1,899,975 acres, an area "too much for a county and too insignificant for a province."[51] De Brahm was not present at Fort Picolata and obviously not aware of the stipulation which extended the East Florida-Creek boundary south from the Oklawaha River and the upper St. Johns River to its source. This omission, plus the lack of any mention of the tidal limit boundary for the remainder of the province, seriously detracts from the value of De Brahm's otherwise extremely interesting and informative map.

A better-informed source of information about the Southern Indian Boundary Line in East Florida was John Stuart, the superintendent for Indian affairs in the Southern District. For this reason, the maps prepared by this division of the colonial administration, rather than those of the surveyor general's office, represent the best eighteenth-century sources for the reconstruction of the East Florida-Creek boundary. Suart was responsible for several manuscript maps illustrating this section of the Southern Indian Boundary Line that were invaluable in the preparation of Figure 25, which depicts it on a present-day map base.[52]

50. *Ibid.,* p. 67.
51. *Ibid.*
52. The maps are: C. O. 700, Maps, North America General/12; M.R. 919, P.R.O.; C. O. 700, Maps, North America General/15; "A Map of the Southern Indian District of North America," 1775, Newberry Library, Chicago, Ill., Edward E. Ayer Collection; Manuscript copy of C. O. 700; Maps, N.A.G./15, in National Archives, Washington, D.C.; Map No. U.S. 113, Record Group 77, Records of the Office of the Chief of Engineers.

While the Stuart maps of the East Florida-Creek boundary line indicate, with captions, that the boundary from the head of the St. Johns River and around the peninsula was determined by "the flowing of the Tide," they in no way indicate a precise location of this tidal boundary. In fact, the physical location of this section of the Southern Indian Boundary Line was not accurately determined and illustrated on a map until 1963.

THE EAST FLORIDA-CREEK BOUNDARY LINE ON THE

PRESENT-DAY MAP

In connection with a petition filed by the Seminole Indians in 1950, alleging that they held title to all lands in the present state of Florida (excepting three designated tracts), the United States Department of Justice requested William P. Cumming to make a detailed study of the Southern Indian Boundary Line in Florida.[53] Cumming conducted a thorough study of documents and maps in archives of England and Spain and, "based upon his study of all available maps, records and reports, he determined the physical location of the Indian boundary line around the Florida peninsula."[54] In connection with his work, Cumming prepared a map of the Florida Indian Boundary Line which was presented before the Indian Claims Commission as Defendant's Exhibit 128.[55]

Cumming's map showed the section of the East Florida-Creek boundary line to the source of the St. Johns River as it had been delineated at the Fort Picolata congress in 1765. This section is identified in the terms of the treaty by recognizable geographic features and so presents no great problem of reconstruction. The remainder of the boundary line is, however, far more difficult to reconstruct since it was delineated only with the phrase, "all the sea coast as far as the tide flows in the manner settled with the

53. *Before the Indian Claims Commission, Docket No. 73, The Seminole Indians of the State of Florida, Petitioner, v. United States of America, Defendant . . . Defendant's Requested Findings of Fact, Objections to Petitioners Proposed Findings, and Brief* (Washington, 1963), p. 69.

54. *Ibid.*

55. The author is indebted to Professor Cumming for providing original notes and other materials connected with his work and to Ramsey Clark, Assistant Attorney General, Lands Division, and Ralph A. Barney, Chief, Indian Claims Section, of the U. S. Department of Justice, who allowed him to duplicate the only copy of Defendant's Exhibit 128 for use in this study. To assist in this duplication they generously provided a copy of U. S. Department of the Interior Geological Survey Map, *State of Florida,* 1:500,000, which was the base for Cumming's exhibit.

English by the great Tomachiche."[56] This section of the Florida Indian boundary can be referred to as the tidal limit boundary, since it defined a ribbon of territory around the coast of Florida reaching inland as far as the tidal influence was discernible on the rivers and streams. Such a limitation to settlement had earlier been imposed on the whites of Oglethorpe's Georgia by the Creeks during Tomachiche's time. Little if any effort was made to demarcate this tidal limit boundary during the British Period in Florida so that it shows only as an inscribed caption on the Stuart maps mentioned above.

When Cumming began to prepare his own map after studying the contemporary cartographic and documentary sources, he quickly recognized the impossibility of fixing this section of the Florida-Creek boundary line with any accuracy from the materials available. The services of a civil engineer were employed to prepare a detailed report and maps showing the mean high tide lines on several Florida rivers.[57] For the section of the East Florida-Creek boundary line which has been referred to above as the tidal limit boundary, Cumming adopted the physical location of these mean tide lines as reference points in the preparation of his own map.[58] Cumming's map showed the tidal limit boundary as it is depicted on the inset of Figure 25, where the boundary is indicated "Boundary determined by tidal limit."

In conclusion, it may be stated that the reconstruction of the East Florida-Creek section of the Southern Indian Boundary Line presented in this chapter owes a great deal to Cumming's efforts on behalf of the U.S. Department of Justice. It might also be stated that these efforts have resulted in a far more accurate reconstruction than would otherwise have been possible. As a consequence, the reader of today may form a more clear impression of the true physical location and significance of this important boundary than could contemporaries active during the period of its evolution.

56. *Supra*, p. 139.
57. William H. Richards, civil engineer.
58. *Before the Indian Claims Commission* . . . , p. 70.

IX · The West Florida-Indian Boundary Line

As in the case of its sister "infant colony," the first discussions of an Indian boundary line for West Florida were broached by Indian delegates to the congress at Augusta in 1763. In introducing this topic, the Indians anticipated the establishment of a British civil government over the Gulf Coast. A Creek spokesman at Augusta stated: "That no settlement should be made by the white people at Pensacola, but within the ebbing and flowing of the tide. Mobile to be settled in the same manner, the tide to determine the line."[1] Since no civil government had, at that date, been established in the area south of Georgia the Indians were told that any discussions on this topic would have to await the arrival of the new governor. As illustrated in the preceding chapter, it would seem probable that the Indians failed to appreciate this postponement and felt that their terms, once stated at Augusta, were binding on the new colonies of East and West Florida.

Not only was there a prelude of misunderstanding on the important topic of a boundary line to confound the problem for the British when they finally occupied the soil of their new colony, there was the additional problem that, in West Florida more than anywhere else in the Southeast, the Indians were in a position of virtually unchallengeable strength. Thomas Pownall had drawn attention to the Indian strength in the vicinity of Mobile in 1755 when he quoted from a French document relating the reasons for the need of such a large garrison there. "It is necessary to fix this number here [at Mobile, i.e., 8 French and 1 Swiss companies] on account of the proximity of Pensacola on one part, & the English on the other, as also to influence the Indians: and as there are at our meeting & treaty held here annually with the Indians

1. *Journal of the Congress* . . . , p. 27.

sometimes two sometimes three thousand Indians present."[2] It can be seen that in addition to their large military establishment, the French also bore the expense of annual Indian congresses where the Choctaw multitudes were feasted and satisfied with presents of trade goods. This was a burden which their English successors were forced to assume, with reluctance, when they finally established their control over the area east of Louisiana.

West Florida occupied a position which brought it closely into contact with both the truculent Creek Confederation and the multitudinous Choctaw "Nation." The superintendent of Indian affairs, John Stuart, reported that the tribes bordering on West Florida were "more numerous than all the tribes to the northward put together."[3] The problem of establishing a boundary line, within which West Florida could develop as a flourishing and populous colony, was clearly bipartite. Congresses and negotiations would have to be held with the two dominant Indian tribes, the Creeks and the Choctaw, if sufficient territory was to be freed of Indian claim to allow West Florida to become a viable colony on the pattern set by those of the Atlantic seaboard.

British military forces assumed control of West Florida from the French at Mobile and Spanish at Pensacola during the late summer and early autumn of 1763 and immediately became involved in the vexing problem of establishing a policy for dealing with the Indians there. Among other things, the new British commander at Mobile ill-advisedly promised the Indians that their new British neighbors intended to continue with the French device of annual conferences and gift distributions.[4] This promise was not in keeping with general British policy and was to engender misunderstanding and cause considerable embarrassment to the civil government in later years.[5] At Pensacola the commander held conferences with the Creek Indians and during September, 1764, reached an agreement with their leader, Wolf King, regarding a land cession. This earliest cession of Indian land to West Florida was described as: "ten miles in depth from Deer

2. Letter from Mr. Vandreuil to the Court, quoted by T. Pownall, C. O. 5-18, p. 305.

3. C. O. 5-582, p. 190.

4. Stuart wrote in 1765 from Mobile: "When the French Governor assembled them [the Choctaw] at this place and paid up presents for Two Years which were due to them, Colonel Robertson, who then commanded in this country, found it necessary for quieting their minds to make some promises which have never till now been complied with." Quoted from C. O. 5-66, p. 32.

5. Alden, *John Stuart*, p. 195.

Point, opposite to the Island of Saint Rose, quite round the Bay of Pensacola, and to extend along the sea coast, to the point of Mobile Bay, from thence up the east side of Mobile Bay, till it comes opposite the town of Mobile [and including] all the settlements formerly possessed by the Yamassas, and eight miles round."[6] Although this cession was confirmed with a large addition at the congress held by the new governor and Indian superintendent at Pensacola during the following spring, it was of doubtful legality since both the British officer and Indian chief concerned probably exceeded their authority in the matter.[7]

Clearly, the military force of occupation had become involved, albeit not happily, in the Indian land problem of West Florida. The situation concerning land was at best muddled and far from satisfactory when the colony's first governor, George Johnstone, arrived at Pensacola on October 21, 1764.[8] From his arrival onward, Indian land and boundary problems were largely the concern of the civil government of the new royal colony of West Florida. In a joint letter the new governor and superintendent of Indian affairs summarized the chaotic state of the problem which faced them early in 1765, as they began their endeavors with the Indian tribes to fix a boundary line in the West Florida frontier. They reported:

The facts were, when we came to the province, our boundary with the Creeks was confined to the little brook which surrounded this town [Pensacola], at a distance of three hundred yards; with a prohibition of any goods being sent into that nation from this province, under the penalty of death. The former inhabitants on the east side of Mobile, had been threatened with destruction, if they did not remove from the land which the Creeks said had only been lent to the French. The boundary with the Chactaws was not at all defined; that nation was in so bad a temper, that the Bloody Hatchet, their symbol of war has even been sent thro' the nation since our arrival; and the Creeks have also committed two several murders, besides killing the cattle of the Inhabitants, in the most insolent and wanton manner.[9]

It can be seen that the pivotal problem was the land and how to gain the permission of the Indians to allow its occupation by George III's white subjects who might be tempted thither.

6. *Ibid.*, quoted from the Gage MSS.
7. C. O. 5-66, p. 361. Alden, *John Stuart*, p. 194.
8. Cecil B. Johnson, *British West Florida, 1763-1783* (New Haven, 1943), p. 24.
9. C. O. 5-582, p. 187.

In West Florida, as in neighboring East Florida, the military force available in the event of a conflict with the Indians was almost non-existent. Stuart and Johnstone wrote that they feared a general Indian uprising in the Southeast and stated: "To such hostile Dispositions we had nothing to oppose, but Embassies, fair Promises, Presents, entering into the Policy of their Nations, creating Jealousies amongst themselves, and using these Engines in the best manner."[10] These Machiavellian stratagems were made necessary by "the debilitated state of our Troops [which] left them incapable of protecting the Country against such powerful Tribes, being hardly sufficient to defend the pitiful Fortresses, if attacked."[11]

There was, of course, no doubt in the Indian superintendent's mind as to the overwhelming significance of the land problem to the successful establishment of a viable British colony in West Florida. In an observation similar to one he made in reference to his negotiations with the Indians upon his first arrival in East Florida he indicated that in West Florida, too, he made an ally of Bacchus to reveal the fundamental motivations of the Indians. He met with a group of Creeks soon after he arrived at Pensacola in October, 1764, and reported: "They staid with me till the 28th and drank freely which gave me an opportunity of discovering their temper and disposition, and every circumstance convinced [me] that all their uneasiness proceeds from jealousy on account of their lands."[12] *In vino veritas* seems an axiom frequently applied in dealings with the aboriginal Americans.

THE DELINEATION OF THE WEST FLORIDA-CHOCTAW
BOUNDARY LINE

Significantly, the first of the great Indian congresses held in West Florida following the establishment of a British government took place in the colony's western center, Mobile. It was felt that a congress with the Choctaw and Chickasaw should be held immediately because of the proximity of these tribes to the French and Spanish, who were strongly suspected of fomenting anti-English feeling among them. The first congress at Mobile was called "Immediately after Governor Johnstone's arrival in this Country, the first necessary step towards the Settlement of it

10. *Ibid.*
11. *Ibid.*
12. C. O. 5-66, p. 3. Stuart arrived at Pensacola on October 4, after visiting St. Augustine and Fort Apalachie in East Florida.

appeared to be gaining the Friendship and Confidence of the Neighbouring Indian Tribes and obtaining from them Grants of Land with Boundaries distinctly ascertained, to avoid all future Contests."[13]

The congress was delayed in convening, first by the Indians who were loathe to shorten their hunting season, and then by the traders who wanted to purchase their stocks of fur and leather before the Indians were showered with presents by the governor and superintendent. Finally, on March 26, 1765, some 2,000 Indians met with Governor Johnstone, Superintendent of Indian Affairs John Stuart, and most of the Europeans of the western parts of West Florida to discuss the establishment of a boundary line and other matters of importance.

Although often referred to as the Choctaw Congress, it was attended by a large delegation of Chickasaw Indians as well. The Chickasaw were primarily interested in trade regulations and played no direct role in the negotiations for a West Florida Indian boundary line. The Chickasaw were, however, very concerned about certain traders to their "Nations" who had been cultivating plantations and grazing stock on their lands. In his opening address the governor reassured the Chickasaw by reading that portion of the Proclamation of 1763 which ordered the removal of settlements made on the Indian lands.[14] He followed this recitation of guarantees to the Indians in regard to their lands by requesting that they, as "a wise and reasonable people," grant to West Florida a cession of land in the king's name.[15] After pointing out how necessary land was to the whites if they were to be in a position to supply the needs of their Indian neighbors, the governor observed:

you all know the Lands on the Sea Coasts are so poor they will produce nothing & you must also be sensible we must have some place to produce Corn & Rice, otherwise we shall hardly be able to meet you again for as I told you before we were obliged to send for the little you have now eaten from over the Great Waters, which might have been lost on the passage, by many dangerous accidents.[16]

On the topic of a boundary line to mark clearly the extent of the lands which the Indians should surrender, the governor stated:

13. *Ibid*, p. 31.
14. C. O. 5-582, p. 221.
15. *Ibid*.
16. *Ibid*.

Whatsoever Line shall now be fixed before so many Great Chiefs & Venerable Warriors, we shall most strictly abide by, & we expect your Young Men will also adhere to the agreement on their part & that they will not disturb any Settlers within that Line, Neither kill any of the cattle, nor steal any of the Horses belonging to the Inhabitants which has been too much practiced. We farther Expect you will agree to bring in any Negroes who may desert their Masters Service for which a proper reward will be allowed. . . . Here are the principles on which we wish to Establish a Lasting Peace between the White & the Red Children of the King.[17]

The superintendent of Indian affairs echoed the governor's contentions in his own address to the assembled Indians and admonished them to "consider this matter maturely and point out clearly the limits of the Land you shall judge proper to give us."[18]

Speaking in reply to the governor and superintendent, the Choctaw chief, Tomatly Mingo, reminded the English that if they intended to replace the French they "must act the part of a father in supplying my [the Indian] wants by proper presents and also by furnishing a plentiful Trade."[19] The Indian leader concluded his address on a note pleasant to English ears by stating, "as it is acting the parts of brothers mutually to supply each others wants, we are determined amongst ourselves to give you lands which you may plant."[20] He described the area which the tribe had agreed to cede as follows: "The Limits of the Land which we give is a Straight Line from Atchatickpe on Tombeckbe River to the source of the Baccatane River which falls into the Pascagoula."[21] In elaboration of this description, the Choctaw leader also stated that it was hoped that the white settlers would never pass beyond "Cent Iboue" (present-day Santa Bogue Creek) and that the "Lands from Nameaba to Old Tome" were excluded from the cession and reserved for the Nameaba and Mobillian Indians.[22]

This preliminary address was followed with another delivered by the Choctaw leader who had been often linked with no less a figure than Pontiac. It was Alibamo Mingo who observed:

17. *Ibid.*
18. C. O. 5-66, p. 45.
19. C. O. 5-582, p. 232.
20. *Ibid.*
21. *Ibid.*
22. The locations of "Cent Iboue" (Santa Bogue Creek) and Nameaba (Naniabe Is.) can be found on panel D of Fig. 27. The Nameaba and Mobillian Indians probably evacuated the area when the Choctaw-Creek War broke out.

I am not of the opinion that in giving land to the English, we deprive ourselves of the use of it, on the contrary, I think we shall share it with them, as for example the house I now speak in was built by the white people on our land, yet it is divided between the white and red people. Therefore we need not be uneasy that the English settle upon our lands as by that means they can more easily supply our wants.[23]

With this endorsement in favor of a cession from Alibamo Mingo, several other chiefs followed with a series of talks in support of the proposition. Governor Johnstone's and Superintendent Stuart's negotiations with the Choctaw were crowned with a success which more than offset the large expense of the first Indian congress at Mobile.

The "Treaty for the Preservation and Continuance of a Perfect Peace and Friendship . . . ," which was concluded between the Indians and English at Mobile on March 26, 1765, described a vast cession of land made by the Choctaw and Chickasaw tribes to "His Majesty King George the Third . . . In Consideration of the great Marks of Friendship benevolence and Clemency Extended to us. . . ."[24] The Indians, however, added one extremely important condition to the terms of the cession by stating, "none of His Majestys white subjects shall be permitted to settle on Tombeckby River to the northward of the rivulet called Centibouck."[25] This last phrase of the treaty article established the northernmost limits to white settlement in the Choctaw country at the present-day Santa Bogue River near the Washington-Choctaw County boundary in the state of Alabama. Santa Bogue Creek had been mentioned by the Chief Tomatly Mingo in the early phases of the congress and may be located on panel C of Figure 27.

The delineation of the West Florida-Choctaw boundary line was completed and the "infant colony" was now free to begin the exploitation of a large tract from the environs of Mobile up the Mobile River valley to the interior as far as Santa Bogue River and Buckatunna Creek, down the Chickasawy River (Pascagoula) to a point reckoned to be twelve leagues from the sea and then due west by a straight line "as far as the Choctaw Nation have a right to grant."

23. C. O. 5-582, pp. 234-35.
24. C. O. 5-66, p. 50. Dunbar Rowland (ed.), *English Dominion*, Vol. I, *Mississippi Provincial Archives, 1763-1766* (Nashville, Tenn., 1911), p. 215, reprints this lengthy treaty article in full.
25. C. O. 5-66, p. 51.

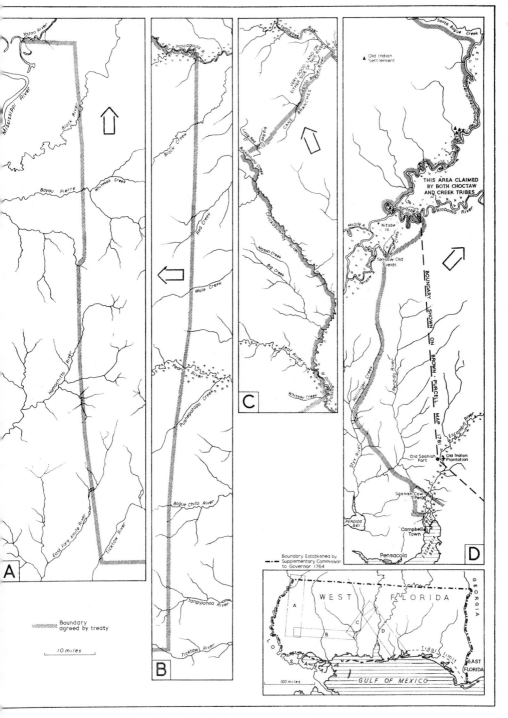

Fig. 27. The West Florida section of the Southern Indian
Boundary Line. Arrows on map panels indicate North.

In their joint dispatch on the conclusion of the Mobile congress the governor and superintendent reported:

The Effect of the whole has been . . . by the Congress at Mobile to gain the principal men of the Choctaw Nation; to induce the whole to give up their French Medals and Commissions, and accept of others from His Majesty; to grant to the Province a tract of rich convenient, and extensive territory; to agree to render blood for blood; to restore Negroes and Deserters, and to refrain from plundering the Inhabitants to submit to the Regulations of Trade prescribed and realy, to their honor be it said, tho' they were near two months at Mobile from first to last, and often two thousand men together; yet no Damage worthy of notice was committed."[26]

There was little time for the colonial administrators to reflect on their success in dealing with the Choctaw and Chickasaw since affairs with the Creeks in the eastern section of the colony remained in a parlous state.

THE DELINEATION OF THE WEST FLORIDA-CREEK BOUNDARY LINE

The Indian congress at Pensacola began exactly two months after the signing of the Chickasaw-Choctaw Treaty and, as had been the case at Mobile, the discussions quickly turned to the subject of a land cession and boundary line. In introducing this topic to the assembled Creeks, Governor Johnstone stated:

We really expect that you will yield us some part to Subsist on, both to Supply our wants & yours when you come among us; for you are sensible, nothing can be produced in this land; but we are far from asking any large tract of country; what we wish most is to avoid Disputing; to fix a certain limit rather than large possessions. I hope it will never be said that this place we have all met, this day with so much joy, has been deserted for want of food. At present we subsist only by supply's from over the Great Waters or Cattle from Mobile. I am sure the Generosity of the Creeks will not allow it to be said, that we shall feed their hungry hunters by the produce of another land, but I am far from prescribing what their limits should be, your wisdom will direct the Line, whatever you fix I shall take care our people shall adhere to.[27]

This appeal to the Creek sense of pride and fair play was followed by a similarly worded exhortation from the superintendent of Indian affairs.

26. C. O. 5-582, p. 189.
27. *Ibid.*, p. 196.

After lengthy preliminary talks by the Creek leaders, the discussion turned to the pivotal question of a land cession and boundary delineation. The chief called The Mortar voiced the Creek point of view on this question when he stated:

As to the proposed boundary line, I acknowledge I did not clearly understand its situation but am informed by Monsieur Montbereau that it runs along by the Forks of the Alibamont [Alabama] and Tombeckbe [Tombigbee] opposite to the interpreters house.

I readily concur in the promise the Wolf King made at Augusta during the late Congress [1763] held there and am far from wishing to alter the line he fixed on that occasion.

(Here the governor wanted to describe to him the Boundary already fixed by the Wolf King, which he prevented by saying) [transcriber's original note]

If the peace and friendship now concluded between the white and red people continued for four years, then there will be an addition made to the lands already granted, but your exceeding the present limits before that time will occasion great disturbances in the Nations for that was the real cause of the Spaniards being killed who attempted to settle on the Indian territories without permission.[28]

On the following day The Mortar again addressed the Congress in terms which shed considerable light on the Creek motives underlying their decision to allow West Florida a cession of land. He stated:

The King of England knows his Red Children are very Numerous & must be cloathed, they are all indigent & I hope the King, the Governor, the Superintendent & all other White people are sensible that they are so, & as I have this day considered the conveniency of the English in granting them land to plant, so I expect they will in return consider me and my people, this land was formerly part of our hunting ground, but now many of us are grown old and incapable to kill deer enough to purchase cloathing: We had formerly good success in hunting but are now obliged to cross to Cherokee [Tennessee] River for game, which considerations induce me to desire, that as deer skins are be-

28. *Ibid.*, p. 202. The Mortar's sagacity was amply displayed by placing the English "on their good behavior" for four years before a future land cession would be forthcoming. It is little wonder that his name had been linked with those of Pontiac and Alabama Mingo as "three very superior characters." The "Monsieur Montbereau" mentioned was a French gentleman who remained in West Florida following the British occupation. He was correctly known as Chevalier De Montault Montbéraut. He served as a deputy Indian superintendent under Stuart for a time. See Alden, *John Stuart*, pp. 210-11.

come scarce, the trade may be reduced in proportion so that we may be enabled to clothe & maintain our Families. . . .[29]

Clearly the Creeks were expecting something more than simply a lump sum compensation for the cession they were prepared to make to West Florida. They were demanding a general lowering in the exchange value of manufactured goods being traded for their deer skins and furs, which were growing increasingly scarce. The Mortar introduced a lengthy list of trade items with the rates at which they should be made available to the Indians, such as a pair of boots for two pounds of leather.[30]

The superintendent of Indian affairs replied to The Mortar's address by stating that the English were well satisfied with the land cession being proposed and wished only that its boundaries should be precisely described in order to prevent misunderstanding and future disputes. He concluded by promising that once the boundary was marked the English would not punish the murders of any people illegally settling beyond it on the Indian land.[31]

The West Florida-Creek boundary line was delineated in detail in the "Treaty for the preservation & continuance of a perfect peace & friendship . . ." which was signed at Pensacola on May 28, 1765. The boundary ran as follows:

[Beginning] at the dividing path going to the Nation and Mobile where is a creek, that it shall run along the side of that creek until its confluence with the river which falls into the bay, then to run round the bay and take in all the plantations which formerly belonged to the Yammassee Indians, that no notice is to be taken of such cattle or horses as shall pass the line; that from the said dividing paths towards the west the boundary is run along the path leading to Mobile to the Creek called Cassaba and from thence still in a straight line to another creek or great branch within forty miles of the ferry, and so to go up to the head of that creek and from thence turn round towards the river, so as to include all the French settlements at Tassa; the eastern line to be determined by the flowing of the sea as was settled at Augusta.[32]

In their report to their superiors, the governor and superintendent described the Creek cession to West Florida in the following terms: "They have given us a tolerable large boundary tho'

29. C. O. 5-582, p. 204.
30. *Ibid.*
31. *Ibid.*, p. 207.
32. *Ibid.*, p. 210.

not all which we could have wished being only about fifteen miles back, which does not reach the rich soil, and so around the sea coast, up along the east side of the Bay of Mobile, as high as the confluence of the River Alibamont [Alabama]."[33]

Although termed a "tolerable large boundary," this first Creek land cession to West Florida was clearly inadequate in the eyes of the colony's leaders. It was almost entirely limited to the sandy coastal belt of infertile soils which were to prove insufficient as the population of West Florida began to grow.

THE DEMARCATION OF THE WEST FLORIDA-INDIAN
BOUNDARY LINES

The small population of West Florida during the years immediately following the great Indian congresses of 1765 created no pressing need for a demarcation of the boundary lines delineated during that year. There seemed to be land enough to accommodate the colony's pioneer settlers until about 1768, when an influx of immigrants from the northern colonies began to swell the population. The provincial surveyor reported in that year that many settlers from the "back country" of Virginia, who had encountered serious difficulties in transporting their produce over the mountains to the seaboard, had visited West Florida with a view to settling along the Mississippi and Mobile rivers.[34]

Johnson wrote that "by . . . the summer of 1770 the movement of settlers from the colonies on the Atlantic seaboard to the fertile lands of West Florida had assumed substantial proportions."[35] In 1771, Bernard Romans reported "a great many plantations" on the fertile islands located at the confluence of the Tombigbee and Alabama rivers.[36] The location of these plantations, as well as a number of land surveys in the area, is shown on an excellent manuscript map prepared by David Taitt in 1771.[37] Significantly, a number of the surveys shown were on the Indian side of the boundary which had been delineated with the Creeks in 1765.

Nor were the Indians themselves oblivious of the increasing white population of West Florida, although the war between the Choctaw and Creeks was a serious distraction. In 1772 the super-

33. *Ibid.,* p. 190.
34. C. O. 5-69, p. 443.
35. Johnson, *British West Florida, 1763-1783,* p. 136.
36. Bernard Romans, *A Concise Natural History of East and West Florida,* p. 332.
37. M.P.G. 6, P.R.O.

intendent reported that "all the Indian Nations seem much alarmed at the emigrations of the back inhabitants of Virginia across their hunting grounds to the Mississippi. . . ."[38] Proof of the seriousness of this alarm was provided by Bartram, who, while on the trail between Pensacola and the Creek towns, reported: "A few days before we arrived at the Nation we met a company of emigrants from Georgia: a man, his wife, several young children and three stout young men, with about a dozen horses loaded with their property. They informed us their design was to settle on the Alabama, a few miles above the confluence of the Tombigbee." A short while later Bartram met a "young white man, in great haste and seeming confusion" fleeing from a band of Choctaw who had taken the Georgia emigrants captive.[39]

Events and developments such as these were soon reflected in a growing desire by colonial officials to call Indian congresses for the purpose of extending West Florida's areal base. The governor of West Florida informed the superintendent of Indian affairs in 1769 that he wished to obtain additional land cessions from the Indians.[40] He stated that the colony desired: (1) from the Creeks a four-mile strip along each bank of the rivers which flowed across West Florida from eighty to one hundred miles inland from the sea, and (2) from the Choctaw the east bank of the Mississippi from the Iberville to the Yazoo River.

In reporting the desires of West Florida for an enlarged land cession the superintendent wrote:

the cession of lands from the Choctaws was as formal and specific as it could be without an actual survey; and is indeed a great and very valuable territory.

The land on the Mississippi below Yazoo River and as far as Ibborville is not claimed by the Choctaws but by the small tribes who have villages upon them; who must be satisfied for giving it up which I believe may be effected with little difficulty.

On the side of Pensacola, West Florida is much confined, the Upper Creek Towns are not distant above 180 miles from the Bay; these Indians are extremely tenacious of their land and will not easily be prevailed upon to cede more in that quarter.[41]

Fortunately the Creeks had not entirely forgotten their promise to demarcate the boundary with West Florida. In 1769 an ap-

38. C. O. 5-73, p. 403.
39. Harper, *Bartram's Travels,* pp. 280-81.
40. Alden, *John Stuart,* p. 319.
41. British Museum, Additional MSS. 21,672, fol. 1.

parent schism in the tribe provided an opportunity to renew discussions on the topic of a boundary line. Emistisiguo, The Mortar's chief rival for pre-eminence in the Creek Confederation, stated "that the line should be as a great brick wall not to be passed by his [the governor's] people and I find they have not."[42] The Indian went on to mention that the war with the Choctaw then underway made it extremely dangerous for the Creeks to undertake the demarcation. He promised that when peace was restored "the headmen will show the governor of Pensacola where the line runs." He ended by chiding the Floridians for their impatience in the matter saying that "the land will not rot or go."[43]

Clearly, conditions were ripe for a reopening of the whole question of a larger Indian land cession to West Florida as the colony began to burgeon during the seventh year of its existence. On the one hand, the colony's attractiveness was becoming recognized by white settlers who were already moving from the more northerly colonies. On the other, there seemed little Indian resistance to the expanding white settlements along the Mississippi between the Iberville and Yazoo rivers. Control of the land here was nominally in the hands of the "Small Tribes" who were few in total number and could be expected to offer little if any resistance to a purchase of their rights. The Choctaw boundary, which had been delineated in 1765, seemed satisfactory and needed only demarcation to insure its easy identification to prevent accidental violations of it by surveyors and settlers. To the east of the Mobile River and Bay, however, the Creeks held sway and although ready to demarcate the boundary of 1765, they were not going to surrender additional land inland from Pensacola willingly. It should be kept in mind that the Creeks were being importuned to surrender portions of their hunting grounds on three separate fronts—in Georgia, in East Florida, and in West Florida. They were a numerous and warlike people who might have been expected to resist such a threat to their chief resource, their hunting grounds.

The troubled conditions of West Florida were, of course, a major concern to colonial officials on the spot but often overlooked or ignored by the Crown in distant London. Repeated Indian crises in West Florida, coupled with the growing tension arising from the Anglo-Spanish controversy over the Falkland Islands,

42. C. O. 5-70, p. 262.
43. *Ibid.*

prompted officials in London to issue permission in 1770 for a new series of Indian congresses to solve the West Florida Indian problem, which largely concerned land and trade.

The first of these congresses was convened at Pensacola on October 29, 1771, with Emistisiguo as the chief spokesman for the Creeks. The usual grievances over trade conditions, complaints about cattle drovers crossing tribal lands, and encroachments by settlers were eloquently aired by the Creeks. The governor and superintendent, too, followed a familiar path of denouncing the various excesses and unlawful acts which the Creeks had committed against the white people. Little time was lost, however, in getting to the central theme of the congress, which was land.

The governor repeated earlier complaints about the barrenness of the environs of his small capital in the hope that the Creeks would be persuaded to cede more land to the colony in this area. He also reported the removal of all the settlers who had established themselves along the Alabama River beyond the 1765 boundary. These encroachments he explained were the result of misunderstanding because the boundary had not been demarcated. The superintendent of Indian affairs, John Stuart, followed with an address in which the following paragraph was included. It is a clear statement of the intentions of West Florida regarding a land cession:

We do not want to get your hunting grounds, we are not hunters, we are planters, an hundred miles of pine land would be of no value to us, what we ask you can easily spare. It is the lands on both sides the Scambia as far up as a Boat can go and we want no more than five miles back from the River and as far up as the River is navigable.[44]

Such a cession was not acceptable to the Creeks since, as Romans pointed out, "the heads of these rivers are all within a few miles of the savage towns."[45] Rather than risk a rupture which would cause the congress to break up prematurely, Emistisiguo claimed that he and the other Creek delegates lacked the authority necessary to cede away any land and that the whole Creek Nation's approval would be required. He did, however, promise to under-

44. C. O. 5-589, p. 90. Bartram gave some clue to the navigability of the Escambia in his *Travels*. He stated: "There are several rivers which run into this great bay [Escambia] from the continent, but none of them navigable, for large craft, to any considerable distance into the country, the Shambie [Escambia] is the largest, which admits shallops some miles up, and perreauguers upwards of fifty miles" (p. 263).

45. Romans, *A Concise Natural History of East and West Florida*, p. 303.

take the long-promised demarcation of the boundary line during the following spring. In another of his statements he shed light on an important aspect of intertribal boundaries, which were little understood by the English. He referred to the earlier Choctaw cession in the area of the Tombigbee-Alabama confluence: "They may give land on the other side of Tombeckby, but on this side [east] of it the land belongs to us."[46]

On the day following (and probably after much behind-the-scenes pressuring) Emistisiguo relented slightly and said that he would "lend" the English more land for plantations:

On both sides of the River Cancia [or] Scambia as far up as the Old Spanish Cowpen, The Spaniards upon their first coming to this land settled a Boundary with us, but they did not take care to keep within the limits [and] made a fort upon Cancia beyond the line; the consequence of which was a war between them and us. . . . The Spanish old fort is upon our land and it is our intent to Build a town at the old field opposite to said fort upon Cancia as soon as peace can be concluded with the Chactaws. I again explain the distance I now offer which is to the old Cowpen and further we cannot take upon us to give.[47]

The superintendent replied by stating that what Emistisiguo was proposing was only an alteration of four miles in the line and took in only a small quantity "of very poor land upon the banks of Cancia and it is not worth the trouble of altering the old lines and drawing a new treaty for such a trifle."[48] On the topic of the Creek-Choctaw debate over the triangular area formed by the Tombigbee and Alabama rivers, the superintendent agreed that the English would await the outcome of discussions between the tribes before they would accept the area from either side. This area continued to be shown as disputed ground on the maps prepared by the Indian Department throughout the British period of control in West Florida.[49]

A treaty was signed at Pensacola which described both the old boundary of 1765 in detail as well as a "Further Cession of Land"

46. C. O. 5-589, p. 94.
47. *Ibid.*, p. 95.
48. *Ibid.*, p. 96.
49. The locations of the disputed area, "Spanish Old Fort" and "Cowpen," are shown on panel D of Fig. 27. Romans, *A Concise Natural History of East and West Florida*, p. 73, stated that the Choctaw had drawn back from their eastern frontier to consolidate their strength in the Creek war and that "they have deserted many of their eastern frontier towns since the present war with the Creeks."

which the Creeks had reluctantly surrendered. This "Further Cession" was to include

all the land lying between Coosa River and a line to run from Bryar Creek above Major Farmar's Plantation at Tassa—miles distant from and parallel to, the Tassa Branch of Coosa River to the great River formed by the confluence of Coosa and Tombeckby River and then to extend along the high land by the Edge of the Swamp on the eastern side of Coosa River above the confluence with Tombeckby River and afterwards the line is to Run by the Eastern Bank of Coosa River to the mouth of the Branch called by the Chactaws Byuck Cannonga and by the Creeks Hetisia.[50]

It can be seen on panel D, Figure 27, that this "Further Cession" extended the northern end of the West Florida-Creek boundary line from its previous termination at Tensaw Old Fields to a point several miles farther north on the Alabama River.

The alteration to the southern end of the line has already been described and was not mentioned in the formal treaty, since the English were hopeful of obtaining a much larger cession on the Escambia River. This same reason delayed the demarcation of the West Florida-Creek boundary. David Taitt, whose journals are invaluable commentaries on the geography of the Creek country, was sent as deputy Indian superintendent to the Creeks in an effort to persuade the tribe to grant a larger cession on the Escambia during the winter of 1771-1772.[51] Although Taitt's efforts were vastly productive in the sphere of geographical knowledge, he accomplished very little in the way of persuading the Creeks to part with their lands along the Escambia River. The Creeks were increasingly alarmed by the preliminaries to the "New Purchase" scheme which were disturbing their Georgia frontier. It soon became apparent that West Florida's hope for a territorial increase at the expense of the Creeks was in serious danger of being frustrated by the gathering momentum behind the drive for a similar increase by Georgia. It might be safely said that as the fortunes of Georgia's "New Purchase" waxed, those of West Florida's Escambia Cession scheme waned.

Added to the influence of the events presaging the "New Purchase" on the Creek's attitude toward the Escambia valley lands was the tribe's apparently growing interest in the area. In

50. C. O. 5-589, p. 113.
51. C. O. 5-73, pp. 290-309. Taitt's journals have been reprinted in Newton D. Mereness, *Travels in the American Colonies* (New York, 1916), pp. 493-565.

a talk dated April 19, 1772, Emistisiguo repeated his assertion that the tribe itself intended to occupy the land desired by West Florida. He stated:

I likewise told the Governor that he might build his fire at Penssacola, but go no further, and if ever his people went beyond the line we would tell them their error which we have done . . . we told you that the path should be your boundary like a stone wall or a tree which you are not to climb over . . . as for the boundary it is true it is not run but the days are not all gone yet, It is at the Tansa Old Fields and we mean to run it there and no further, as for the lands on Scambia we cannot give it, for as soon as we have peace with the Choctaws we mean to settle that ourselves, they told us that the land was ours and all the deer and beaver upon it which we think very right.[52]

From this statement and the similar assertion made at the congress held at Pensacola during the previous year, it would seem that in West Florida arose the unique situation of an Anglo-Indian controversy over land which both sides wished to occupy and settle on a permanent basis. In all other land controversies influencing the evolution and location of the Southern Indian Boundary Line, the frontier was shown to be moving from the seaboard toward the interior. On the one hand, the boundary line frequently indicated the shrinking areal base of the Indian tribes and the expanding areal base of the English colonies on the other. In the Escambia Valley both frontiers—Indian and white—were expanding and an impasse resulted.

The superintendent of Indian affairs did not seem to lend much credence to the expressed ambitions of the Creeks to occupy this area. Rather, he blamed their refusal to cede the contested Escambia lands on the machinations of those who were pressing the Creeks to accede to the "New Purchase." In June, 1772, after the Creeks had again refused to make the desired cession to West Florida, he wrote: "The Upper Creeks . . . refused to cede the lands which was asked of them upon the river Scambia, which Mr. Taitt attributes to the machinations of the Traders who grosly insulted him in the presence of all the Indian Chiefs upon a supposition that he was to oppose the cession of lands in their favor [in Georgia]."[53]

The impasse over the Escambia cession was not overcome, and

52. C. O. 5-73, p. 272.
53. *Ibid.*, p. 156.

West Florida continued to forestall the demarcation of the boundary line with the Creeks throughout the period of this study. The West Florida-Choctaw boundary line was demarcated following the congress held at Mobile during December, 1771, and January, 1772. As already indicated, West Florida seemed quite satisfied with the extent of the cession which the Choctaw had granted in 1765, so there was no need to press for an enlargement of it as had been the case with the Creeks at Pensacola. Most of the time of the congress was spent in discussing problems of trade which were relatively easily dealt with by the governor and superintendent. The boundary line was introduced by reading and explaining the treaty article which had been signed in 1765. The superintendent followed this recitation by stating: "I am not come to ask for more land and a new line but to confirm the old one. I therefore desire you will pitch upon a certain number of your people as deputies from you to attend Mr. Charles Stuart my deputy and such persons as may be appointed . . . in marking said boundary."[54]

The congress was concluded and on January 16, 1772, Charles Stuart with a party of thirty Indians and a surveyor set out to demarcate the West Florida-Choctaw boundary line. The demarcation began smoothly and the party proceeded up the Tombigbee River to a point downstream from Santa Bogue Creek and overland paralleling the Santa Bogue, where trouble soon developed. The Indians refused to continue the survey claiming that the course of the boundary in the vicinity of Buckatunna Creek was all "morasses and sunken grounds," which they termed impassable at that season.[55] The governor of West Florida doubted their reason for abandoning the demarcation and felt rather that they were making an excuse to leave an unpleasant task.

In the absence of the Indian members of the demarcation party, the deputy Indian superintendent and his assistants perservered and carried the boundary down the Buckatunna Creek and Chickasawhay River to the spot on the Pascagoula River which was reckoned to be "twelve leagues from the sea." The demarcation of the boundary from the confluence of the Tombigbee and Alabama rivers to the Pascagoula River was thus completed in the early months of 1772. The remainder of the Southern Indian Boundary Line from the Pascagoula west to the Mississippi was not demar-

54. *Ibid.*, p. 76.
55. C. O. 5-579, p. 1.

cated until 1779 and so falls outside the limits of this study. Since this last and most westerly section of the Southern Indian Boundary Line resulted from the forces set in motion during the period of the study in hand, it is shown on Figures 27 and 29.

THE WEST FLORIDA INDIAN-BOUNDARY LINES ON EIGHTEENTH-CENTURY MAPS

The West Florida section of the Southern Indian-Boundary Line appeared on several eighteenth-century manuscript maps, which serve as indispensable sources in efforts aimed at tracing its evolution and location. By virtue of their original purpose, these maps fall into two major groups. The first group portrays the colony of West Florida or rather portions of it at a relatively large scale, while the second group portrays the Southern Indian District and as a result shows the West Florida section of the boundary line as one part of the whole Southern Indian Boundary Line. This discussion, however, will not attempt a description or analysis of all eighteenth-century maps which impinge on the subject of the West Florida section of the boundary line. Rather, only those which proved of the greatest value in the preparation of Figure 27 will be of concern here. Figure 27 shows the West Florida section of the Southern Indian Boundary Line as reconstructed from the documentary and cartographic sources examined in connection with this study. As the inset of Figure 27 indicates, it was a boundary of great length paralleling the coastline of the Gulf of Mexico from East Florida to the Mississippi River. On the eve of the American Revolution only those areas between the Gulf and Mississippi and the boundary line were available for white settlement.

Unlike other sections of the Southern Indian Boundary Line, that section in West Florida was a composite, evolving as it did between the colony and two distinct and separate Indian nations. Just as the documentary evidence already presented reflects this fact in the separate records of congresses held at Mobile and Pensacola, so too does the detailed cartographic evidence which depicts the contemporary geographical setting of the West Florida section of the Southern Indian Boundary Line. Probably the best source of information on the geography of the West Florida-Creek part of the boundary line is the manuscript map by David Taitt, which bears the following lengthy and descriptive title in the style of his day:

A Plan
of part of the Rivers
Tombecbe, Alabama, Tensa, Perdito, & Scambia—
—In the Province of—
West Florida

. . . with a sketch of the boundary between the Nation of upper Creek Indians and that part of the Province which is contiguous thereto, as settled at the Congresses at Pensacola in the Years 1765 & 1771.— Collected from different Surveys at the desire of the Honble John Stuart Esquire Sole Agent and Superintendant of Indian Affairs for the Southern district of North America.[56]

Parish pointed to the great value of this map in his essay "John Stuart and the Cartography of the Indian Boundary Line," but it does not appear that the map has been exposed to scholars in any published form as yet.[57] This map alone could be the subject of several pages, but it must suffice here to say that it is an invaluable source of detailed information regarding the Indian boundary line and the geography of West Florida from Pensacola and the Escambia valley on the east to Mobile and the Tombigbee River on the west. Much of the detail which appears on panel D of Figure 27 is derived from this source.

While Taitt's map of the Creek section of the boundary clearly illuminates the vagaries of the loosely worded treaty articles signed at Pensacola, the Choctaw section must be reconstructed in a cartographic twilight. It will be recalled that the Choctaw boundary was demarcated by the deputy superintendent and a West Florida surveyor in the early months of 1772. Unfortunately, the original map titled "A Plan of the Indian Boundary Lin[e] [section torn away] From Atchtickpi to the Buckatanne; and from the Line at Buckatanne to the Pascagoula River; the road to Mobile [torn] Surveyed 17th Feby 17 [72]" has been badly torn and shows none of the actual boundary line in its present condition.[58]

56. M.P.G. 6, P.R.O.
57. Parish, *The Persistence of the Westward Movement and Other Essays,* pp. 142-43.
58. William L. Clements Library, No. 668 (Clinton Papers, Clinton Map 341). Christian Brun, *Guide to Manuscript Maps,* p. 162, incorrectly dates this map 1771. Clearly it should be 1772, since the demarcation party did not set out until Jan. 16, 1772.
    While studying this map in the Clements Library, the author noted the following on a card clipped to the map folder: "John C. Parish HistDept. U.C.L.A.

Fortunately this gap in the cartographic fabric can be effectively patched by employing another manuscript map, one probably prepared within a few years of the demarcation of the Choctaw boundary line.[59] This map is untitled but listed in the *Catalogue of the Maps, Plans and Charts in the Library of the Colonial Office 1910* as a "Survey of the Bay and River Mobile. With list and references to the lands granted, the proprietors names etc. [1775]." The Choctaw boundary line is clearly shown on this map in red ink beginning at "Alchatickpe" on the "Tombecbe" and to "Buckatanne," a tributary of the "Pascagoula River." An inscription on the map stated:

The Line stained Red shews the Chactaw Indian Boundary Line as it was marked by the Indians after the Congress held at Mobile in the Month of December 1772 [actually 1771] being a confirmation of their former cession by which all the land southward of the boundary Line as far as the Sea Shore, included between the Rivers Mobile or Tombecbe, and Pascagoula belong to the English.[60]

The portion of the Choctaw boundary line reconstructed as panel C of Figure 27 is derived largely from this source.

Panels A and B of Figure 27 show the westernmost section of the Southern Indian Boundary Line which was not demarcated from the Pascagoula to the Mississippi River until 1779. Although not strictly within the period of this study, it is included here because it was an outcome of those forces and programs which were set in motion during the twelve-year span from 1763 to 1775. It will be recalled that the boundary to the west of the Pascagoula River was to be marked by a due-west line as far as the Choctaw had a right to grant.

In 1777, a congress was held with the Chickasaw and Choctaw to insure their allegiance to England in the conflict which had broken out with the Atlantic colonies. At this congress the Choc-

will verify this as being the work of David Tait Deputy Indian Agent—see N. D. Mereness 'Travels in So.Cols.' "

There is no date for this identification by Parish, and he makes no mention of the map in his essay mentioned above. A comparison of the Taitt original and photostatic copy of the map in the Clements Library fails to confirm Parish's identification. Indeed, Brun makes no mention of Taitt in connection with this map. It would appear that Charles Stuart or the West Florida surveyor who accompanied him on the demarcation of the Choctaw boundary line was the author of the Clements map.

59. C. O. 700, Maps, Florida/51.
60. *Ibid.*

taw agreed to a boundary which was to run south from the mouth
of the Yazoo River toward the Gulf Coast and then east to the
Pascagoula River.[61] This boundary line was demarcated and
mapped by Joseph Purcell in 1779, and it is on his excellent maps
that panels A and B of Figure 27 are based.[62]

The several manuscript maps which were prepared explicitly
to illustrate the Southern Indian District and Southern Indian
Boundary Line have been discussed at length in other sections of
this study and will be only briefly mentioned here. They are the
series of maps prepared under the direction of the Indian superintendent, John Stuart, and executed by the draftsman and surveyor
Joseph Purcell.[63] On the map which Purcell completed in 1781
most of the West Florida section of the Southern Indian Boundary
Line agrees closely with the detail of Figure 27. In one respect,
however, this map, usually referred to as the Brown-Purcell, shows
a significant difference in the location of the boundary line. This
is the section of the line which extends from the Escambia to the
Alabama River. It has been indicated on panel D of Figure 27 as
Purcell located it on his map. No evidence to support this boundary line, which takes in the whole of the Perdido River Valley,
has been found in the materials studied. It may be that Purcell
was illustrating what the English desired in this area and not the
true location of the boundary. In the following paragraphs it will
be shown that this map may have caused an error in a recent reconstruction of this section of the Southern Indian Boundary Line.

THE WEST FLORIDA-INDIAN BOUNDARY LINES ON THE
PRESENT-DAY MAP

The present-day state of Florida is bounded on the west by
the Perdido River and so includes much of the territory which
formed the British colony of West Florida. On his map, described
above, Cumming included a reconstruction of the West Florida-
Creek boundary line from the tidal streams and marshes east of
Pensacola Bay to a point on the Perdido River.[64] In the set of
explanatory notes, "Florida Boundary Lines According to British-
Indian Treaties of 18th Century," Cumming stated that this sec-

61. Parish, *The Persistence of the Westward Movement and other Essays*, p. 143.
62. C. O., 700 Maps, Florida/56, 1 and 2.
63. C. O. 700 Maps, North America General/12, M.R. 919, and C. O., 700,
Maps, North America General/15.
64. Defendant's Exhibit 128, *Before the Indian Claims Commission, Docket
No. 73*.

tion of the boundary to the Perdido River could be followed on the Purcell 1781 map.[65] Thus Cumming, by following the Brown-Purcell map of 1781, seems to have located the West Florida-Creek boundary line about ten miles too high up the much-contested Escambia River valley. This can be observed on panel D of Figure 27.

The middle section of the West Florida Indian boundary line received the attention of the frequently quoted interpreter of the early Gulf Coast, Peter J. Hamilton.[66] As Parish has already pointed out, Hamilton's attempted reconstructions of the Southern Indian Boundary Line "are in a large part wrong" and seriously in need of correction.[67] Figure 27 should provide a helpful source of reference to anyone attempting to understand Hamilton's writing on the Indian boundary lines.

The last and westernmost section of the boundary line, which extends from the Pascagoula River west to the Ticktaw River and north to the confluence of the Yazoo with the Mississippi River, has not been the subject of detailed research in the preparation of this study, since its demarcation occurred after the American Revolution began. It is, however, an intensely interesting boundary line and deserves further study. For example, a comparison of Purcell's map of 1779 with the present-day map reveals interesting evidence of a major change in the channel of the Mississippi River just upstream of the city of Vicksburg, which could be of value to geomorphologists and hydrographers.[68] Also, a number of present-day county boundaries seem to have been based on Purcell's earlier Indian boundary line demarcated in 1779 while the area was still a part of the British empire. Purcell was an accomplished surveyor and took great pains to indicate on his map the type of natural vegetation which he observed in the area traversed by the boundary Line he demarcated. This information would be invaluable to the historical geographer who would attempt to recreate the landscape of this part of North America during the latter eighteenth century.

65. From a copy provided by Professor Cumming.
66. Peter J. Hamilton, *Colonial Mobile* (Boston and New York, 1910).
67. Parish, *The Persistence of the Westward Movement and Other Essays*, p. 142.
68. C. O., 700 Maps, Florida/56, 1 and 2.

X · The Boundary on an "Accurate General Map"

Interest in the frontier congresses, surveys, and demarcations which lent form and substance to the Southern Indian Boundary Line was not restricted to Indian campfire councils and colonial governmental bodies alone. On the contrary, the foremost political and administrative minds of Britain were focused closely on the events transpiring thousands of miles away in the forests of the Southern Indian District. As Crown officers in London attempted to piece together the frequently contradictory mass of treaty articles, verbal descriptions, surveyor's sketches, and maps to form a meaningful impression of the boundary line, the shortcomings of the available maps of the American Southeast became painfully apparent.

The reader of this study would, at this point, doubtlessly sympathize with Lord Hillsborough, secretary of state for the Southern Department in 1769, as he grappled with the problem of clearly and concisely explaining the location and significance of a boundary line through an uncharted American wilderness to his interested and inquisitive monarch. Early in that year, Lord Hillsborough addressed the following request to John Stuart: "[We] desire that you will employ a skillfull person to lay down upon some accurate general map of America, in order to be transmitted to me, for His Majesty's information, the several Lines agreed upon and marked out, for the want of which it is difficult to distinguish with precision in what manner the several lines unite and the courses they follow."[1] Stuart undertook his assigned task with his usual alacrity.

In a letter written more than two years later, he provided an eloquent testimonial of the immense difficulties that were to beset anyone attempting the ambitious project of preparing "an accu-

1. C. O. 5-70, p. 177.

rate general map" of the Southeast during the eighteenth century. The following extract from this letter is lengthy but worthy of inclusion here since it provides perspective from which Stuart's final map can be more clearly viewed. He wrote:

I beg pardon for not having complyed with my promise . . . of 30th July 1769, of furnishing your Lordship with the boundary lines marked on an accurate map by some good hand, . . . not . . . from inattention . . . but from the impossibility of performing it with such a degree of accuracy as to convey a just idea of our boundaries upon any of the printed maps that I have seen, in all of which the natural boundaries specified in the different treaties are either erroneously laid down or entirely left out and [obliterated] the possibility of forming a precise idea of the extent of the different cessions made by the Indians, until natural boundaries are accurately explored and properly laid down; as the lines particularly behind this Province are determined by the courses and confluence of brooks and rivers, with which we are not by any means well acquainted; I have sent a proper person to accomplish surveying and marking the Indian Boundaries before I leave West Florida, which with the materials that I have collected will enable one to make a good map of this country; and as there will be actual surveys of the lines behind Virginia, North and South Carolina and Georgia accomplished before my return to Charles Town [*sic*], I flatter myself with the expectation of having it in my power to lay before your Lordship a map of my department which may be depended upon.[2]

Stuart forwarded a map of the "Boundary Line Dividing the Lands Reserved by The Different Nations of Indians From Those Ceded to His Majesty," on February 25, 1773.[3] This was, however, merely a copy of John Mitchell's engraved and printed map of 1755, with the boundary lines inked on it. It was not an original map and was, by Stuart's admission, imperfect. Although imperfect, this annotated map met with approval in London where any map from America seemed better than none. Stuart however, was not satisfied. It will be recalled that he was personally possessed of considerable cartographic ability.

He, with the aid of his department's most talented cartographer, Joseph Purcell, continued in the effort to produce a more accurate and reliable general map of his district. In February, 1776, Stuart notified Lord Dartmouth of the completion of his map of the

2. C. O. 5-72, p. 334.
3. C. O. 5-74, p. 62. This map has not been located to date.

Southern Indian District.[4] He had found the task of compiling it to be far more difficult than he had first imagined when he began the undertaking seven years before. This map, probably completed late in the year 1775, is inscribed: "A Map of the Southern Indian District of North America Compiled under the Direction of John Stuart, Esqr. His Majesty's Superintendant of Indian Affairs and by him Humbly Inscribed to the Earl of Dartmouth His Majesty's Secretary of State for the Colonies, etc., etc."[5] It is a very large manuscript map, measuring seventy-four inches by seventy-six inches, and shows the Southeast in greater detail and clarity than any other map of its period. The scale is about 14 miles: 1 inch. Surveys and maps produced by such individual figures as Bernard Romans, David Taitt, John Donelson, Joshua Fry, Peter Jefferson, John Pickins, William DeBrahm, Henry Yonge, Samuel Savery, Philip Yonge, Andrew Way, Samuel Lewis, and Charles Stuart, as well as others, were collated and utilized by Stuart and Purcell, in the light of their own considerable knowledge, to prepare this valuable map.

The reader of the present day, like Lord Hillsborough two centuries ago, can better appreciate the Southern Indian Boundary Line when it is viewed as a continuous whole. To provide this opportunity Figure 28 has been prepared. Figure 28, "The Southern Indian Boundary Line as depicted on the Stuart-Purcell map of 1775 (P.R.O., C. O. 700—N.A. GEN./12)," is based on a tracing made from the original Stuart-Purcell map. The great degree of reduction necessary to reproduce this six-by-six-foot map here has necessitated the omission of a large amount of the rich detail which covers the original. This tracing, inadequate as it is, summarizes Stuart's six-year effort to show the Southern Indian Boundary Line on "an accurate general map." While it is not without error, the reader of the present day would probably join Lord Germain, who observed (of the original) that, "as it appears to be executed with great accuracy it will be useful in furnishing us with just ideas of that country."[6]

This map, interesting as it is, is not adequate as a cartographic summarization for the reader of the present study. To serve this end, Figure 29, a map of the Southern Indian Boundary Line

4. C. O. 5-77, p. 36.
5. C. O. 700, Maps, North America General/12. See the Bibliography, Selected Manuscript Maps, at the end of this study for references to other extant copies of this map.
6. C. O. 5-77, p. 36.

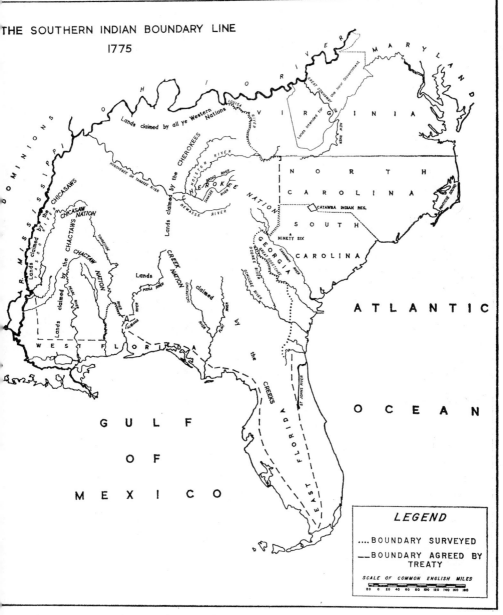

Fig. 28. The Southern Indian Boundary Line as depicted on
the Stuart-Purcell map of 1775. (P.R.O., C. O. 700, Maps, North
America General/12.)

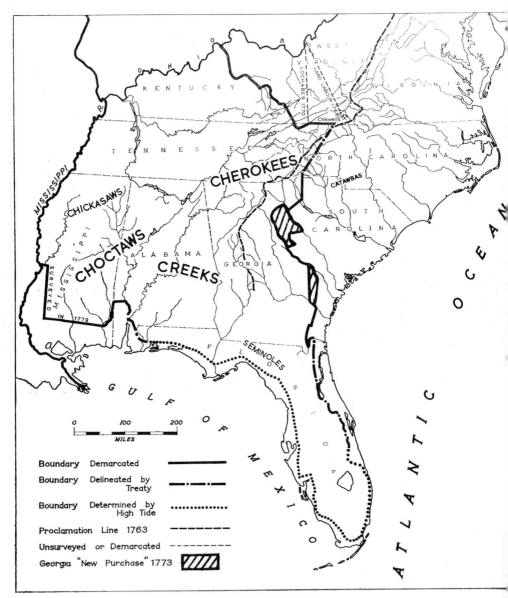

Fig. 29.   The Southern Indian Boundary Line.

based on present-day planimetric knowledge, has been prepared. It portrays the Southern Indian Boundary Line against the lineaments of the Southeast with a reasonable degree of accuracy. To assist in the orientation and location of salient features, the names and outlines of the present-day states of the region along with the courses of the major streams are included. To add perspective, the general locations of the major Indian tribes of the Southeast are shown. Figure 29 is a recreation of the Southern Indian Boundary Line on the map base of the present day. This is a valuable aid to understanding when it is recalled that in many respects the boundary line evolved in a manner which was earlier likened to "a set of separate colonial links only loosely welded into a chain by the British Crown." The separate colonial "links" have been discussed at length and depicted on the maps accompanying those discussions. Figure 29 along with Figure 28 depicts the "chain."

Over much of its great length the Southern Indian Boundary Line evolved, in clearly marked stages, from a hazy administrative concept to a geographic reality boldly demarcated across the landscape of America's first west. Through the remainder of its length it was the subject of detailed delineation in eighteenth-century Indian congress, documents, and maps and formed an equally significant conceptual reality.

Needless to say, the Southern Indian Boundary Line was a factor of the greatest moment to the Indians, pioneer settlers, and British administrators concerned with America's first west, since it was a restrictive barrier beyond which European settlement was not allowed to extend. All along the Southeastern frontier the major motif was westward expansion. This motif was equally present in those areas where the boundary had been demarcated, as well as those where it has been delineated only (the southern extremity and western coast of the Florida peninsula excepted). A lengthy study could result from an examination of the numerous attempts, successful and unsuccessful, which were made by Europeans to circumvent the strictures of the boundary line and gain possession of the Indian hunting grounds beyond. These considerations are, however, too lengthy to be included in detail here and must remain topics for future study.

In conclusion, it should be stated that the Southern Indian Boundary Line was conceived of as an entity in the minds of British statesmen as early as the year 1763. A continuous boundary did emerge in the space of little more than a decade, albeit with many modifications to the original concept. Its evolution was, in many respects, the result of a large number of *ad hoc* compromises bearing little, if any, relation to one another or to any imperial design. Haphazard as its evolution might seem, the Southern Indian Boundary Line was a very real and potent fact of frontier life for Indian and European alike during the ante bellum period which saw its appearance in the Southeast. It helped to moderate the pace and alter the direction of the tide of white pioneers moving from the seaboard toward the Indian hunting grounds.

The existence of a continuous Indian boundary line would have doubtlessly influenced the course of British settlement in the Southeast far more profoundly had not the political break between colony and Crown followed so quickly on its completion. Indeed, the British continued their efforts to formalize the boundary in the colonies which remained loyal and the westernmost segment in the province of West Florida was finally demarcated in 1779. Still further proof of the significance and vigor of the idea of an Indian boundary line is to be found in the fact that the newly formed state governments and Continental Congress adopted programs to prevent the encroachment of Indian land which were essentially identical to those which the Crown of Britain had evolved during the twelve-year period covered by this study. In many respects, the relations between the Continental Congress, early federal government, and the Southern States concerning Indian land matters were identical to the relations which had existed between the British Crown and the colonies. In the relationships between federal government, states, and Indian tribes in the Southeast, a boundary line similar in all respects to the Southern Indian Boundary Line continued to be of major significance even after Britain had withdrawn from the region.

Bibliography

BOOKS

Abernethy, Thomas Perkins. *From Frontier to Plantation in Tennessee.* Chapel Hill, N.C.: University of North Carolina Press, 1932.
———. *Three Virginia Frontiers.* Baton Rouge: Louisiana State University, 1940.
———. *Western Lands and the American Revolution.* New York: Appleton-Century Co., Inc., 1937.
Acts Passed by the General Assembly of the Colony of Georgia, 1755 to 1774. Wormsloe, Ga.: Privately printed, 1886.
Adams, Percy G. (ed. and trans.). *Crevecoeur's Eighteenth-Century Travels in Pennsylvania and New York.* Lexington, Ky.: University of Kentucky Press, 1961.
The Advantages of A Settlement Upon the Ohio in North America. London, 1763 [1773].
Alden, George Henry. *New Governments West of the Alleghanies Before 1780.* ("Bulletin of the University of Wisconsin Historical Series," Vol. II, No. 1.) Madison, Wis.: University of Wisconsin Press, 1897.
Alden, John Richard. *General Gage in America: Being Principally A History of His Role in the American Revolution.* Baton Rouge: Louisiana State University Press, 1948.
———. *John Stuart and the Southern Colonial Frontier.* Ann Arbor, Mich.: University of Michigan Press, 1944.
Alexander, J. B. *The History of Mecklenburg County From 1740 to 1900.* Charlotte, N.C.: Observer Printing House, 1902.
Alvord, Clarence Walworth. *The Mississippi Valley in British Politics.* 2 vols. Cleveland: Arthur H. Clark Co., 1917.
Alvord, C. W., and Bidgood, L. *The First Explorations of the Trans-Allegheny Region by the Virginians, 1650-1674.* Cleveland: Arthur H. Clark Co., 1912.
American Husbandry: Containing an Account of the Soil, Climate, Production and General Agriculture of the British Colonies in North America and the West Indies. 2 vols. London, 1775.

Anburey, Thomas. *Travels Through the Interior Parts of America; In a Series of Letters by An Officer.* 2 vols. London: W. Lane, 1789.

Andrews, Evangeline W., and Andrews, Charles M. (eds.). *Journal of a Lady of Quality. . . .* New Haven: Yale University Press, 1934.

Asbury, Rev. Francis. *The Journal of Rev. Francis Asbury.* 3 vols. New York: Lane and Scott, 1852.

Ashe, Samuel A'Court. *History of North Carolina.* 2 vols. Greensboro, N.C.: Charles L. Van Noppen, 1908.

Bailey, Kenneth P. *The Ohio Company of Virginia and the Westward Movement.* Glendale, Cal.: Arthur H. Clark Co., 1939.

————. *The Ohio Company Papers, 1753-1817.* Ann Arbor, Mich.: Edwards Bros., 1947.

Bakeless, John. *The Eyes of Discovery.* New York: Dover Publications, 1961.

Bartram, William. *Travels Through North and South Carolina, Georgia, East and West Florida, The Cherokee Country. . . .* Philadelphia: James & Johnson, 1791.

Basye, Arthur H. *The Lords Commissioners of Trade and Plantations, 1748-1782.* New Haven: Yale University Press, 1925.

Benson, Adolph B. *The America of 1750: Peter Kalm's Travels in North America, the English Version of 1770.* 2 vols. New York: Wilson-Erickson, Inc., 1937.

Bidwell, P. W., and Falconer, J. I. *History of Agriculture in the Northern United States, 1620-1860.* Washington, D.C.: The Carnegie Institution, 1925.

Billington, Ray A. *Westward Expansion: A History of the American Frontier.* New York: Macmillan Co., 1949.

Blumenthal, Walter H. *American Indians Dispossessed: Fraud in Land Cessions Forced Upon the Tribes.* Philadelphia: George S. MacManus Co., 1955.

Boggs, S. Whittemore. *International Boundaries—A Study of Boundary Functions and Problems.* New York: Columbia University Press, 1940.

Bowen, Eliza A. *The Story of Wilkes County Georgia.* Edited, annotated, indexed with an introduction by Louise F. Hayes. Marietta, Ga.: Continental Book Co., 1950.

Boyd, Julian P. *The Indian Treaties Printed by Benjamin Franklin, 1736-1762.* Philadelphia: The Historical Society of Pennsylvania, 1938.

Brown, John P. *Old Frontiers: The Story of the Cherokee Indians from Earliest Times to the Date of Their Removal to the West 1838.* Kingsport, Tenn.: Southern Publishers, Inc., 1938.

Brown, Lloyd A. *Early Maps of the Ohio Valley.* Pittsburgh: University of Pittsburgh Press, 1959.

Brown, Ralph H. *Historical Geography of the United States.* New York: Harcourt Brace, 1948.
———. *Mirror for Americans: Likeness of the Eastern Seaboard, 1810.* (American Geographical Society Special Publication No. 27.) New York: American Geographical Society, 1943.
Byrd, Col. William. *History of the Dividing Line and Other Tracts.* 2 vols. Richmond, Va., 1866.
———. *The Westover Manuscripts: Containing the History of the Dividing Line, A Journey to the Land of Eden, 1733 and A Progress to the Mines.* Petersburg, Va., 1844.
———. *The Writings of Colonel William Byrd.* Ed. Spencer Bassett. New York: Doubleday, Page & Co., 1901.
Calder, Isabel M. (ed.). *Colonial Captivities, Marches and Journeys.* New York: The Macmillan Co., 1935.
Callaway, James E. *The Early Settlement of Georgia.* Athens, Ga.: University of Georgia Press, 1948.
Candler, Allen D. (ed.). *The Colonial Records of the State of Georgia.* 19 vols. Atlanta: Franklin Printing and Publishing Co., 1904-1911.
Carter, Clarence E. (ed.). *The Correspondence of General Thomas Gage with the Secretaries of State, 1763-1775.* 2 vols. New Haven: Yale University Press, 1931.
Cartwright, John. *American Independence, The Interest and Glory of Great Britain.* London, 1775.
Caruso, John A. *The Appalachian Frontier: America's First Surge Westward.* Indianapolis and New York: The Bobbs-Merrill Co., 1959.
Catesby, Mark. *The Natural History of Carolina, Florida, and the Bahama Islands.* Revised by Mr. Edwards. 2 vols. London, 1754.
Chalmers, Lionel. *An Account of the Weather and Diseases of South Carolina* 2 vols. London: Edward and Charles Dilly, 1776.
Chatelaine, Verne E. *The Defenses of Spanish Florida 1565 to 1763.* (Carnegie Institution of Washington, Publication 511). Washington, D.C., 1941.
Clark, Walter (ed.). *The State Records of North Carolina.* 16 vols. (XI-XXVI). Winston, N.C.: M. I. and J. C. Stewart, Printers to the State, 1895-96; Goldsboro, N.C.: Nash Brothers, Book and Job Printers, 1898-1905.
Cluny, Alexander. *The American Traveller; or Observations on the Present State, Culture and Commerce of the British Colonies in America. . . . By an Old and Experienced Trader.* London: Edward and Charles Dilly, 1769.
Coleman, Kenneth. *The American Revolution in Georgia, 1763-1789.* Athens, Ga.: University of Georgia Press, 1958.
Cooper, Thomas, and McCord, David J. (eds.). *Statutes at Large of South Carolina.* 10 vols. Columbia, S.C.: A. S. Johnston, 1838-1841.

Corbitt, David L. *The Formation of the North Carolina Counties, 1663-1943.* Raleigh, N.C.: State Department of Archives and History, 1950.

Corkran, David H. *The Cherokee Frontier: Conflict and Survival, 1740-1762.* Norman, Okla.: University of Oklahoma Press, 1962.

Corry, John P. *Indian Affairs in Georgia, 1732-1756.* Philadelphia: University of Pennsylvania Press, 1936.

Coulter, E. Merton. *Georgia: A Short History.* Chapel Hill, N.C.: University of North Carolina Press, 1947.

Crane, Verner W. *The Southern Frontier, 1670-1732.* Durham, N.C.: Duke University Press, 1928.

Cruickshank, Helen G. *John and William Bartram's America.* ("The Natural History Library," Anchor Books.) Garden City, N.Y.: Doubleday & Co., Inc., 1961. (Published in co-operation with the American Museum of Natural History.)

Cumming, William P. *The Southeast in Early Maps.* 2nd ed. Chapel Hill, N.C.: University of North Carolina Press, 1962.

Darlington, William M. *Christopher Gist's Journals with Historical, Geographical and Ethnological Notes and Biographies of His Contemporaries.* Pittsburgh: Weldin & Co., 1893.

De Brahm, John Gerar William. *History of the Province of Georgia with Maps of the Original Surveys.* Wormsloe, Ga.: Privately printed, 1849. (Limited to forty-nine copies.)

De Voto, Bernard A. *The Course of Empire.* Boston: Houghton Mifflin Company, 1952.

A Digest of the Laws of the State of Georgia, From its First Establishment As a British Province Down to the Year 1800, Inclusive. Philadelphia: R. Aitken, 1801.

Doddridge, Joseph. *Notes on the Settlement and Indian Wars of the Western Parts of Virginia and Pennsylvania from 1763 to 1783, Inclusive, Together with a Review of the State of Society and Manners of the First Settlers of the Western Country.* Pittsburgh: John S. Ritenour and Wm. T. Lindsey, 1912.

Douglas, Edward M. *Boundaries, Areas, Geographic Centers and Altitudes of the United States and the Several States.* (Department of the Interior, Geological Survey, Bulletin 689.) Washington, D.C.: Government Printing Office, 1923.

Douglass, William. *A Summary, Historical and Political of the First Planting, Progressive Improvements and Present State of the British Settlements in North America.* London: R. Baldwin, 1755.

Drayton, John. *Memoirs of the American Revolution.* 2 vols. Charleston, S.C.: A. E. Miller, 1821.

Duke, Cecil A. "The Indian Boundary Line South of the Ohio, 1763 to 1802." Master's thesis, Vanderbilt University, 1930.

Easterly, J. H. (ed.). *The Journal of the Commons House of Assembly,*

September 12, 1739-March 26, 1741: *The Colonial Records of South Carolina.* Columbia, S.C.: The Historical Commission of South Carolina, 1952.

Evans, Lewis. *Geographical, Historical, Political, Philosophical and Mechanical Essays, The First Containing an Analysis of a General Map of the Middle British Colonies in America; and of the Country of the Confederate Indians. . . .* Philadelphia: B. Franklin and D. Hall, 1755.

Fenton, William N. *American Indian and White Relations to 1830: Needs and Opportunities for Study.* (Published for the Institute of Early American History and Culture, Williamsburg, Va.) Chapel Hill, N.C.: University of North Carolina Press, 1957.

Fenton, William N., and Gulick, John (eds.). *Symposium on Cherokee and Iroquois Culture.* (Smithsonian Institution, Bureau of American Ethnology, Bulletin 180.) Washington, D.C.: Government Printing Office, 1961.

Fernow, Berthold. *The Ohio Valley In Colonial Days. . . .* Albany, N.Y.: J. Munsell's Sons, 1890.

Fite, Emerson D., and Freeman, Archibald. *A Book of Old Maps.* Cambridge, Mass.: Harvard University Press, 1926.

Fleming, Barry. *Autobiography of a Colony: The First Half Century of Augusta, Georgia.* Athens, Ga.: University of Georgia Press, 1957.

Folmsbee, Stanley J., *et al. History of Tennessee.* 4 vols. New York: Lewis Historical Publishing Company, Inc., 1960.

Forbes, James G. *Sketches, Historical and Topographical, of the Floridas; More Particularly East Florida.* New York: C. S. Van Winkle, 1821.

Force, Peter. *Tracts and Other Papers.* 4 vols. Washington, D.C.: P. Force, 1836.

Ford, Worthington Chauncey. *The Writings of George Washington.* 14 vols. New York and London, G. P. Putnam's Sons, 1889-1893.

Fries, Aldelaide L. (ed.). *Records of the Moravians in North Carolina.* 8 vols. ("Publications of the North Carolina Historical Commission.") Raleigh, N.C.: Edwards & Broughton Printing Company, 1922-1954.

Friis, Herman R. *A Series of Population Maps of the Colonies and the United States, 1625-1790.* (American Geographical Society Mimeographed Publication, No. 13.) New York: American Geographical Society, 1940.

Frontiers of the Future. (Lectures delivered under the auspices of the Committee on International Relations on the Los Angeles Campus of the University of California, 1940.) Berkeley and Los Angeles: University of California Press, 1941.

Fundaburk, Emma L. (ed.). *Southeastern Indians: Life Portrait, A*

Catalogue of Pictures, 1565-1860. Luverne, Ala.: Emma L. Funda-
burk, Publisher, 1957.
Gipson, Lawrence H. *Lewis Evans.* Philadelphia: The Historical
Society of Pennsylvania, 1939.
Glen, James. *A Description of South Carolina.* . . . London: R & J
Dodsley, 1761.
Gray, Lewis C. *History of Agriculture in the Southern United States
to 1860.* 2 vols. Washington, D.C.: The Carnegie Institution, 1933.
Gregg, Alexander. *History of the Old Cheraws.* Columbia, S.C.: The
State Co., 1925.
Griffin, Clarence W. *History of Old Tryon and Rutherford Counties
North Carolina, 1730-1936.* Asheville, N.C.: Miller Printing Co.,
1937.
———. *Western North Carolina Sketches.* Forest City, N.C.: The
Forest City Courier, 1941.
Hale, John P. *Trans-Allegheny Pioneers: Historical Sketches of the
First White Settlers West of the Alleghenies 1748 and After.* 2nd
ed. Charleston, W. Va.: The Kanawha Valley Publishing Co., 1931.
Hall, James. *Sketches of History, Life, and Manners in the West.*
Philadelphia: H. Hall, 1835.
Hamilton, Peter J. *Colonial Mobile: An Historical Study Largely
from Original Sources.* . . . Boston and New York: Houghton
Mifflin Co., 1910.
Hamilton, Stanislaus Murray (ed.). *Letters to Washington and Other
Papers.* 5 vols. Boston and New York: Houghton Mifflin and
Company, 1898-1902.
Harmon, George D. *Sixty Years of Indian Affairs: Political, Economic
and Diplomatic, 1789-1850.* Chapel Hill, N.C.: University of North
Carolina Press, 1941.
Harper, Francis (ed.). *The Travels of William Bartram: Naturalist's
Edition.* New Haven: Yale University Press, 1958.
Harwell, Richard B. (ed.). *The Committee of Safety of Westmoreland
and Fincastle.* Richmond, Va.: Virginia State Library, 1956.
Hawes, Lilla M. (ed.). *The Papers of Lachlan McIntosh 1774-1779.*
("Collections of the Georgia Historical Society," Vol. XII.) Sa-
vannah, Ga.: For the Society, 1957.
——— (ed.). *The Proceedings and Minutes of the Governor and
Council of Georgia, October 4, 1774 through November 7, 1775, and
September 6, 1779 through September 20, 1780.* ("Collections of
the Georgia Historical Society," Vol. X.) Savannah, Ga.: For the
Society, 1952.
Haywood, John. *The Civil and Political History of the State of
Tennessee.* (An exact reprint of the 1823 edition.) Nashville, Tenn.:
W. H. Haywood, 1891.
Haywood, Marshall D. *Governor William Tryon and His Administra-*

tion in the Province of North Carolina, 1765-1771. Raleigh, N.C.: E. M. Uzzell, 1903.

Henderson, Archibald. *The Conquest of the Old Southwest.* New York: The Century Company, 1920.

Hewatt, Alexander. *An Historical Account of the Rise and Progress of the Colonies of South Carolina and Georgia.* 2 vols. London: Alexander Donaldson, 1779.

Hiden, Martha W. *How Justice Grew—Virginia Counties: An Abstract of Their Formation.* Williamsburg, Va.: The Virginia 350th Anniversary Celebration Corporation, 1957.

Hinkhouse, Fred J. *The Preliminaries of the American Revolution as Seen in the English Press 1763-1775.* New York: Columbia University Press, 1926.

A History of the Erection and Dedication of the Monument to Gen'l. James Edward Oglethorpe, Unveiled in Savannah, Ga., November 23, 1910. ("Collections of the Georgia Historical Society," Vol. VII, Pt. 2.) Savannah, Ga.: For the Society, 1911.

The History of North America with the Present State of the Different Colonies. London, 1776.

Hodge, Fred W., and Lewis, Theodore H. *Spanish Explorer in the Southern United States, 1528-1543.* New York: C. Scribner's Sons, 1907.

Hooker, Richard J. *The Carolina Backcountry on the Eve of the Revolution: The Journal and Other Writings of Charles Woodmason, Anglican Itinerant.* Chapel Hill, N.C.: University of North Carolina Press, 1953.

Howe, Henry. *Historical Collections of Virginia.* Charleston, S.C.: Babcock & Co., 1845.

Hutchins, Thomas. *The Courses of the Ohio River Taken by Lt. T. Hutchins Anno 1766. . . .* Ed. Beverly W. Bond, Jr. Cincinnati: Historical and Philosophical Society of Ohio, 1942.

———. *An Historical Narrative and Topographical Description of Louisiana and West Florida. . . .* Philadelphia: R. Aitken, 1784.

———. *A Topographical Description of Virginia, Pennsylvania, Maryland, and North Carolina.* Reprinted from the original edition of 1778 and ed. Frederick C. Hicks. Cleveland: Burrows Bros., 1904.

Imlay, Gilbert. *A Topographical Description of the Western Territory of North America.* New York: S. Campbell, 1793.

Jacobs, Wilbur R. (ed.). *Indians of the Southern Colonial Frontier: The Edmund Atkin Report and Plan of 1755.* Columbia, S.C.: University of South Carolina Press, 1954.

———. *Diplomacy and Indian Gifts: Anglo-French Rivalry Along the Ohio and Northwest Frontiers, 1748-1763.* Stanford, Cal.: Stanford University Press, 1950.

Jefferson, Thomas. *Notes on the State of Virginia.* With an introduction by Thomas Perkins Abernethy. ("Harper Torchbooks," The University Library.) New York: Harper & Row, 1964.

Jenson, Merrill (ed.). *American Colonial Documents to 1776.* Vol. IX of *English Historical Documents.* London, Eyre & Spottiswoode, 1955.

Jillson, Willard R. (ed.). *Filson's Kentucke.* (Filson Club Publications, No. 35.) Louisville, Ky., 1930.

Johnson, Cecil B. *British West Florida, 1763-1783.* New Haven: Yale University Press, 1943.

Johnston, J. S. *First Explorations of Kentucky: Dr. Thomas Walker's Journal also Col. Christopher Gist's Journal.* (Filson Club Publications, No. 13.) Louisville, Ky., 1898.

Jones, Charles C. *The Dead Towns of Georgia.* ("Collections of the Georgia Historical Society," Vol. IV.) Savannah, Ga.: For the Society, 1878.

Kappler, Charles J. *Indian Affairs—Laws and Treaties.* 4 vols. Washington, D.C.: Government Printing Office, 1903-1929.

Koontz, Louis K. *The Virginia Frontier, 1754-1763.* Baltimore: Johns Hopkins University Press, 1925.

Labaree, Leonard W. (ed.). *Royal Instructions to British Colonial Governors, 1670-1776.* 2 vols. New York: D. Appleton-Century Co., Inc., 1935.

Landrum, John B. O. *Colonial and Revolutionary History of Upper South Carolina.* Greenville, S.C.: Shannon & Co., 1897.

————. *History of Spartanburg County.* Atlanta: Franklin Printing and Publishing Co., 1900.

Laney, Francis B., and Wood, Katherine H. *Bibliography of North Carolina Geology, Mineralogy, and Geography With a List of Maps.* ("Bulletin of the North Carolina, Geological and Economic Survey," No. 18.) Raleigh, N.C.: E. M. Uzzell & Co., 1809.

Lefler, Hugh T. *A Guide to the Study and Reading of North Carolina History.* Chapel Hill, N.C.: University of North Carolina Press, 1955.

————. *North Carolina History Told by Contemporaries.* Chapel Hill, N.C.: University of North Carolina Press, 1934.

Le Page Du Pratz. *The History of Louisiana, or the Western Parts of Virginia and Carolina.* (Translated from French.) London, 1763.

Letters From General Oglethorpe to the Trustees of the Colony and Others, from October, 1735 to August, 1744. ("Collections of the Georgia Historical Society," Vol. III.) Savannah, Ga.: For the Society, 1873.

Letters of Benjamin Hawkins, 1796-1806. ("Collections of the Georgia Historical Society," Vol. IX.) Savannah, Ga.: For the Society, 1916.

The Letters of Hon. James Habersham, 1756-1775. ("Collections of the Georgia Historical Society," Vol. VI.) Savannah, Ga.: For the Society, 1904.

Letters of Joseph Clay, Merchant of Savannah, 1776-1793. ("Collections of the Georgia Historical Society," Vol. VIII.) Savannah, Ga.: For the Society, 1913.

Lewis, George E. *The Indiana Company 1763-1798: A Study in Eighteenth Century Frontier Land Speculation and Business Venture.* Glendale, Cal.: Arthur H. Clark Co., 1941.

Livermore, Shaw. *Early American Land Companies: Their Influence on Corporate Development.* New York: Columbia University School of Law, 1939.

Lunny, Robert M. *Early Maps of North America.* Newark, N.J.: The New Jersey Historical Society, 1961.

McCall, Hugh. *The History of Georgia: Containing Brief Sketches of the Most Remarkable Events Up to the Present Day.* 2 vols. Savannah, Ga.: Seymour Williams, 1811.

McCrady, Edward. *The History of South Carolina Under the Royal Government, 1719-1776.* New York: Macmillan Co., 1899.

MacDowell, William L. (ed.). *Documents Relating to Indian Affairs, May 21, 1750-August 7, 1754.* Columbia, S.C.: Archives Department, 1958.

McIlwaine, H. R., and Kennedy, John P. (eds.). *Journals of the House of Burgesses of Virginia, 1619-1776.* 13 vols. Richmond, Va.: The Colonial Press, E. Waddey Co., 1905-1915.

McLendon, Samuel G. *History of the Public Domain of Georgia.* Atlanta: Foote & Davis Co., 1924.

MacLeod, William C. *The American Indian Frontier.* London: Kegan, Paul, French, Trubner & Co., Ltd., 1928.

McPherson, Robert G. (ed.). *The Journal of the Earl of Egmont.* ("Wormsloe Foundation Publications," No. 5.) Athens, Ga.: University of Georgia Press, 1962.

Marschner, F. J. *Land Use and Its Patterns in the United States.* (U.S. Department of Agriculture Handbook No. 153.) Washington, D.C.: Government Printing Office, 1959.

Martin, Lawrence (ed.). *The George Washington Atlas.* Washington, D.C.: United States Washington Bicentennial Commission, 1932.

Mereness, Newton D. *Travels in the American Colonies.* New York: The Macmillan Company, 1916.

Meriwether, Robert L. *The Expansion of South Carolina, 1729-1765.* Kingsport, Tenn.: Southern Publishers, Inc., 1940.

Merrens, Harry Roy. *Colonial North Carolina In the Eighteenth Century: A Study In Historical Geography.* Chapel Hill, N.C.: University of North Carolina Press, 1964.

Miller, [David] Hunter (ed.). *Treaties and Other International Acts* of the United States. Washington, D.C.: U.S. Government Printing Office, 1931.

Miller, John C. *The Colonial Image: Origins of American Culture.* New York: George Braziller, 1962.

Milling, Chapman J. *Red Carolinians.* Chapel Hill, N.C.: University of North Carolina Press, 1940.

Mitchell, John. *The Present State of Great Britain and North America with Regard to Agriculture, Population, Trade and Manufacturing.* London: T. Becket & P. A. de Hondt, 1767.

Mohr, Walter H. *Federal Indian Relations, 1774-1788.* Philadelphia: University of Pennsylvania Press, 1933.

Monette, John W. *History of the Discovery and Settlement of the Valley of the Mississippi. By the Three Great European Powers . . . and Extension of Civil Government by the United States until the Year 1846.* 2 vols. New York: Harper & Bros., 1846.

Mooney, James. *Myths of the Cherokee.* ("Nineteenth Annual Report of the Bureau of American Ethnology, To the Secretary of the Smithsonian Institution, 1897-1898," Pt. I.) Washington, D.C.: Government Printing Office, 1900.

Moore, Francis. *A Voyage to Georgia, Begun in the Year 1735. . . .* ("Collections of the Georgia Historical Society," Vol. I.) Savannah, Ga.: For the Society, 1840.

Mowat, Charles L. *East Florida as a British Province, 1763-1784.* Berkeley and Los Angeles: University of California Press, 1943.

Mulkearn, Lois (ed.). *George Mercer Papers Relating to the Ohio Company of Virginia.* Pittsburgh: University of Pittsburgh Press, 1954.

Myer, William E. *Indian Travels of the Southeast.* ("Forty-Second Annual Report of the Bureau of Ethnology to the Secretary of the Smithsonian Institution, 1924-1925.") Washington, D.C.: Government Printing Office, 1928.

Nettel, Curtis P. *The Roots of American Civilization: A History of American-Colonial Life.* New York: F. S. Crofts and Company, 1938.

A New and Accurate Account of The Provinces of South Carolina and Georgia. London: J. Worrall and J. Roberts, 1732 [?].

A New Voyage to Georgia. By a Young Gentleman. Giving an Account of His Travels to South Carolina, and Part of North Carolina. . . . ("Collections of the Georgia Historical Society," Vol. II.) Savannah, Ga.: For the Society, 1842.

North America and the West Indies. London: Carington Bowles, 1764.

Nugent, Nell M. *Cavaliers and Pioneers: Abstracts of Virginia Land Patents and Grants 1623-1800.* 5 vols. Richmond, Va.: Dietz Printing Co., 1934.

Ogilby, John. *America: Being the Latest and Most Accurate Description of the New World.* . . . London, 1671.

Parish, John C. *The Persistence of the Westward Movement and Other Essays.* Berkeley and Los Angeles: University of California Press, 1943.

Patton, Sadie S. *Sketches of Polk County History.* Asheville, N.C.: Miller Printing Co., 1950.

Paullin, Charles O. *Atlas of the Historical Geography of the United States.* Washington, D.C.: The Carnegie Institution, 1932.

Peckham, Howard H. *Pontiac and the Indian Uprising.* Princeton, N.J.: Princeton University Press, 1947.

Phillips, Paul Chrisler. *The Fur Trade.* 2 vols. Norman, Okla.: University of Oklahoma Press, 1961.

Phillips, P. L. (ed.). *A Descriptive List of Maps of the Spanish Possessions Within the Present Limits of the United States 1502-1820, By Woodbury Lowery.* Washington, D.C.: Government Printing Office, 1912.

————. *Notes on the Life and Works of Bernard Romans.* Deland, Fla.: The Florida State Historical Society, 1924.

Pickett, Albert J. *History of Alabama and Incidentally of Georgia and Mississippi, From the Earliest Period.* Sheffield, Ala.: R. C. Randolph, 1896.

Pittman, Captain Philip. *The Present State of the European Settlements on the Mississippi with a Geographical Description of that River....* London, 1770.

Pomeroy, Kenneth B., and Yoho, James G. *North Carolina Lands.* Washington, D.C.: The American Forestry Association, 1964.

Pownall, Thomas. *A Topographical Description of the Dominions of the United States of America.* . . . Ed. Lois Mulkearn. Pittsburgh: University of Pittsburgh Press, 1949.

Price, A. G. *White Settlers and Native Peoples: An Historical Study of Racial Contacts Between English-Speaking Whites and Aboriginal Peoples in the United States, Canada, Australia and New Zealand.* Cambridge: Cambridge University Press, 1950.

Pugh, R. B. *The Records of the Colonial and Dominions Offices.* ("Public Record Office Handbooks," No. 3.) London: H. M. Stationery Office, 1964.

Ramsey, J. G. M. *The Annals of Tennessee.* Charleston, S.C.: John Russel, 1853.

Ranck, George W. *Boonesborough: Its Founding, Pioneer Struggles, Indian Experiences, Transylvania Days and Revolutionary Annals....* (Filson Club Publications, No. 16.) Louisville, Ky.: John P. Morton & Co., 1901.

Report of the Lords Commissioners for Trade and Plantations on the

Petition . . . For a Grant of Lands on the River Ohio . . . For the Purpose of Erecting a New Government. London, 1772.

Rights, Douglas L. *The American Indian in North Carolina.* 2nd ed. Winston-Salem, N.C.: John F. Blair, 1957.

Roberts, William. *An Account of the First Discovery and Natural History of Florida . . . Collected from the Best Authorities. . . .* London: T. Jeffrey's, 1763.

Romans, Bernard. *A Concise Natural History of East and West Florida.* (A facsimile reproduction of the 1775 edition with an introduction by Rembert W. Patrick.) Gainesville, Fla.: University of Florida Press, 1962.

Rowland, Dunbar (ed.). *English Dominion.* Vol. I. *Mississippi Provincial Archives, 1763-1766.* Nashville, Tenn.: Mississippi Department of Archives & History, 1911.

Royce, Charles C. *The Cherokee Nation of Indians.* ("Fifth Annual Report of the Bureau of American Ethnology to the Secretary of the Smithsonian Institution, 1883-1884.") Washington, D.C.: Government Printing Office, 1887.

————. *Indian Land Cessions In the United States.* ("Eighteenth Annual Report of the Bureau of American Ethnology to the Secretary of the Smithsonian Institution, 1896-1897.") Washington, D.C.: Government Printing Office, 1899.

Salley, A. S. *The Boundary Line Between North Carolina and South Carolina.* (Bulletin of the Historical Commission of South Carolina, No. 10.) Columbia, S.C.: The State Company, 1929.

———— (ed.). *Journal of the Commons House of Assembly of South Carolina January 8, 1765-August 9, 1765: The Colonial Records of South Carolina.* Columbia, S.C.: Historical Commission of South Carolina, 1949.

Saunders, William L. (ed.). *The Colonial Records of North Carolina.* 10 vols. Raleigh, N.C.: P. M. Hale, 1886-1890.

Skaggs, Marvin L. *North Carolina Boundary Disputes Involving Her Southern Line.* Chapel Hill, N.C.: University of North Carolina Press, 1941.

A State of the Province of Georgia Attested Upon Oath In the Court of Savannah, November 18, 1740. ("Collections of the Georgia Historical Society," Vol. II.) Savannah, Ga.: For the Society, 1842.

Stewart, George R. *Names on the Land.* New York: Random House, 1945.

Sutherland, Stella H. *Population Distribution in Colonial America.* New York: Columbia University Press, 1936.

Swanton, John R. *Early History of the Creek Indians and Their Neighbors.* (Bureau of American Ethnology, Smithsonian Institution, Bulletin 73.) Washington, D.C.: Government Printing Office, 1922.

————. *Indian Tribes of the Lower Mississippi Valley and Adjacent Coast of the Gulf of Mexico.* (Bureau of American Ethnology, Smithsonian Institution, Bulletin 43.) Washington, D.C.: Government Printing Office, 1911.

————. *The Indian Tribes of North America.* (Bureau of American Ethnology, Smithsonian Institution, Bulletin 145.) Washington, D.C.: Government Printing Office, 1952.

————. *The Indians of the Southeastern United States.* (Bureau of American Ethnology, Smithsonian Institution, Bulletin 137.) Washington, D.C.: Government Printing Office, 1946.

Thwaites, Reuben G. *Early Western Travels, 1748-1846.* 32 vols. Cleveland: A. H. Clark Co., 1904-1907.

Thwaites, Reuben G., and Kellogg, Louise P. *Documentary History of Dunmore's War 1774.* Madison, Wis.: Wisconsin Historical Society, 1905.

Timberlake, Lt. Henry. *Memoirs.* London, 1765.

U.S. Bureau of the Census. *A Century of Population Growth: From the First Census of the U.S. to the Twelfth, 1790-1900.* Washington, D.C.: Government Printing Office, 1901.

U.S. Department of Agriculture. *Atlas of American Agriculture: Physical Basis, Including Land Relief, Climate, Soils, and Natural Vegetation of the United States.* Washington, D.C.: Government Printing Office, 1936.

Urlsperger, S. *Ausfuhrliche Nachrichten von den Salzburgischen.* Vol. I. Halle, 1735-1752.

Vail, R. W. G. *The Voice of the Old Frontier.* Philadelphia: University of Pennsylvania Press, 1949.

Vance, Rupert B. *Human Geography of the South: A Study in Regional Resources and Human Adequacy.* Chapel Hill, N.C.: University of North Carolina Press, 1932.

Waddell, Alfred M. *A Colonial Officer and His Times, 1754-1773.* Raleigh, N.C.: Edwards & Broughton, 1890.

Wallace, David L. *The History of South Carolina.* New York: The American Historical Society Inc., 1934.

————. *The Life of Henry Laurens: With a Sketch of the Life of Lt. Col. John Laurens.* New York and London: G. P. Putnam's Sons, 1915.

Ware, Ethel K. *A Constitutional History of Georgia.* New York: Columbia University Press, 1947.

Washington—Wilkes, The Story of. Compiled and written by workers of the Writers' Program of Works Projects Administration in the State of Georgia. Athens, Ga.: University of Georgia Press, 1941.

Waynick, Capus. *North Carolina Roads and Their Builders.* Raleigh, N.C.: The Superior Stone Co., 1952.

Weeks, Stephen B. (ed.). *The Colonial Records of North Carolina.* 4 vols. Raleigh, N.C.: P. M. Hale, 1909-1914.

Wheat, Carl S. *Mapping the Transmississippi West.* 5 vols. San Francisco: The Institute of Historical Cartography, 1957.

Williams, Samuel C. (ed.). *Adair's History of the American Indians.* Johnson City, Tenn.: The Watauga Press, 1930.

————. *Dawn of Tennessee Valley and Tennessee History.* Johnson City, Tenn.: The Watauga Press, 1937.

————. *Early Travels in the Tennessee Country, 1540-1800.* Johnson City, Tenn.: The Watauga Press, 1928.

————. *Tennessee During the Revolutionary War.* Nashville, Tenn.: Tennessee Historical Commission, 1944.

Withers, Alexander Scott. *Chronicles of Border Warfare.* Cincinnati: The R. Clarke Company, 1895.

Woodward, Grace Steele. *The Cherokees.* Norman, Okla.: University of Oklahoma Press, 1963.

Wyman, Walker D., and Kroeber, Clifton B. *The Frontier in Perspective.* Madison, Wis.: University of Wisconsin Press, 1957.

Young, Arthur. *Observations on the Present State of the Waste Lands of Great Britain. . . .* London: W. Nicoll, 1773.

ARTICLES AND PAPERS

Alden, John R. "The Albany Congress and the Creation of the Indian Superintendencies," *The Mississippi Valley Historical Review,* XXVII (September, 1940), 193-210.

————. "John Stuart Accuses William Bull," *The William and Mary Quarterly,* Third Series II (July, 1945), 315-20.

Alvord, Clarence W. "The British Ministry and the Treaty of Fort Stanwix," *Wisconsin Historical Society Proceedings,* January, 1908, pp. 165-83.

Baer, Harold M. "An Early Plan for the Development of the West," *The American Historical Review,* XXX (April, 1925), 537-43.

Bartram, John. "Diary of a Journey Through the Carolinas, Georgia and Florida from July 1, 1765, to April 10, 1766," ed. Francis Harper, *Transactions of the American Philosophical Society,* n.s. XXXIII, Pt. 1 (December, 1942).

Bartram, William. "Travels in Georgia and Florida, 1773-74: A Report to Dr. John Fothergill," annotated by Francis Harper, *Transactions of the American Philosophical Society,* n.s. XXXIII, Pt. 2 (November, 1943).

Boyd, Mark F. "From a Remote Frontier: San Marcos de Apalache, 1763-1769," *The Florida Historical Quarterly,* XIX and XX (January, July, October, 1941 and January, 1942), 179-212, 82-92, 203-9, 293-310.

──────. "A Map of the Road from Pensacola to St. Augustine, 1778," *The Florida Historical Quarterly,* XVII (July, 1938), 15-24.

Brown, Ralph H. "The DeBrahm Charts of the Atlantic Ocean, 1772-1776," *Geographical Review,* XXVIII (January, 1938), 124-32.

Corry, John P. "The Houses of Colonial Georgia," *The Georgia Historical Quarterly,* XIV (September, 1930), 181-201.

Corse, Carita D. "DeBrahm's Report on East Florida, 1773," *The Florida Historical Quarterly,* XVII (January, 1939), 219-26.

Crane, Verner W. "Hints Relative to the Division and Government of the Conquered and Newly Acquired Countries in America," *The Mississippi Valley Historical Review,* VIII (March, 1922), 367-73.

──────. "The Origin of Georgia," *The Georgia Historical Review,* XIV (June, 1930), 93-110.

Crittendon, Charles C. "Inland Navigation in North Carolina, 1763-1789," *The North Carolina Historical Review,* VIII (April, 1931), 145-54.

──────. "Means of Communication in North Carolina, 1763-1789," *The North Carolina Historical Review,* VIII (October, 1931), 373-83.

──────. "Overland Travel and Transportation in North Carolina, 1763-1789," *The North Carolina Historical Review,* VIII (July, 1931), 239-57.

Cumming, William P. "Geographic Misconceptions of the Southeast in the Cartography of the 17th and 18th Centuries," *Journal of Southern History,* IV (November, 1938), 476-92.

De Vorsey, Louis. "The Donelson Line in East Tennessee and Kentucky," *Memorandum Folio,* Southeastern Division, Association of American Geographers, XIV (1962), 16-26.

──────. "The Pre-Revolutionary Southeast On 'An Accurate General Map,'" *Memorandum Folio,* Southeastern Division, Association of American Geographers, XVII (1965), n.p.

──────. "The Virginia-Cherokee Boundary of 1771," *East Tennessee Historical Society's Publications,* XXXIII (1961), 17-31.

Downes, Randolph C. "Cherokee-American Relations in the Upper Tennessee Valley, 1776-1791," *East Tennessee Historical Society's Publications,* VIII (1936), 35-53.

Farrand, Max. "The Indian Boundary Line," *The American Historical Review,* X (July, 1905), 782-91.

Flippin, Percy S. "The Royal Government in Georgia, 1752-1776," *The Georgia Historical Quarterly,* X (March, 1926), 1-25.

Ford, Worthington C. "Early Maps of Carolina," *Geographical Review,* XVI (April, 1926), 264-73.

Forsyth, Gideon C. "Geological, Topographical and Medical Information Concerning the Eastern Part of the State of Ohio," *The Medical Repository,* Second Hexade VI (November, 1808), 350-58.

Franklin, W. Neil. "Virginia and the Cherokee Indian Trade, 1673-

1752," *East Tennessee Historical Society's Publications,* IV (1932), 3-21.

Gamble, Thomas. "Colonial William Bull—His Part in the Founding of Savannah," *The Georgia Historical Quarterly,* XVII (June, 1933), 111-26.

Hamer, Philip M. "The British in Canada and the Southern Indians, 1790-1794," *East Tennessee Historical Society's Publications,* II (1930), 107-34.

———. "John Stuart's Indian Policy During the Early Months of the American Revolution," *The Mississippi Valley Historical Review,* XVII (December, 1930), 351-66.

———. "The Wataugans and the Cherokee Indians in 1776," *East Tennessee Historical Society's Publications,* III (January, 1931), 108-26.

Henderson, Archibald. "The Creative Forces in Westward Expansion: Henderson and Boone," *American Historical Review,* XX (October, 1914), 86-107.

———. "Richard Henderson: The Authorship of the Cumberland Compact and the Founding of Nashville," *Tennessee Historical Magazine,* II (October, 1916), 155-74.

———. "The Treaty of Long Island of Holston, July 1779," *North Carolina Historical Review,* VIII (January, 1931), 55-116.

Hinsdale, B. A. "The Western Land Policy of the British Government from 1763 to 1775," *Ohio Archaeological and Historical Publications,* I (December, 1887), 207-29.

Hofer, J. M. "The Georgia Salzburgers," *The Georgia Historical Quarterly,* XVIII (June, 1934), 99-117.

Horsman, Reginald. "American Indian Policy in the Old Northwest, 1783-1812," *The William and Mary Quarterly,* XVIII (January, 1961), 35-53.

Howard, C. N. "The Military Occupation of British West Florida, 1763," *The Florida Historical Quarterly,* XVII (January, 1939), 181-99.

Jackson, George B. "John Stuart: Superintendent of Indian Affairs for the Southern District," *Tennessee Historical Magazine,* III (September, 1917), 165-91.

James, Alfred P. "The First English-Speaking Transappalachian Frontier," *The Mississippi Valley Historical Review,* XVII (June, 1930), 55-71.

Jones, Howard M. "The Colonial Impulse: An Analysis of the Promotion Literature of Colonization," *Proceedings of the American Philosophical Society,* XC (May, 1948), 131-61.

Jones, Stephen B. "Boundary Concepts in the Setting of Place and Time," *Annals of the Association of American Geographers,* IL (September, 1959), 241-55.

Kirk, William. "Problems of Geography," *Geography*, XLVIII (November, 1963), 357-71.
Kristof, Ladis K. D. "The Nature of Frontiers and Boundaries," *Annals of the Association of American Geographers*, IL (September, 1959), 269-82.
Leowald, Klaus G., Starika, Beverly, and Taylor, Paul S. (eds.). "Johann Martin Bolzius Answers a Questionnaire on Carolina and Georgia," *The William and Mary Quarterly*, Third Series XIV (April, 1957), 218-61.
"A List of Early Land Patents and Grants Petitioned for in Virginia up to 1769," *The Virginia Magazine of History and Biography*, V (October, 1897, and January, 1898), 173-80 and 241-44.
McKinstry, Mary T. "Silk Culture in the Colony of Georgia," *The Georgia Historical Quarterly*, XIV (September, 1930), 225-35.
Mikesell, Marvin W. "Comparative Studies in Frontier History," *Annals of the Association of American Geographers*, L (March, 1960), 62-74.
Minghi, Julian V. "Boundary Studies in Political Geography," *Annals of the Association of American Geographers*, LIII (September, 1963), 407-28.
Mood, Fulmer. "The English Geographers and the Anglo-American Frontier in the Seventeenth Century," *University of California Publications in Geography*, VI (1944), 362-96.
Mowat, Charles L. "St. Augustine Under the British Flag, 1763-1775," *The Florida Historical Quarterly*, XX (October, 1941), 131-50.
————. "That Odd Being DeBrahm," *The Florida Historical Quarterly*, XX (April, 1942), 323-45
Nelson, Howard J. "Walled Cities of the United States," *Annals of the Association of American Geographers*, LI (March, 1961), 1-22.
Newton, Hester W. "The Agricultural Activities of the Salzburgers in Colonial Georgia," *The Georgia Historical Quarterly*, XVIII (September, 1934), 248-63.
————. "The Industrial and Social Influences of the Salzburgers in Colonial Georgia," *The Georgia Historical Quarterly*, XVIII (December, 1934), 335-53.
Norona, Delf. "Cartography of West Virginia," *West Virginia History*, IX (January, 1948), 99-127, 187-223.
———— (ed.). "Joshua Fry's Report on the Back Settlements of Virginia (May 8, 1751)," *The Virginia Magazine of History and Biography*, LVI (January, 1948), 22-41.
"Oglethorpe's Treaty with the Lower Creek Indians," *The Georgia Historical Quarterly*, IV (March, 1920), 3-16.
Pargelles, Stanley (ed.). "An Account of the Indians in Virginia," *The William and Mary Quarterly*, Third Series XVI (April, 1959), 228-43.

Pounds, Norman J. G. "The Origin of the Idea of Natural Frontiers in France," *Annals of the Association of American Geographers,* XLI (June, 1951), 146-57.

Reed, Susan M. "British Cartography of the Mississippi Valley in the Eighteenth Century," *The Mississippi Valley Historical Review,* II (September, 1915), 213-24.

Reps, John W. "Town Planning in Colonial Georgia," *The Town Planning Review,* XXX (January, 1960), 273-85.

Rights, D. L. "The Trading Path of the Indians," *The North Carolina Historical Review,* VIII (October, 1931), 403-26.

Roberts, Lucien E. "Sectional Problems in Georgia During the Formative Period, 1776-1798," *The Georgia Historical Quarterly,* XVIII (September, 1934), 208-27.

Rothrock, Mary W. "Carolina Traders Among the Overhill Cherokees, 1690-1760," *East Tennessee Historical Society's Publications,* I (1929), 3-18.

Rowland, Kate M. "The Ohio Company," *William and Mary College Quarterly Historical Papers,* I (April, 1893), 197-207.

Sauer, Carl O. "Historical Geography and the Western Frontier," *Papers Read at a Conference on the History of the Trans-Mississippi West,* 1930.

Siebert, Wilbur H. "The Loyalists in West Florida and the Natchez District," *The Mississippi Valley Historical Review,* II (March, 1916), 465-83.

Sioussat, St. George L. "The Breakdown of the Royal Management of Lands in the Southern Provinces, 1773-1775," *Agricultural History,* III (April, 1929), 67-98.

Sosin, Jack M. "The Yorke-Camden Opinion and American Land Speculators," *The Pennsylvania Magazine of History and Biography,* LXXXV (January, 1961), 38-49.

Smith, Daniel. "The Journal of Daniel Smith," introduction by St. George L. Sioussat, *Tennessee Historical Magazine,* I (March, 1915), 40-65.

Spykman, Nicholas John. "Frontiers, Security, and International Organization," *The Geographical Review,* XXXII (July, 1942), 436-47.

Turner, Frederick J. "Western State-Making in the Revolutionary Era," *The American Historical Review,* I (October, 1895), 70-87.

Trudeau, Jean Baptiste. "Remarks on the Manners of the Indians Living High Up the River Missouri," trans. Samuel L. Mitchell, *The Medical Repository,* Second Hexade VI (May, 1809), 52 and 120.

Webber, Mabel L. "An Indian Land Grant in 1734," *The South Carolina Historical and Genealogical Magazine,* XIX (October, 1918), 157-61.

White, Dr. J. E. "Topography of Savannah and Its Vicinity; A Report to the Georgia Medical Society, May 3, 1806," *The Georgia Historical Quarterly,* I (September, 1917), 236-42.

Williams, Samuel C. "Henderson and Company's Purchase Within the Limits of Tennessee," *Tennessee Historical Magazine,* V (April, 1919), 5-27.

———. "Stephen Holston and Holston River," *East Tennessee Historical Society's Publications,* VIII (1936), 26-34.

Wilson, Samuel M. "West Fincastle—Now Kentucky," *The Filson Club Quarterly,* IX (January, 1935), 65-94.

BIBLIOGRAPHICAL GUIDES, DOCUMENTS, AND UNPUBLISHED MATERIALS

Abbott, Phyllis R. "The Development and Operations of an American Land System to 1800." Unpublished Ph.D. dissertation, University of Wisconsin, 1959.

Adams, Randolph G. *British Headquarters Maps and Sketches . . . A Descriptive List of the Original Manuscripts and Printed Documents in the William L. Clements Library. . . .* Ann Arbor, Mich.: The William L. Clements Library, 1926.

Andrews, Charles M. *Departmental and Miscellaneous Papers.* Vol. II of *Guide to the Materials for American History to 1783, In the Public Record Office of Great Britain.* Washington, D.C.: The Carnegie Institution, 1914.

———. *The State Papers.* Vol. I of *Guide to the Materials for American History to 1783, In the Public Record Office of Great Britain.* Washington, D.C.: The Carnegie Institution, 1912.

Andrews, C. M., and Davenport, F. C. *Guide to the Manuscript Materials for the History of the United States to 1783, In Minor London Archives and In the Libraries of Oxford and Cambridge.* Washington, D.C.: The Carnegie Institution, 1908.

Before the Indian Claims Commission. Docket No. 73, The Seminole Indians of the State of Florida, Petitioner; Docket No. 151, The Seminole Nation of Oklahoma, Petitioner, Versus United States of America, Defendant. Defendant's Requested Findings of Fact, Objections to Petitioners' Proposed Findings, and Brief. Washington, D.C.: Government Printing Office, 1963.

Brun, Christian. *Guide to the Manuscript Maps in the William L. Clements Library.* Ann Arbor, Mich.: University of Michigan, 1959.

Catalogue of Maps, Plans and Charts in the Map Room of the Dominion Archives. ("Publications of the Canadian Archives," No. 8.) Ottawa: Canadian Government Printing Bureau, 1912.

Cumming, William P. "Cartography of Colonial Carolina." Address delivered at the formal opening of the Kendall Memorial Room, South Caroliniana Library, University of South Carolina, October 29, 1961.

Davidson, George. "Explanation of an Indian Map of the Rivers, Lakes, Trails and Mountains from the Chilkaht to the Yukon, Drawn by the Chilkaht Chief Kohklux, in 1869." Reprinted from *Mazama* (Portland, Oregon), April, 1901.

Derthick, Lawrence G. "The Indian Boundary Line in the Southern District of British North America, 1763-1779." Unpublished Master's thesis, University of Tennessee, 1930.

Drake, Samuel G. *Early History of Georgia, Embracing the Embassy of Sir Alexander Cummings to the Country of the Cherokees, in the Year 1730.* Reprint of a paper read before the New England Historic, Genealogical Society, February, 1872. Boston: David Clapp & Son, 1872.

Journal of the Congress of the Four Southern Governors, and the Superintendent of That District, with the Five Nations of Indians, At Augusta, 1763. Charles-Town, S.C.: Peter Timothy, 1764. (Photographic copy of journal bound with C. O. 323-17, P.R.O., London.)

Karpinski, Louis C. "Manuscript Maps of American European Archives," *Michigan History Magazine*, XIV (Winter, 1930), 5-14.

————. "Manuscript Maps Relating to American History in French, Spanish and Portuguese Archives," *The American Historical Review*, XXXIII (January, 1928), 328-30.

————. *MS. Maps in French, [Spanish], & Portuguese Archives.* Library of Congress Geography and Map Division, n.d. (photo copy of typescript).

Kelsay, Laura E. (comp.). *List of Cartographic Records of the Bureau of Indian Affairs.* (Record Group 75.). *Special Lists, No. 13.* The National Archives, National Archives and Records Service, General Services Administration. Washington, D.C.: National Archives, 1954.

———— (comp.). *List of Cartographic Records of the General Land Office.* (Record Group 49.) *Special Lists, No. 19.* The National Archives, National Archives and Records Service, General Services Administration. Washington, D.C.: National Archives, 1964.

List of Colonial Office Records Preserved in the Public Record Office. London: Public Record Office, 1911.

List of National Archives Microfilm Publications, 1961. The National Archives, National Archives and Records Services Administration. Washington, D.C.: National Archives, 1961.

Manuscript Maps, Charts and Plans, and Topographical Drawings in the British Museum. Vols. I-III. London: Department of Manuscripts, B. M., n.d.

The New World: A Catalogue of an Exhibition of Books, Maps, Manuscripts and Documents Held at Lambeth Palace Library Be-

tween 1 May and December 1957. London: Lambeth Palace Library, 1957.

"North Carolina Items from the South Carolina and American General Gazette: May 30, 1766—December 20, 1780." North Carolina Historical Commission, N.C. Department of Archives and Records, n.d. (typed).

Palmer, William P. (ed.). *Calendar of Virginia State Papers and Other Manuscripts, 1652-1781, Preserved in the Capitol at Richmond.* 11 vols. Richmond, Va.: State of Virginia, 1875.

Paullin, C. O., and Paxson, F. L. *Guide to the Materials in London Archives for the History of the United States Since 1783.* Washington, D.C.: The Carnegie Institution, 1914.

Petty, Julian P. *A Bibliography of the Geography of the State South Carolina.* ("University of South Carolina Publications, Series II, Physical Sciences," Bulletin No. 2.) Columbia, S.C.: Research Committee, University of South Carolina, 1952.

Rhoads, James B., and Ashby, Charlotte M. (comps.). *Preliminary Inventory of the Cartographic Records of the Bureau of the Census.* (Record Group 29.) *Preliminary Inventories, No. 103.* The National Archives, National Archives and Records Service, General Services Administration. Washington, D.C.: National Archives, 1958.

Swem, Earl G. *Maps Relating to Virginia in the Virginia State Library and Other Departments of the Commonwealth.* ("Bulletins of the Virginia State Library," Vol. 7, Nos. 2 and 3.) Richmond, Va.: D. Bottom, superintendent of Public Printing, 1914.

Thomas, Bradford L. (comp.). "A Bibliographical List of Cartographers, Engravers, and Publishers of the XVI to XIX Century Maps in the University of Kansas Library." Lawrence, Kan.: The University of Kansas Department of Geography, 1961 (mimeographed).

Vindel, Francisco. *Mapas De America y Filipinas En Los Libros Espanoles De Los Siglos XVI al XVIII. . . .* Madrid, 1959.

———. *Mapas De America En Los Libros Espanoles De Los Siglos XVI al XVIII.* Madrid, 1955.

Wroth, Lawrence C. "Source Materials of Florida History in the John Carter Brown Library of Brown University," *The Florida Historical Quarterly,* XX (January, 1940), 3-46.

MANUSCRIPTS

British Museum, London.
Additional Manuscripts.
King George III's Topographical Collection.
King's Manuscripts.

Library of Congress, Washington, D.C.
Manuscript and Photo Copied Maps.
North Carolina Department of History and Archives, Raleigh, N.C.
Various Manuscript Maps and Papers.
Public Record Office, London. Colonial Office Records.
America and West Indies (original correspondence, etc.). C. O. 5 ([1606] to 1807). 1,450 volumes and bundles.
Colonies General. C. O. 323 (1689 to 1943). 1,868 volumes.
Maps and Plans. C. O. 700 (17th to 19th centuries). *Ca.* 1,600 maps.
William L. Clements Library, Ann Arbor, Mich.
Manuscript Maps.

SELECTED MANUSCRIPT MAPS

Southeast and General

"A Map of the Cherokee Country," John Stuart. 1761. **British** Museum, Additional MSS. 14,036, fol. e.

"A Map of the Southern Indian District 1764," John Stuart. 1764. British Museum, Additional MSS. 14,036, fol. d.

"A Map of the Indian Nations In the Southern Department, 1766," [De Brahm or Stuart]. 1766. Clements Library, No. 564.

"A Map of the Southern Indian District of North America: Compiled Under the Direction of John Stuart Esqr. His Majesty's Superintendent of Indian Affairs and by Him Humbly Inscribed to the Earl of Dartmouth . . . ," Joseph Purcell. [1775]. P.R.O., C. O. 700, North America General/12; Library of Congress, Photo Copy.

Ibid. (another copy). P.R.O., M.R. 919. (In the course of research connected with this study, the author identified two separately catalogued map fragments as portions of another copy of the Stuart-Purcell map of 1775. These fragments are now joined and catalogued under the number given here.)

"A Map of the Southern Indian District of North America: Compiled Under the Direction of John Stuart Esq. His Majesty's Superintendent of Indian Affairs," Joseph Purcell. [1775]. Ayer Collection, Newberry Library, Chicago. (This is essentially another copy of the Stuart-Purcell map of 1775. It lacks the dedication to Dartmouth and is incorrectly dated 1773).

"A New Map of the Southern District of North America from Surveys taken by the Compiler and Others, from Accounts of Travellers and from the Best Authorities etc. etc. Compiled in 1781 for Lieut. Colonel Thomas Brown, His Majesty's Superintendent of Indian Affairs etc.," Joseph Purcell. 1781. P.R.O.,

C. O. 700, North America General/15; Library of Congress, Photo Copy.

Ibid. (another copy, without title). National Archives, Washington, D.C., Map No. U.S. 113, Record Group 77, Records of the Chief of Engineers. (The author has identified this as a manuscript copy of the Brown-Purcell map. It includes several notes not found on the original.)

Virginia

"A Plan of the Line Between Virginia and North Carolina, From Peters Creek to Steep Rock Creek, Ran In the Year of Our Lord, 1749 . . . ," Joshua Fry, Peter Jefferson, Wm. Churton, and Danl. Weldon. 1749. P.R.O., M.P.G. 361; Library of Congress, Photo Copy.

"Map of the Lands Purchased At Fort Stanwix, and Those Which Remain to be Purchased of the Cherokees In Order To Secure Peace [Western Virginia]," Anon. 1768. P.R.O., C. O. 700, Virginia/18.

"A Sketch of the Cherokee Boundaries with the Province of Virginia etc.," John Stuart. 1771. P.R.O., M.P.G. 348.

"Boundary Line Between the Colony of Virginia and the Cherokee Hunting Grounds," John Donelson. 1771. P.R.O., C. O. 700, Virginia/19; Library of Congress, Photo Copy.

The Carolinas

"Boundary Line Between the Province of South Carolina and the Cherokee Indian Country, Marked Out In Presence of the Head Men of the Upper, Middle and Lower Cherokee Towns, Whose Hands and Seals are Affixed . . . ," John Pickens. 1766. P.R.O., C. O. 700, Carolina/26; Library of Congress, Photo Copy.

"Map of Lands Near the Salud River Showing Reservations made for Cherokee Half Breeds: With Surveyors Certificate," Patrick Calhoun. 1770. P.R.O., M.P.G. 338.

Georgia

"A Map of Georgia and Florida Taken From the Latest and Most Accurate Surveys. Delineated & Drawn by a Scale of 69 English Miles to a Degree of Latitude," Thomas Wright. 1763. P.R.O., C. O. 700, Georgia/13; Library of Congress, Photo Copy.

"A Map of the Sea Coast of Georgia & the Inland Parts Thereof Extending to the Westward of that Part of Savannah Called Broad River . . . ," Henry Yonge & Wm. G. De Brahm. August 20, 1763. Clements Library, No. 635 (Clinton Map 329); Library of Congress, Photo Copy.

Ibid. (another copy). British Museum, Additional MSS. 14,036, fol. g.; Library of Congress, Photo Copy.

"Georgia . . . Sketch of the Boundary Line as It Is Now Mark'd Between the . . . Province and the Creek Indian Nation," Samuel Savery. 1769. P.R.O., C. O. 700, Georgia/14; Library of Congress, Photo Copy.

"Georgia . . . Sketch of the Boundary Line as It Is Now Mark'd Between the . . . Province and the Creek Indian Nation (a certified copy)," Bernard Romans. 1769. P.R.O., M.P.G. 337.

"Georgia—By the Surveyor General," [De Brahm]. [1771]. British Museum, Additional MSS. 14,036, fol. f.; Library of Congress, Photo Copy.

[Map of Georgia showing boundaries with Indians], Anon. 1771. P.R.O., M.P.G. 20 (Removed from C. O. 5-661, p. 437. This map was used in London to illustrate the Board of Trade representation to the Crown concerning the New Purchase.)

"The Lands Which the Cherokees Have Assigned for Payment of Their Debts," John Stuart. 1772. P.R.O., M.R. 18; Library of Congress, MS Copy.

"A Map of the Lands Ceded to His Majesty by the Creek and Cherokee Indians at a Congress Held in August the 1st June 1773 . . . Containing 1,616,298 Acres," Philip Yonge. 1773. P.R.O., M.P.G. 2.

"The Boundary Line Between the Province of Georgia and Nation of Creek Indians From Altamaha to Ogeechee Rivers," Andrew Way. 1773. P.R.O., C. O. 5-663, p. 113.

The Floridas

"Map Showing Location of Spanish Land Grants In East Florida— Drawn From the Original Plan of John Gordon Esqr. Given to Governor Grant," James Moncrief, Engineer. *Ca.* 1763. P.R.O., C. O. 700, Florida/7; Library of Congress, Photo Copy.

"Field Survey of the River Mobile and Part of the Rivers Alabama and Tensa with the Different Settlements and Lands Marked Thereon. The Old Settlements Made by the French are Marked with Black. Those Granted to the English are Marked Red," Durnford. 1770. P.R.O., C. O. 700, Florida/40.

"Map of the General Surveys of East Florida Performed from the Year, 1766 to 1770 . . . ," William Gerard De Brahm. *Ca.* 1771. British Museum, King's MSS. 211, fol. 3 (1); Library of Congress, Photo Copy.

"A Plan of Part of the Rivers Tombicbe, Alabama, Tensa, Perdito & Scambia In the Province of West Florida," David Taitt. 1771. P.R.O., M.P.G. 6.

"Plan of the Rivers Mississippi, Iberville, Mobile, and Bay of

Pensacola . . . Shewing the Situation and Extent of the Lands Granted by the English Thereon from the Surveys of Elias Durnford, Surveyor General of West Florida," Samuel Lewis. 1772. British Museum, King George III's Topographical Collection, CXXII, 90; Library of Congress, Photo Copy.

"A plan of the Indian Boundary Line [section missing] From Atchtickpi to the Buckatanne; and From the Line at [torn] Buckatanne to the Pascagoula River; the Road to Mobile . . . ," Charles Stuart. 1772. Clements Library, No. 668 (Clinton Map 341); Library of Congress, Photo Copy.

"A New Map of West Florida, Georgia & South Carolina; With Part of Louisiana . . . by Order of John Stuart, Esqr: Superintendent of Indian Affairs . . . ," Samuel Lewis. 1774. British Museum, King George III's Topographical Collection, CXXII, 89; Library of Congress, Photo Copy.

"East Florida East of the 82nd degree of Longitude from Meridian of London . . . ," William Gerard De Brahm. *Ca.* 1775. P.R.O., C. O. 700, Florida/3; Library of Congress, Photo Copy (1770).

"A Survey of the Part of the Eastern Coast of East Florida from St. Mary's Inlet to Mount Halifax. Showing the Ascertained Boundary Between East Florida and the Creek Indians," [William G. De Brahm]. *Ca.* 1775. P.R.O., C. O. 700, Florida/53; Library of Congress, Photo Copy.

"Survey of the Bay and River Mobile With List and References to the Lands Granted, The Proprietors Names etc.," Anon. [1775]. P.R.O., C. O. 700, Florida/51; Library of Congress, Photo Copy.

"That Part of the Chactaw Indian Boundary Line Lying between Yazo and Pascagoula Rivers In [West Florida] . . . ," Joseph Purcell. 1779. P.R.O., C. O. 700, Florida/56, 1 and 2; Library of Congress, Photo Copy.

SELECTED TOPOGRAPHIC MAPS

The student interested in conducting a detailed examination of the Southern Indian Boundary Line would find the maps listed below valuable. They are published and distributed by the United States Geological Survey in the series "United States 1:250,000." The 1:250,000 scale (about 1 inch = 4 miles) provides sufficient detail to allow the Southern Indian Boundary Line to be located with a fair degree of accuracy through its whole length. The price of each map is 50 cents. Prepayment is required and may be made by money order or check, payable to the Geological Survey. The sheet names and numbers listed are sufficient identification for ordering. Further information as well as an index map showing the location of the individual sheets may be obtained from the Map Information Office, Geological Survey, Washington 25, D.C.

Andalusia	NH 16-2
Apalachicola	NH 16-9
Athens	NI 17-7
Augusta	NI 17-8
Baton Rouge	NH 15-6
Bluefield	NJ 17-8
Brunswick	NH 17-2
Charlotte	NI 17-2
Daytona Beach	NH 17-8
Fort Pierce	NG 17-2
Gainesville	NH 17-7
Greenville	NI 17-4
Hattiesburg	NH 16-1
Jackson	NI 15-12
Jacksonville	NH 17-5
Jenkins	NJ 17-7
Johnson City	NJ 17-10
Knoxville	NI 17-1
Macon	NI 17-10
Miami	NG 17-8
Mobile	NH 16-4
Natchez	NH 15-3
Orlando	NH 17-11
Pensacola	NH 16-5
Plant City	NH 17-10
Savannah	NI 17-1
Spartanburg	NI 17-5
Tallahassee	NH 16-6
Tampa	NG 17-1
Valdosta	NH 17-4
Waycross	NH 17-1
West Palm Beach	NG 17-5
Winston-Salem	NJ 17-11

Index

A

Abbeville, S.C., 112
Abbeville County, S.C., 134
Abbott, Phyllis R., 39
Abernethy, Thomas P., 90
Ahoya (The Cowkeeper), 187
Alabama, 5n, 210
Alabama River, 215, 220
Albany Convention, 7
Alden, John R., describes Atkin
  Report, 9; on British economic
  strength, 11; summarizes Virginia
  argument to extend settlement, 59;
  first to employ Donelson Map, 91;
  suggests misunderstanding between
  Cherokee and whites, 125; expansion
  of Georgia cause for Indian disputes,
  145; map of Georgia boundary, 179;
  mentioned, 62, 65, 89
Aleck. See Captain Aleck
Alibama Indians, 9
Alibamo Mingo, 209, 210
Alvord, Clarence W., 90
American Revolution, 14
Anderson County, S.C., 134
Anglo-Cherokee, relations reviewed, 60;
  crises, 118
Anglo-French conflict, 120
Anglo-Indian relations, 8
Anglo-Spanish controversy, 217
Apalachicola River, 182
Apalachie, formal meeting with Creeks
  held, 188
Appalachian Mountains, 5; as western
  limit of colonies, 36
Appalachian Valley, 5
Altamaha River, 141, 143, 171, 173,
  175
Athens, Ga., 171
Atkin, Edmund, observations on tribal
  locations, 10; Report and Plan of
  1755, 10n; mentioned, 9, 12
Atlantic Coast, 5

Attakullakulla (Little Carpenter), in-
  troduces topic of Cherokee-Virginia
  Boundary, 48; gives reason for altering boundary, 83; motives for alteration, 84-85; leads peace delegation, 122; states Cherokee attitude
  toward advancing S.C. frontier, 124;
  mentioned, 61, 79
Augusta County, Va., 48
Augusta, Ga., 39, 140, 171

B

Bailey, Kenneth P., 53
Bartram, John, 191
Bartram, William, describes Indian vil-
  lage, 17; describes Indian agriculture,
  18; joins boundary survey, 170; at-
  tends Indian congress, 191
Beards Creek, 178
Big Sandy River, 87
Black Creek, 193
Blue Grass region, 5
Blue Ridge, 51, 59, 119
Board of Trade, prohibited westward
  growth of Virginia, 27; map shows
  1763 Indian boundary, 32-34; Re-
  port of 1748, 54; prohibits land
  grants, 58; expresses confidence in
  Governor of Georgia, 168; map of
  Indian cession in Georgia, 175; on
  disposition of French and Spanish
  territory, 182
Boggs, S. W., 44
Bolzius, the Reverend Johann M., 144
Boone, Governor Thomas, 124
Botetourt, Lieutenant Governor, 69, 78
Boundary, defined, 44; Indian under-
  standing of, 45
Briar Creek (Bryar Creek), 143, 156
British Public Record Office, 7n, 43
Broad River, 162, 169, 175
Buckatunna Creek (Baccatane, Bucka-
  tanne), 209, 210, 222, 224, 225
Bureau of American Ethnology, 13

C

Calhoun, Patrick, 105, 124
Callaway, James E., 144
Cameron, Alexander, 76, 79, 97, 102, 128, 130, 132
Caneecatee (Old Hop), 117
Canoochee River, 156
Captain Aleck, delegated to settle boundary with Georgia, 152-53; complains of disorderly frontiersmen, 160; modifies Creek boundary proposal, 193
Carrollton, Kentucky, 86
Cartwright, John, 29
Catawba Indians, census by Atkin, 9; elected chief of, 16; number and location in 1764, 20; at Augusta Congress in 1763, 40
Catawba Path, 113
Catawba River, 86
Charleston, S.C. (Charles Town) delegation of Cherokee visit, 118; mentioned, 115, 117
Chattahoochee River, 20, 182, 184
Chehaws Square, 153
Cherokee County, S.C., 98
Cherokee hunting grounds, 48, 115
Cherokee Indians, census by Atkin, 9; tribal subdivisions, 16; number and location in 1764, 19-20; propose boundary with Virginia, 60; describe North Carolina-Cherokee Boundary, 94; complain of encroachments, 94; alarmed by advance of white settlers, 95; inform of epidemic, 100; meet Governor of N.C., 101; land cessions to S.C., 112n; involved with French and Indian enemies, 116; alarmed by S.C. frontier advance, 116-17; indicate preference for English over French, 118; meet Oglethorpe, 141; cede land to traders, 162-63
Cherokee Path, 115
Cherokee War, of 1760, 121; at peace with Georgia during, 148
Cherokee River. *See* Tennessee River
Chickasaw Indians, census by Atkin, 9; number and location in 1764, 22; town near Augusta surveyed, 140; meet Oglethorpe, 141; included at Choctaw Congress, 208
Chickasawy River, 210
Chiswell, John, 57, 58n

Chiswell's Lead Mine, 57, 58n, 61, 64, 65, 99
Choctaw Congress, 208
Choctaw-Creek War, influence on East Florida, 195; a distraction to the tribes, 215
Choctaw Indians, census by Atkin, 10; number and location in 1764, 22; meet Oglethorpe, 141; contacts with West Florida, 205; cede territory at Mobile, 210
Coleman, Kenneth, 179
Colonial and Dominions Offices Records, 7n, 43
The Commons House of Assembly of S.C., 124
Continental Congress, 234
Cook, James, 113
Coosa River, 20
Corner Creek. *See* Devises Corner Brook
Coronaka (Coronacre, Corn Acre) S.C., 113, 115
Coronaka Creek, 113
Coulter, E. Merton, 143
Coweta Town, 140-41
Cowkeeper, The. *See* Ahoya
Crackers, creating problems, 125; defined, 168
Creek Indians, census by Atkin, 9; internal political life complex, 16; number and location in 1764, 20-21; Lower Division of, 39; withdraw from Georgia, 136; reaffirm treaty with Oglethorpe, 141; attend Congress with Georgia in 1757, 146; create disturbances in Georgia, 153; at war with Choctaw, 161; claims in East Florida, 199; contacts with West Florida, 205
Cripple Creek, 57
Croghan, George, 73
Cumberland Front, 5
Cumberland Plateau, 5, 56, 86
Cumming, William P., prepared map of Florida's Indian Boundary Line, 202; determined location of tidal limit boundary, 203; reconstruction of West Florida-Creek Boundary, 226-27; mentioned, 173
Cusseta Town, 141

D

Dartmouth, Lord, 229
De Brahm, William G., description of Cherokee land, 17n; comment on

Indian cartography, 47; *Report of the General Survey* . . . , 160n, 200; map of East Florida, 200; suspended as surveyor of East Florida, 201; mentioned, 157, 230

Declaration of Independence, 39

Defendant's Exhibit 128, presented before the Indian Claims Commission, 202

Derthick, Lawrence G., 90

Devises (Dewises, Dewitt's Duet's) Corner Brook, 98, 114, 128n, 129

De Voto, Bernard A., 42, 43, 44

Doctor's Town, 178

Donelson, John, map of Virginia-Cherokee Line, 79-91 *passim*; mentioned, 76, 110, 230

Donelson Line, the demarcation of, 79-85 *passim*; an evaluation of, 85-92 *passim*; retraced in 1774, 89

Dunmore, Governor John M., 87, 88

E

East Florida, colony of, 21; a result of the Proclamation of 1763, 181; boundaries adjusted, 184; discussed at Augusta Indian Congress, 184-85; population of, 198; mentioned, 35, 150, 152

East Florida-Creek Boundary, delineation of, 190-198 *passim*; not demarcated, 195; ratified, 197; on eighteenth-century maps, 198-202; on present-day maps, 202-3

East Florida-Creek hunting grounds, 191-92

Ebenezer, Ga., 143, 173

Egremont, Lord, on an Indian policy, 27-28; requests that Indian reserve be included in provincial bounds, 33-34

Ellis, Governor Henry, 28-29, 146

Emistisiguo, 217, 218, 219

Escambia River, 220

Escambia Valley, Anglo-Indian controversy concerning, 221

Evans, Lewis, 25

F

Falkland Islands, controversy over prompts new series of Indian Congresses, 217

Farrand, Max, omits mention of Donelson Line, 90; map of Southern Indian Boundary Line, 179

Fauquier, Lieutenant Governor Francis, 59n, 62, 68

Fleming, Berry, 179

Flint-Apalachicola River system, 182

Flint River, 20, 32, 182

Flippin, Percy S., 139

Florida, 5n

Florida Peninsula, 32

Fort Barrington, 141, 173, 178

Fort Duquesne, 27, 58

Fort Loudon, 118, 121

Fort Picolata, Indian Congress convened, 191; treaty between East Florida and Creek Indians signed, 194; second Congress called, 196

Fort Prince George, 94, 119, 120, 122, 125, 128

Fort Stanwix, Indian Congress held, 65-66

Fort Stanwix Cession, seen as extinguishing Indian claims south of Ohio River, 69; affects frontiersmen, 71; accelerates westward expansion, 73

Fort Stuart Military Reservation, 153

Franklin, Benjamin, 39, 89

French, territory along Gulf of Mexico, 181; Congress with Indians of Gulf Coast, 205; *See also* Propagandists

French and Indian War, The, 25-26, 58

Friis, Herman R., 116

Frohock, John, 102

Frontier, 44-45n

Fry, Joshua, discusses Virginia-Indian relations, 49-52; Report on the Back Settlements of Virginia, 50n; quoted, 55; mentioned, 110, 230

G

Galphin, George, 160

Gentleman's Magazine, The, 36

Georgia, Colony of, contacts with Creek Indians, 21; pioneers moving into, 26; allowed to extend limits, 148; flow of new settlers into, 157; concern about character of frontier settlers, 169; mentioned, 20

Georgia-Creek Boundary, of 1739, 141, 172; delineation of, 149-51; demarcation in 1768, 151-57 *passim*

Georgia, General Assembly of, 146, 160

Georgia-Indian Boundary, on eighteenth-century maps, 172-78 *passim*; on present-day maps, 178-80

Germany Creek, 159

Gist, Christopher, 53

Glen, Governor James, 46, 115, 119
Goose Ponds, 153
Grant, Governor James, leads force in Cherokee War, 122; on East Florida-Georgia boundary, 184n; arrives at St. Augustine, 189; requests an Indian Congress, 190; advocates military strength, 190; desires additional land, 195; delays demarcation, 197
Great Creek, 159
Great Valley of Virginia, 55
Greeks, 198
Greenbrier River, 57, 71
Greenville County, S.C., 99, 105
Greenville-Spartanburg County boundary, 107
Greenwood, S.C., 112, 115
Gulf Coast, 5

H

Haldimand, General, 135
Halifax, Lord, 34
Hamer, Philip M., 110, 111
Hamilton, Peter J., 227
Hard Labour, S.C., 64, 133
Hard Labour Line, The, named, 65; Virginia seeks to extend, 67, 76; on map, 78; mentioned, 74
Henderson, Archibald, 90
Henderson, Richard B., 90, 111
Heron, Benjamin, 109
Hillsborough, Lord, 228, 230
Hinsdale, B. A., 39
Hite, Jacob, 134
Holston River, 48, 52, 55, 62, 75, 110
Holston Valley, pioneers ordered to leave, 38; Virginia pioneers settle, 74

I

Iberville River, 181, 216
Illinois country, 5
Indentured servants, 198
Indians, Southeastern, chief fears of, 8; dilemma of, 11-12; need for location maps on, 13; lands claimed by in 1763, 14; tribal organization, 15; political maturity of, 15; location and strength of, 15-23 *passim*; reliance on agriculture, 17-18; concept of boundaries, 43-47 *passim*; cartographic capabilities of, 45-47
Indian Congresses, journals of, 4
Indian hunting grounds, 31, 234
Indian traders, 64, 169
Indian treaties, 43

Irish Settlement, in Georgia, 160
Iroquois, Federation of, 7; claims to land behind Virginia, 50; raids on Catawba Tribe, 50; decline in strength of, 51; mentioned, 15
Italians, 198

J

Jefferson County, Ga., 160
Jefferson, Peter, 230
Jessup, Ga., 152
Johnson, Sir William, accepts southern territory from Iroquois, 66; mentioned, 73
Johnstone, Governor George, arrives at Pensacola, 206; negotiations with Choctaw 210; informs Indians of land needs, 212
Jud's Friend (Ustenaka), 101

K

Kanawha River, 32, 66
Kanawha Valley settlements, 59, 64
Kentucky, 5n, 26, 66
Kentucky River, followed by Donelson, 84; several names of, 86, 87n; mentioned, 5
Keowee, 119, 123, 124
Keowee River, 119
Kingsport, Tenn., 61, 83
Kirk, William, 44

L

Lake County, Fla., 199
Lake George, 199
Lake Greenwood, 115
Lake Maurepas, 181
Lake Ponchartrain, 182
Lancaster, Pa., 71
Land speculation, in western Virginia, 53
Laurens County, S.C., 105
Lead Mines. *See* Chiswell, John
Levisa Fork, 86
Lewis, Samuel, 230
Lexington Plain, 5
Little River (Ga.), 153, 156
Little River (S.C.), 116
Little Tennessee River, 121
Lochaber, 76
Lochaber Indian Congress, 77
Lochaber Line, 77, 78, 79
Loggstown, 71
Long Canes Boundary Line, 113, 116, 124
Long Canes Creek, 112, 115, 116, 121

Long Island of the Holston, 61, 77, 79
Louisa River, 83, 84, 86
Louisiana, 5n, 182
Louisville, Ga., 159

M

McCall, Hugh, 139
McDuffie County, Ga., 159
McGillivrary, Lachlan, 160
McIntosh, Roderick, 156
Maps and plans, in British Public Record Office, 8n
Maryland, 5n
Meriwether, Robert L., 115
Merrens, Harry R., 109
Minorcans, 198
Mississippi River, western limit of Georgia, 148; settlements along, 181; land along desired, 216; change in channel, 227
Mississippi, State of, 5n
Mitchell, John, 55, 229
Mobile, 204; British replace French in, 205; new commander to continue Indian policies, 205; first Indian Congress called, 207; land cession made, 210
Mobile Bay, 182
Mobile River, 210
Mobillian Indians, 209
Mohawk spokesman, 7
Monroe County, Tenn., 121
Mooney, James, 45
Moravians, of North Carolina, 77, 110
Mortar, The, 213, 217
Mosquito Inlet, 199
Mount Pleasant, 143; trail from, 173
Mulkearn, Lois, 53

N

Nameaba Indians, 209
Nelson, William, 78
New-Kanawha River system, 38, 52
New Orleans, 181
New Purchase, description of, 171; maps of, 175; affects West Florida, 220
New River, 38, 62; valley of, 37, 38; low land prices, 55; site of Chiswell's Mine, 57
Ninety-Six, S.C., 113, 115, 121
Nolachucky River, 75
North Carolina, 5n, 20; Moravians of, 77; populous colony, 93; retarded growth of Indian trade, 93; frontiers of, 99, 111; pioneers cross Indian boundary, 110; Presbyterians petition for Georgia land, 168
North Carolina-Cherokee Boundary, 93-111 *passim*; delineation of, 100-2; demarcation of, 102-7; proclamation concerning, 108-9
North Carolina-South Carolina Colonial Boundary, 93, 105
North Carolina-Virginia boundary, 110
Nothern Indian District, 5

O

Oakfuskie River, 20
Oconostota, 65, 76-77, 92
Ogeechee River, 139, 145, 148, 156, 159, 171, 175, 191
Oglethorpe, James, 136, 137, 140
Ohio Company of Virginia, 53
Ohio River, 5, 59
Oklawaha River, 199
Old Hop. *See* Caneecatee
Ossabaw (Osabow) Island, Ga., 141

P

Palmer, Robert, 102
Pamunky Indians of Virginia, 8-9
Parish, John C., 4, 224, 227
Parishes, Georgia divided into, 146
Pascagoula River, 22, 210, 227
Patton, James, 49n, 57
Peace of Paris (1763), 3, 12, 14, 181; Board of Trade report regarding, 30-34
Pearis, Richard, 134
Pearl River, 22
Pensacola, 182, 204; British replace Spanish in, 205; conference with Creeks held, 205; Indian Congress held, 212; West Florida Boundary delineated, 214; second Indian treaty, 219
Perdido River, 226
Phenhollaway Swamp, 152
Phoenix City, Ala., 141
Pickins, John, 130, 230
Piedmont, 5
Pipe Maker's Bluff, 141
Pitt, William, 145
Pittsburgh, 58
"Plan for the Future Management of Indian Affairs" (1764), 41-42, 94
Ponce de Leon Inlet, 199
Pontiac, 5, 34; leads Indian uprising,

36; Rebellion of, 57; mentioned, 38, 151

Powell River, 75

Pownall, Thomas, 10, 27, 204; on British commercial superiority, 11; on Indian cartographic skill, 46; on Indians in Anglo-French conflict, 56

Proclamation of 1763, The, 59, 162; purpose of, 34-35; effects on evolution of Indian Boundary Line, 35-40 *passim*; a provisional arrangement, 62-63; Cherokee invoke provisions of, 95; Cherokee refuse to obey, 163; portions read at Mobile, 208

Proclamation Line, The, 38, 39, 40

Propaganda, campaign waged by French and Spanish, 27

Propagandists, Spanish and French, 148

Purcell, Joseph, map of West Florida-Choctaw Boundary, 226; cartographer, 229

Q

Quakers, settled in Georgia, 159

Quebec, 35

Queensborough (Queensburg), Ga., 160

R

Rae, John, 160

Ramsey, J. G. M., 73

Records of the Moravians in North Carolina, 38

Reedy River, 93-109 *passim*, 133

Regulators, of North Carolina, 111

"Report to the Crown on the Management of Indian Affairs in America, A" (1768), 62

Reynolds, Robert L., 42

Roanoke River, 50

Romans, Bernard, 18, 21, 215, 218, 230

Royce, Charles C., 91, 178

Rutherford, John, 102

S

Saint Augustine, 136, 187, governor arrives, 189

St. Brides Church (London), 137

St. Catherine Island, Ga., 141

St. Johns River, 193

St. Mark's at Apalache, 187

St. Marks River, 187

St. Marys River, 184, 193

Sallouih (Saluy), 124, 125n

Saluda Old Town, 117, 120, 121

Saluda River, 105

Salzburgers, of Georgia, ordered off Indian land, 144

Santa Bogue Creek (River), 209, 210

Sapelo Island, Ga., 141

Savannah, Ga., 138

Savannah River, 22, 113, 132, 136, 139, 143, 148, 173, 191

Savery, Samuel, 156, 157, 174, 230

Scotch-Irish, settled in Georgia, 159

Scottish Highlanders, 140

Sea Isles, Ga., 139, 173

Seminole, meaning of name, 20-21

Sempoyasse, 192

Small Tribes, of Lower Mississippi valley, 22-23, 217

Smith, James, 71

South Carolina, 5n, 20; demand for frontier land, 113; sphere of influence, 136

South Carolina-Cherokee Boundary, 93, 94; preliminaries to, 112; delineation of, 126-29; area described, 132; demarcation of, 130-33; on present-day map, 133-35

South Carolina Gazette, 124

Southern Indian Congress at Augusta, Ga., The (1763), 40, 149

Southern Indian District, The, 5

Spanish Florida, 181; surrender of, 148; Creeks explain Spanish tenure in, 188, 189n; map showing grants in, 199

Spanish, in Georgia, 136

Spanish Louisiana, 182

Spartanburg County, S.C., 98, 99 105

Spykman, Nicholas J., 44

Stalnaker, Samuel, 57; settlement of, on upper Holston, 73

Stamp Act Disturbances, 41

Stuart, Charles, 222, 230

Stuart, John, 12; "Report" and map of 1764, 13-14; explains Indian land tenure, 18-19; on Indian cartographic skill, 46; guided by "Plan" of 1764, 41; forwards map of suggested boundary, 68; informs Governor of N.C., 97; criticizes S.C., 127; prosecutes violators, 134; prepares map of Georgia lands, 174; report on tribes in W. Fla., 205; forwards map, 229; mentioned, 44, 152, 156, 201, 207, 218, 228

Stuart-Purcell Map, 115, 178, 230, 231

Superintendent for Indian Affairs, 5

Superintendent for Indian Affairs in

the Southern District of America, 9, 186, 187

T

Taitt, David, 215, 220, 230; manuscript map, 223-24
Tallechea (Telletsher), 150 184, 192n
Taylor, Michael, 113, 115
Telletsher. *See* Tallechea
Tellico River, 121
Tennessee, 5n, 26, 93
Tennessee (Cherokee) River, 66, 67
Tennessee Valley Authority, 121
Tensaw Old Fields, 220
Ticktaw River, 227
Tidal limit boundary, in Georgia, 139, 146; in Florida, 193, 202, 203, 226
Tiger River, 101
Tomatly Mingo, 209, 210
Tombigbee River, 22, 45, 215
Tomochichi (Tomochiche), 138, 139, 194n
Trustees for Establishing the Colony of Georgia, 137
Transylvania, 111
Tryon, Governor William, 98-109 *passim*
Tryon Mountain, N.C., 105
Tryon Peak, N.C., 107
Turk, John, 113, 115
Turnbull, Dr. Andrew, 198
Twenty-Six Mile Creek, S.C., 122

U

Uchee Indians, of Georgia, 143
United States Department of Justice, 202, 203
Uptons Creek, Ga., 156, 159
Ustenaka (Jud's Friend), 101, 102

V

Van Doren, 43
Vicksburg, Miss., 227
Virginia, 5n, 20; frontier settlement of, 36, 38, 51, 52, 58, 68, 71, 74; proposals for an Indian Boundary, 74-76;

pioneers from moving to West Florida, 216
Virginia-Cherokee Boundary, The, first discussed, 49; negotiations begun, 60; mentioned, 67, 81-92 *passim*
Virginia Council, The, 76
Virginia Gazette, 71
Virginia House of Burgesses, The, 74, 76

W

Wakulla River, 187
Walker, Thomas, 55, 56n
Walpole, Thomas, 89
Warren County, Ga., 159
Washington, George, 39, 89
Washington-Choctaw County boundary, Ala., 210
Watauga River, 75, 110
Watauga settlements, 90, 110
Way, Andrew, 175, 230
West Florida, 21, 35, 150, 181, 184, 215
West Florida-Indian Boundary Lines, preliminaries, 204-7; delineation of Choctaw line, 207-12 *passim*; delineation of Creek line, 212; demarcation of, 215-23 *passim*; on eighteenth-century maps, 223; on present-day map, 226-27
West Virginia, 5n
Whiteoak Mountain, N.C., 107
Wilkinson, Edward, 130, 162
Williams Creek, Ga., 156
Wolf King, 151, 205
Wright, Governor James, 152-72 *passim*
Wrightsborough Township, Ga., 159

Y

Yamassee War, 136
Yazoo River, 184, 216
Yellow Water, 128. *See also* Devises Corner Brook
Yonge, Henry, 230
Yonge, Philip, surveys New Purchase, 175, 230
Yonge-De Brahm map, 172, 173